Hannah Wright was born in 1944 and educated at Birkenhead High School and St Clare's Hall School in Oxford. Her A-level results were so bad that no university would touch her. She left home in an atmosphere of failure and disappointment and, being a keen cook, took a job as general assistant in a posh Wiltshire restaurant. This encouraged her to take the Cordon Bleu Diploma Course in which she came top of her year. She finally landed on her feet as chef/partner in the Spread Eagle Restaurant in Greenwich, where she spent four punishing, profitable years. She later travelled and worked for two years in the Far East and Australasia. Soon after her return home her always defective eyesight dramatically decreased and she was registered blind in 1978. A chef's career now being out of the question, she changed course with surprising ease and great good luck, writing major articles and then a column for the New Statesman on nutrition and the politics of food, and broadcasting weekly on the national radio programme for the blind. In December 1981 she married Neil Fairbairn, a writer and musician. They have two children and live in Essex.

'A veritable encyclopaedia of the soup-maker's craft, international in scope and covering every type of ingredient. A pleasure to cook from.'
The Guardian

Soups

Hannah Wright

Illustrations by Vivien Ashley

ROBERT HALE · LONDON

© *Hannah Wright 1985*
First published in Great Britain 1985
Paperback edition 1986
Reprinted 1986, 1987, 1991
1992 and 1994

ISBN 0 7090 2054 6 (paperback)

Robert Hale Limited
Clerkenwell House
Clerkenwell Green
London EC1R 0HT

British Library Cataloguing in Publication Data

Wright, Hannah
  Soups.
  1. Soups
  I. Title
  641.8'13   TX757

  ISBN 0 7090 2054 6

Printed in Great Britain by
St Edmundsbury Press Limited, Bury St Edmunds, Suffolk.
Bound by WBC Bookbinders Limited

Contents

Acknowledgements

Being in the modern phrase 'print handicapped', my list of acknowledgements is longer and more heartfelt than usual, for without the following people this book would certainly not have been written: Sheila Clarke, Jane MacAskill and Kathleen Luke, who read hundreds of recipes on to tape; Elspeth Milmore, Ferdie McDonald and my father, H. Myles Wright, who corrected the galley proofs; and last and most, Neil Fairbairn, who ate soup for breakfast, dinner, lunch and tea for over a year, corrected thousands of typing errors and hundreds of slipshod sentences, and did all with gaiety, sharp intelligence and great good grace.

I would also like to thank the friends and relatives who regularly worked their way through whole soup dinners, being forced to compare and contrast as they ate.

I am immensely indebted to all the good and great cookery writers who have preceded me, especially Eliza Acton, James Beard, Julia Child *et al.*, Elizabeth David, Jane Grigson, George Lasalle and Constance Spry.

Lastly I would like to thank John Gale, greengrocer, of Royal Hill, Greenwich, for much information about vegetables and their seasons; L. Richards, of Brewer Street, Soho, for information about fish and shellfish; and Harry Schiach, of the National Association of Tripe Dressers, who almost made me like tripe.

Introduction

Soup is the most versatile, nutritious and easily prepared form of food and has never been given an important enough place in British cooking. Soup can be a completely uncooked combination of cucumber, yogurt and herbs; just potatoes, onion, milk and butter with parsley sprinkled on top; an ice-cold, shining amber jelly flavoured with madeira; chunks of different fish and shellfish swimming in a purée of tomatoes, garlic and olive oil; or a whacking great bowlful of vegetables and noodles in a paprika flavoured broth with a foot-long knackwurst balanced across the rim. The only certainty about a soup is that some part of it will have to be eaten with a spoon.

Soup has not had a prestigious history in Britain. Victorian cooks put a lot of labour into gravy and brown Windsor soups without much imagination or knowledge of good eating. The most successful British soups have tended to be regional and poor man's specialities such as Scotch Broth. More recently the tinned and dried soups so massively marketed by the multinational food companies have accustomed most of a generation to smooth and unnaturally coloured liquids whose flavour and texture, founded more on sugar, monosodium glutamate and starch than on vegetables and meat, are steadily ruining the remains of the British taste bud. Both for our health and for our pleasure we need to eat more home-made soups.

A freshly made soup is a far healthier way of eating than frying, roasting or boiling the same ingredients. The excessive heat of frying or roasting kills some vitamins, besides increasing the fat content and calorie count of the food. Up to 90% of the soluble vitamins B and C can be thrown out with the vegetable water after boiling, and even long, slow casseroling tends to damage these vitamins substantially. In soup-making the heat is gentle by comparison and the vitamin loss reduced, especially since the cooking liquid forms part of the dish. Food policists in Britain and the United States are now encouraging us to eat less of all kinds of fat and recommend that more protein should come from vegetable and grains and less from meat. We should also be consuming more liquids which are neither sweet nor alcoholic, more bulky foods such as rice and potatoes and lots of vegetables of all kinds. Soups fit this prescription for preventive medicine quite naturally besides being easy to digest.

The arrangement of this book is different from that in most cookery books. The recipes are given in alphabetical order according to the main ingredient of the soup. Soups with traditional names such as Minestrone or Cock-a-Leekie are listed under these names and then cross-referenced to their place under the main ingredient. Those with a glut of tomatoes in the garden can look up T for Tomato and find 5 main recipes and lots of variations.

Practically all the recipes end with at least a couple of variations. These include variations in the liquid used, in seasonings and spices, minor ingredients and the richness of the soup. The main recipe will generally come as near as possible to the original or traditional recipe while the variations often include cheaper or easier to find alternatives. The variations also contain suggestions for other enrichments, garnishes or methods. (There are separate sections on these subjects and on basic equipment.)

Recipes are never definitive. They must always be adapted to local and seasonal ingredients, time and labour available, the weather, tastes of family and friends and last but not least, income. The variations are intended to help the less experienced cook venture away from a few safe bets and begin to adapt recipes to suit the situation. For the skilled amateur and professional cook, the variations are intended as a reminder and a source of fresh ideas.

Nearly all the recipes and some of the variations are on pages 281-89 according to seven categories. These show which soups freeze well, are easy or slimming, are suitable for a main course or for making in large quantities and so on. I dithered with an eighth category of soups which keep well, but left it out, because most soups keep well for at least 24 hours in the fridge and those that don't (delicate vegetable and fish soups) are fairly obvious. The lists are intended to speed up the finding of a recipe which suits your purpose, so if you want a low calorie or vegetarian soup (or both in one) a quick glance at the right page will give the selection in this book. There is also a list of previously cooked foods, such as rice or beans and what soups they can be used in.

I have tried to make the recipes as detailed as possible and as a result some may seem rather dauntingly long. Length does not necessarily indicate complication. Anyone can write down the bare outline of a recipe, it is the right detail and warnings of possible pitfalls that make a recipe really useful.

This collection of soups, which come from France, Italy, Germany, Russia, America, Africa and the Caribbean as well as the best of British traditional cookery is intended to provide cooks of different skills and tastes with a wide range of precise recipes and stimulating ideas for a most practical and enjoyable art.

Amount of Soup made from the recipes in this book

Unless otherwise specified every recipe makes 1½ pints, 900ml. of soup.

This is enough to feed 2 people substantially including second helpings, 3 people a good-sized bowlful, and 4 or 5 people an appetiser portion of soup.

Where there are a lot of ingredients and the soup is of a chunky main course type, I have doubled the amount to 3 pints, 1.75 litres. This is stated at the beginning of the recipe.

Measurements
All spoon measures in this book are flat unless otherwise specified.

Equipment

Pots and Pans

Aluminium pans are often sturdy, well designed and cheaper than pans made from other metals, but they have their vices. They can bleach green vegetables to an ugly yellow and make peculiar changes in the flavour of some delicate ingredients such as celeriac, and fish cooked with vinegar or lemon. These effects are particularly evident when the soup is a purée.

Stainless steel pans have no such effects on food, but unless the kind with copper bottoms is used, the heat is unevenly distributed and the food burns easily. These pans are very expensive, but are a good investment if carefully chosen.

Aluminium pans with a non-stick coating are perfectly satisfactory for soup-making, but are relatively expensive, and unless you are scrupulously careful the coating does not last long.

Lightweight enamelled pans have the same advantages and drawbacks as non-stick pans. They also catch rather easily on the bottom and are therefore not good for thick soups.

Cast-iron pans without a coating rust easily and should be kept oiled. They are heavy and long-lasting but have an unpleasant effect on the flavour and colour of mixtures containing vinegar, lemon and some alcohols.

Cast-iron pans coated with enamel (the best known are the French Le Creuset range) are heavy and may be a burden to those with weak hands or arms, but otherwise they meet all the requirements for successful soup-making. Because they are also designed for use in the oven, however, they tend to have small iron handles which make pouring an awkward and difficult procedure.

Whatever material you choose, remember that cheap pans with thin bottoms and poorly attached handles are not only a false economy but may also be a dangerous one.

Stockpot and Steamer

A stockpot should have a capacity of at least 8 pints (5 l) and preferably more, so that chickens and pieces of beef can be cooked in it with ease. It should be sturdy, but the metal need not be thick, since the heat underneath will always be low and, if the empty pot is very heavy, it may be dangerously unwieldy when full of hot liquid. Traditionally a stockpot has high, straight sides and a small surface area for its capacity. This shape has certain advantages. Firstly, a small surface area diminishes evaporation; secondly, the pot will occupy less of the stove top and is therefore less of a nuisance during long cooking sessions; and thirdly, with greater depth and smaller surface area more pieces of meat etc. can be submerged in the stock at one time.

A refinement on the basic stockpot is the type that doubles as a steamer. I have one with three perforated metal baskets in tier, fitted inside a metal handle for easy removal from the pot. Though not strictly designed for soup-making, it is very useful for this purpose. A boiling fowl or piece of beef can be put in the bottom basket and, after the stock has been skimmed, the vegetable trimmings and spices can be lowered in another of the baskets and removed and discarded at the end of the cooking time. Alternatively, fish heads and bones and vegetables can be put into the bottom basket and used to make fish stock, and another basket used for poaching or steaming any fillets of fish. The third basket could be used for boiling eggs or skinning tomatoes.

Food Mill

A food mill or pressure sieve is cheaper than a blender, lasts for years, and is a most useful aid to soup-making. They are sold complete with fine, medium and coarse plates and, with the exception of Carrot and Coriander Soup, which really does need a blender to achieve the right velvet texture, can be used to purée every vegetable soup in this book. A food mill, however, is not suitable for making meat or fish purées, though of course it can be used for the vegetable and stock part of the soup, leaving bones, gristle, skin etc. caught in the sieve. Food mills are rather fiddly to wash up but no worse than many a blender, and are altogether most useful items of equipment. They are often known as mouli-légumes.

Blender

A blender is now standard equipment and very useful it is too. Its drawback is that it is too efficient, tending to give all soups the same baby-food texture. Ways of avoiding this are discussed in Blending Soup, p. 19. Blenders come in many shapes and at very different prices. The points to look for are a powerful motor, blades that can be removed for thorough cleaning, and a lid that can be screwed or locked into position (see Blending Soups).

Food Processors

While the food mixer was the prized possession of the 1950s' household, when women did not often have a job and enjoyed making cakes, puddings and bread for the family, the food processor is the labour-saving gadget of today's slimming-conscious working women, and men too.

It is basically a sophisticated electric chopper which, depending on your model, can do anything from liquidize to slice. It also minces, meat and fish, bread, nuts, pulses and most other dry foods. The usefulness of a food processor in soup-making will already be apparent, for it will slice or shred the vegetables when raw, grind meat ball or quenelle mixtures, and purée the final soup in the blender part.

In selecting a food processor, the same criteria apply as in choosing a blender; the strongest possible motor being even more important since it has to cope with grinding fibrous raw meat, etc. The capacity of the food processor is not of major importance – since each task is completed in seconds, repeating it several times is no problem. One or more of the functions of a food processor will prove useful for nearly every soup in this book.

Basic Processes

BLENDING SOUP

Before blending a soup, allow the boiling liquid to cool considerably, or keep half the liquid aside and add it with the boiling soup in equal proportions. If liquids at or near boiling point are blended, during the first few seconds of blending, a large quantity of steam will rise which can blow an insecure lid off the blender and cover you and the kitchen with scalding liquid. The blender will reduce any soup to a perfectly smooth texture, which makes dull eating. There are two ways to avoid this: one is to blend in bursts of one or two seconds, looking at the soup between each burst until the desired texture is achieved; the other is to leave a ladleful of soup unblended and stir it into the smooth, blended portion.

ROUX: FLOUR AND BUTTER SAUCE BASE

Melt the required amount of butter – 1 to 2 oz (30 to 60 g) – in a heavy-bottomed pan; a successful roux is difficult to achieve in a thin or bumpy pan. When it has just melted, stir in the flour, which should be a little less than the amount of butter. All the flour should be absorbed by the butter into a pale yellow dough. If any flour is left, add more butter until it is all absorbed or the soup will be lumpy. Cook this roux for a minute or two over a low heat, stirring all the time. Then add a little of the liquid – not more than a tenth of it – and stir hard until the lump of doughy sauce is quite smooth.

Add another tenth and stir again. These first additions are the problematical ones. If you are at all doubtful about the complete smoothness of the doughy sauce, whisk it, and do not add more liquid until it is quite smooth. A lump ignored at this stage will be difficult to get out later. Go on adding the liquid and stirring the soup smooth. The liquid can be added much more quickly after the first quarter is safely amalgamated, since lumps are unlikely beyond this stage. Leave the thickened soup cooking on a very low heat for at least 15 minutes or it will have a nasty taste of raw flour.

SWEATING VEGETABLES

In cookery to sweat means to cook very gently, usually in fat, in a covered pan so that juices will start to run from the cut-up vegetables, blending with the fat to make a well-flavoured base for the soup. If the heat is high, or the pan left uncovered, the liquid will evaporate as it leaves the vegetables and the surface of the vegetables will fry and harden, sealing in the rest of the juices. Therefore a thick-bottomed pan with a tight-fitting lid should be used. The vegetables to be sweated should be cut into small, evenly-sized pieces or dice and added to the fat as soon as it has melted. The pan should be covered immediately and left on a very low heat. Lift the lid after a minute to stir and check that things are not frying. There should be plenty of steam when the lid is lifted and a gentle, moist sound, not a hard crackle. If you want a low fat soup the vegetables can be sweated dry, or in only a very little fat. If so be even more careful about the heavy-bottomed pan, the tight fitting lid and the very low heat, since sticking and burning will be more likely. Sweating usually lasts 5 to 10 minutes, until the vegetable are limp and semi-cooked. Liquid is then added to the pan and cooking proceeds.

THICKENING SOUPS

Breadcrumbs

Fresh white or wholemeal crumbs can be made instantly from crustless bread in a blender, coffee grinder or food processor. Crumb one slice at a time and stir it into the soup. Judge the increased thickness and crumb more slices if necessary. The soup can be served at once.

Cornflour, Rice Flour or Potato Flour

All these flours must be mixed with cold liquid (slaked) before they are added to hot soup. Stir 1 tablespoon of the flour into 6 tablespoons of the chosen cold liquid or water. When it is quite smooth, whisk it into the boiling soup. Simmer the soup for a minute or so before serving. More thickening can be added in the same way if needed. Cornflour gives rather a gluey consistency.

Egg Yolks, Whole Eggs, Yogurt or Cream

Eggs, yogurt and raw cream will all curdle if added directly to boiling soup; only pasteurized cream can be added in this way. There is a simple technique for dealing with the problem, but it is important not to add these thickening ingredients until the very last moment, when people are seated at the table, since reheating the soup after this point is tricky. Egg is the most prone to disaster, but the process is the same for the other ingredients. Take a balloon whisk and whisk the egg yolks (or whole egg, yogurt or raw cream) to a smooth texture. Bring the soup to just below boiling point. Adjust seasoning and make any other final additions. Then slowly add a ladleful of the soup to the egg mixture, whisking all the time. Transfer the whisk to the saucepan. Move the pan off the heat and, whisking continuously, pour the egg and soup mixture into the soup. It should thicken a little. Serve at once. If you are not sure that the soup has thickened (only a very slight and delicate thickening will take place) put the pan back on a very low heat and cook for another minute, stirring all the time at the bottom of the pan. Egg curdles and cooks at 190°F (90°C), some way below boiling point, so be very careful.

Grated Raw Potato

Grate a small peeled potato, using the coarse side of the grater. Add it to the soup at once or it will discolour, and cook the soup for another 5 to 7 minutes before serving. More grated potato can be added if needed.

Kneaded Butter and Flour: Beurre Manié

Knead together 1 heaped tablespoon flour and $1\frac{1}{2}$ oz (40 g) soft butter to form a smooth lump of dough; this amount will lightly thicken 1 pint (600 ml) of soup, and can be doubled or tripled for a thick soup. When the soup is ready to serve, whisk in the *beurre manié* a little at a time. When it is all amalgamated, serve the soup immediately, if possible, to prevent a raw flour taste from forming. If the soup has to wait the flour flavour must be cooked out for a further 15 minutes.

Rice or Small Pasta

Vermicelli, broken spaghetti, noodles or alphabet pasta can be added to a soup 10 to 12 minutes before serving. White rice can be added in the same way, but brown rice takes at least 45 minutes to cook and is therefore not a satisfactory last-minute thickening unless you have some ready pre-cooked. Stir the rice or pasta a few times after adding to make sure it is well distributed through the soup. Keep the soup boiling gently as it cooks.

THINNING SOUPS

Blending a soup will have the effect of thinning it slightly. Otherwise simply add more liquid, or remove some of the solids from the soup.

Salt, Pepper & Spices

Sodium, a substance contained in salt, is essential to the human body, but so many vegetables and other foods already contain sodium, and so many convenience foods contain large quantities of salt for preservative purposes, that the Western diet generally contains far too much. Excessive intake over the years can lead to high blood pressure, and in 1977 the US Senate Report on Dietary Aims for the American People gave 5 g per day as a recommended intake of salt – that is to say, one flat teaspoon. Since most of us grossly exceed this quantity, discussion of the relative merits of sea salt and table salt is irrelevant. The additives in table salt may be bad, but nothing like so bad as the salt itself. It is sensible to decrease by degrees the salt you add to dishes and to stop putting extra salt on the table.

Pepper can irritate a delicate stomach, but compared with salt its health record is lily-white. Like all other spices, peppercorns lose their flavour very rapidly after grinding and subsequent exposure to warmth, air, light and moisture. It is the black, outer part of a peppercorn which is aromatic. The core, which is the white peppercorn, has more heat than flavour, but is useful for white and creamy soups. Freshly milled black peppercorns have a lovely scent – I sometimes grind a little into my hand just for the pleasure of smelling it – much of which disperses within minutes of grinding, leaving the flat taste which generations assumed to be the only way pepper could taste. It is for this reason that the use of freshly milled pepper is urged throughout the book. If you particularly enjoy the spiciness of pepper, add it just before serving, or even at the table – in this way it will be less integrated but more aromatic.

These comments also apply to all other spices, though in most the deterioration in flavour is not so rapid. Freshly-opened packaged ground spices may have a very good flavour; the question is, how long will it take you to work down the jar or drum? It is a good idea to buy only whole spices, which do keep for years. They can often be used whole and removed before serving the dish, or they can be milled as needed. Some admirable people keep a row of coloured mills, each containing a different spice. Otherwise, spices can be ground successfully in a small electric coffee grinder. Blending whole spices with soups is risky since unpleasantly large chunks may be left intact. The fine or medium plate of a food mill will catch the whole spices, but they may jam under the pressure plate and prevent it turning.

Herbs

In the last few years pretty jars of dried herbs, often fitted snugly into a pine rack, have become a badge to be pinned on the kitchen of the aspiring cook. Having a wide range of herbs in every supermarket and many corner shops is a great convenience, but we pay for it in price and staleness. Dried herbs, even in glass jars, only keep their sweet flavour for about a year, often less, and there is no way of knowing how long they have been on the shelf before you buy them.

The more a herb is ground up, the more surface area is exposed to air, moisture, light and so on, and the more quickly it deteriorates. On the other hand ground herbs are more convenient to use and can be packaged more compactly. Small branches and twigs of dried thyme or rosemary, for instance, retain their flavour longer, but are likely to get damaged in transit from grower to wholesaler to retailer to home.

There is no easy answer, but if you grow or can obtain sprigs of bushy herbs such as thyme, marjoram, oregano, fennel, rosemary and bay they will dry very successfully if hung in small bunches in a warm, dry place. If you do have to buy dried, rubbed herbs in packets or jars, buy them in small quantities only from shops with a fast turnover, and keep your nose alert each time you open the jar.

No herbs at all are better than stale herbs; and any freshly picked herb, even if less appropriate to the recipe, is a great improvement on that musty taste of stale, dried herbs which penetrates all other flavours. It is sometimes difficult to make oneself throw out a nearly new package of herbs, but it is a false economy to add dead-tasting, stale herbs to any dish.

Some of the delicate green herbs such as tarragon, basil and dill dry quite satisfactorily, although the flavour is not so subtle as that of the fresh herb. The very delicate-flavoured herbs such as chives and parsley are a total wash-out.

Many herbs grow happily in pots or window boxes, and are therefore convenient for snipping as and when required. A herb bed at the bottom of the garden, on the other hand, however varied and beautiful, tends to remain unused by the cook.

Attractively designed herb charts have made people rather over-conscious of putting the right herb with the right main ingredient. It is true that there are certain affinities – basil with tomatoes, fennel with fish – but freshness is all-important. Remember to use freshly picked herbs if possible, freshly dried if not. Then experiment and enjoy them.

Garnishes &
Accompaniments

Bread and Pastry

CROÛTONS

Plain croûtons can be fried or baked in the oven. Frying is quicker and uses less fuel, but more difficult in that the croûtons tend to brown unevenly unless your full attention is on them. The baking method is also more successful for cheese, curry and herb croûtons, because these extra ingredients tend to stick to the frying pan and burn.

Plain Fried Croûtons

4 slices bread
2 to 3 tablespoons oil
1 oz (30 g) butter

Remove the crusts and cut the bread into small, even dice. Put 2 or 3 sheets of kitchen paper in the bottom of a flat tin or dish. Heat the oil and butter together in a heavy frying pan, and when the butter stops sizzling add the bread dice. Fry over a moderate heat, stirring and turning the cubes continually until they are an even nut brown –

about 3 minutes. Lift them out at once and leave them to drain on the kitchen paper for a minute. Serve as soon as possible.

Plain Baked Croûtons

4 thin slices bread
1½ oz (40 g) butter

Preheat the oven to 375°F (190°C, Gas 5). Butter both sides of the bread and remove the crusts. Dice the bread, put the cubes on a baking tray and bake for 5 minutes on the top shelf of the oven. Then stir them, and turn the tray round if one side is cooking more quickly than the other. The croûtons will be ready in another 5 minutes or less. They do not need draining and can be left in a low oven for a little while without harm

Variation: Curry Croûtons
Follow the method for plain baked croûtons but add ½ teaspoon curry powder and a squeeze of lemon juice to the softened butter before it is spread on the bread.

Variation 2: Cheese Croûtons
Stir ½ oz (15 g) or more grated Parmesan cheese into the softened butter and continue as for plain baked croûtons.

Variation 3: Herb Croûtons
Stir 1 tablespoon chopped parsley, or mixed parsley and chives, or other young green herbs, into the softened butter. Add a squeeze of lemon and continue as for plain baked croûtons.

HOT HERB AND GARLIC BREAD

4 oz (110 g) butter *or* 8 tablespoons olive oil
grated rind of ½ lemon
2 to 3 cloves garlic, peeled and crushed
3 tablespoons chopped parsley, mixed parsley and chives, or other young green herbs
cayenne
salt
1 small wholemeal or French loaf

Preheat the oven to 375°F (190°C, Gas 5). Mash the butter or olive oil with the grated lemon rind, garlic and herbs. Add a little cayenne and salt. Cut the loaf into thick slices which are still just attached at the base. Spread the butter in between the slices, then push the slices back into shape again. Wrap the loaf in foil and heat for 15 minutes. Serve hot.

PIROSHKIS

These little Russian pasties are traditionally served with the beetroot soup called borscht, but make a lovely accompaniment to almost any thick soup. They are easy to make and lift an ordinary soup snack meal into something sophisticated and delicious.

Makes about 18 2 in (5 cm) Piroshkis:

4 oz (110 g) plain flour
1 teaspoon baking powder
a little salt
3 oz (90 g) butter
a few tablespoons sour cream
1 small onion
2 sticks celery

4 oz (110 g) mushrooms – flat
    ones are best for flavour
salt
freshly milled pepper
ground nutmeg
beaten egg

Mix the flour, baking powder and salt and rub in 2 oz (60 g) butter. Mix in enough sour cream to make a soft dough. Knead until smooth and leave covered in the fridge to relax for 30 minutes while you make the filling.

Preheat the oven to 425°F (220°C, Gas 7). Chop the onion and celery and sweat them gently in the remaining butter for 5 minutes. Chop the mushrooms, add them to the celery and onion mixture and sweat for another 10 minutes or until the mixture is soft and cooked. Season rather highly and leave to cool. Roll out the pastry to $\frac{1}{4}$ in ($\frac{1}{2}$ cm) thick. Cut into 2 in (5 cm) circles with a biscuit cutter, and brush each circle with egg. Put a heaped teaspoon of filling in the centre of each circle. Fold the circles in half and seal their edges. Brush the tops with the beaten egg. Bake for 15 to 20 minutes and serve hot.

Other fillings can be devised using cooked minced meat or fish and vegetables. The fillings should be rather highly seasoned. You need about 8 oz (225 g) of filling or a little less for this quantity of Piroshkis.

Egg Garnishes

EGG THREADS OR DROPS

Beat a whole egg with 1 dessertspoon sifted flour. Bring the broth or soup to the boil and, while it is boiling gently, pour the egg mixture through a sieve into the soup. Simmer for 1 minute and serve. To make egg drops, stir the egg mixture as it enters the pan.

OMELETTE SHREDS

Make a 2-egg omelette seasoned with herbs, cheese, ham or whatever is appropriate to the soup. Cook it a little longer than usual, until the upper surface is quite firm. Roll it up with a fork or spatula and leave to get cool, then cut the roll into thin slices. Add to broth or other thin soup a minute before serving.

PARMESAN BALLS

Grate 1 oz (30 g) Parmesan cheese and mix it well with 2 egg yolks. When the thin soup or broth is just ready to serve, drop $\frac{1}{2}$ teaspoons of the mixture all over the surface of the soup. Leave them for 2 to 3 minutes or until just firm, then serve.

POACHED EGGS

German restaurants have an unpleasant habit of slipping a raw egg into a bowl of hot broth and serving it to you as a poached egg. After only 30 seconds or so in nowhere-near-boiling broth, the egg white is still semi-transparent and mucoid while the yolk is entirely raw. A properly poached egg does, however, turn a broth or other thin soup into a full meal. Heat the broth in a shallow, wide pan, and add 1 dessertspoon wine vinegar or lemon juice per $1\frac{1}{2}$ pints (900 ml) broth. Swirl the broth round and break a very fresh egg into the swirl. Simmer over a very low heat for 2 minutes and leave to stand in the covered pan for a further minute, then serve. With a little practice and the right shape of pan 2 to 3 eggs can be poached at once.

Alternatively the eggs can be poached separately either in salted water or in an egg-poacher and added to the soup on serving.

Vegetable and Nut Garnishes

ALMONDS

Toast 1½ to 2 oz (40 to 60 g) blanched slivered almonds under the grill, watching and stirring them all the time since they burn easily. Scatter the hot almonds on simple vegetable soups and purées. Alternatively the almonds can be fried in 1 oz (30 g) butter or oil.

CHIFFONADE

A chiffonade is generally made from lettuce, but other delicate green leaves such as spinach, beet leaves or Chinese cabbage can also be used. Take about 3 oz (90 g) washed inner leaves, remove any coarse stalks and roll the leaves into a tight cigar shape. Cut across into wafer-thin slices. Add to a boiling broth, consommé or delicate cream soup a minute before serving.

JULIENNE STRIPS

A julienne of vegetables is a mixture of firm vegetables such as carrot, celery, celeriac, Jerusalem artichoke, etc. cut into even, elegant matchsticks and cooked in the soup for a minute or two before serving as a tender but crisp garnish. For 1½ pints (900 ml) soup use 1 small carrot, 1 small stick celery and 1 small Jerusalem artichoke. These should give a peeled weight of 3 to 4 oz (90 to 110 g), which will make a light garnish for a broth or consommé. Strongly flavoured vegetables such as turnip and parsnip should be used only in small quantities, cooked separately in water or stock and added to the soup just before serving.

MUSHROOMS

Take 4 oz (110 g) cup or button mushrooms; flat mushrooms have the best flavour but tend to discolour the soup. Remove the stalks and use them for another dish. According to your preference, slice the mushroom caps very thinly, cut them in quarters, or, if small and even-sized, leave them whole. (If you really get carried away you can scallop the edges.) Add the mushrooms raw to the soup 2 minutes before serving, or sweat them in 1 oz (30 g) butter or oil for a minute or two beforehand.

TOMATOES

Peel and core 2 to 3 large, ripe, red tomatoes. Scoop the seeds out and cut the flesh into fine dice. Add to broth, consommé or simple purées a minute before serving. For a richer flavour, sweat the tomato dice in 1 oz (30 g) butter for a minute or two before adding them to the soup. (For more details on preparing tomatoes see p. 247.)

Dumplings, Meat Balls, Quenelles and Other Floating Objects

SUET DUMPLINGS

1½ oz (40 g) beef suet	salt
2½ oz (75 g) plain flour	freshly milled pepper
1 dessertspoon grated onion	2 to 3 tablespoons cold water
1 dessertspoon chopped parsley	

Mix the suet, flour, onion, parsley, salt and pepper and bind with the water. Knead the dough just enough to blend all the ingredients and roll it into a fat sausage on a floured surface. Cut the sausage into 12 pieces. Roll into balls and poach in the soup for 10 to 15 minutes before serving.

POTATO DUMPLINGS

1 medium large potato – 4 oz
   (110 g) after peeling
salt
½ oz (15 g) butter
1 dessertspoon grated onion
a little grated lemon rind or

nutmeg
1 dessertspoon chopped parsley
   or other green herb
1 egg yolk
1½ tablespoons flour

Cube the potato and boil it in salted water until soft. Mash it with the butter, onion, lemon rind or nutmeg and herbs plus a little more salt. Stir in the egg yolk and 1 tablespoon flour. Roll the mixture into small balls using the remaining flour and poach them in the soup for 10 minutes before serving.

BEEF BALLS

The simplest and meatiest type of beef ball will be found in Meat Ball and Tomato Soup on pps. 81-2. Here is a recipe for half the quantity of small beef balls, containing some breadcrumbs, for use as a garnish. It will make about 20 half-ounce meat balls.

4 oz (110 g) lean raw beef
2 slices wholemeal bread
water or beef stock
a very little grated onion
sprinkle of cayenne
dash of soy sauce

salt
1 dessertspoon finely chopped
   parsley or other fresh herb as
   appropriate (optional)
1 egg

Soak the bread slices in water or beef stock and squeeze nearly dry. If you have no food processor or strong-motored blender, ask the butcher to mince some lean stewing beef twice for you. Pound this mince with the bread and seasonings. If you do have a food processor, cut up the beef and bread in small pieces, put all the ingredients except the egg into the processor, and grind to a smooth pulp. Stir in the egg and form into little balls. Poach in the soup for 10 to 15 minutes and serve.

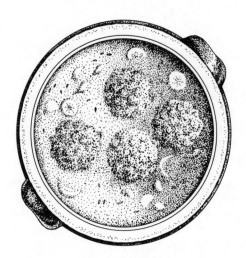

LIVER BALLS

This recipe makes about 14 half-ounce balls.

4 oz (110 g) lamb's or pig's liver
2 slices wholemeal bread without
    crusts
pinch of marjoram

½ clove garlic, peeled and
    crushed with salt
salt
freshly milled pepper

For this recipe a food processor or efficient blender is necessary to achieve the right consistency. Cut up the bread and liver and put them in the food processor or blender with the garlic and seasoning. Blend or grind very thoroughly. Form into little balls and poach for about 8 minutes in the soup. They have a very pleasant, delicate flavour and hold together without egg.

COOKED LAMB AND RICE BALLS

3 to 4 oz (90 to 110 g) freshly
    cooked lamb or mutton
3 tablespoons cooked rice,
    brown or white
1 dessertspoon minced or grated
    onion

1 dessertspoon chopped parsley
salt
freshly milled black pepper
½ teaspoon cumin
1 egg
about 2 tablespoons flour

Grind or pound the meat and rice to a pulp. Stir in the onion and parsley and season rather strongly. Blend in the egg and a little of the flour to make a good, stiff consistency for rolling into balls. Roll the finished balls in the rest of the flour and poach in a little of the soup broth for 10 minutes. Lift them out with a draining spoon and add to the main soup as you serve it.

BREAD AND HERB BALLS

4 slices old wholemeal bread without crusts
water, broth or stock
1 oz (30 g) butter or other fat
1 tablespoon finely minced or grated onion
2 tablespoons finely chopped parsley or other fresh herb
grated rind of ½ lemon
1 beaten egg
salt
freshly milled pepper

Soak the bread in the water, broth or stock and squeeze out. Grind or pound it to a smooth pulp. Fry the onion in the butter, add it with the herbs and lemon rind to the bread and grind or pound again. Stir in the seasoning, add the beaten egg and form into tiny balls. Poach in the soup or broth for 3 minutes and serve.

See also:
Bread and Bacon Balls *under* Hare Soup with Madeira and Bread Balls

QUENELLES OF FISH OR SHELLFISH

2 slices day-old white bread without crusts
milk or fish stock
3½ oz (100 g) skinless raw white fish fillet or any shellfish meat
½ teaspoon anchovy essence *or* 1 anchovy fillet
sprinkle of cayenne
a little finely grated lemon rind
1 egg, separated

Soak the bread in the milk or fish stock and squeeze out. Pound or grind the raw fish or shellfish and bread together to a smooth pulp. It is important that no flakes of fish are left or the quenelle may break up. Preferably pass the mixture through a fine sieve or the fine plate of a food mill. Pound or grind in the lemon rind, anchovy and cayenne. Stir in the egg yolk. When you are ready to poach the quenelles, whip the egg white stiffly and fold it into the mixture.

Poach ½ teaspoons of the mixture in simmering, salted water or fish stock for about 6 minutes.

Cooked fish or shellfish can also be used, but neither the taste nor the consistency will be so good.

RAVIOLI

Fresh little ravioli are the last word in elegant finishing touches in a chicken or beef broth or Mediterranean vegetable soup. They can contain any highly seasoned meat or vegetable filling appropriate to the recipe, but this classic spinach and cream cheese filling is quickly made and easy to use.

Pasta dough:
3 oz (90 g) plain white flour, plus
   a little more if needed
1 tablespoon oil
1 egg
salt

Filling'
good handful fresh spinach
   leaves – 4 oz (110 g) after
   removing the stalks – *or* 2 oz

(60 g) frozen spinach
3 heaped tablespoons ricotta,
   cream cheese or cottage
   cheese
1 egg
1 oz (30 g) grated Parmesan
a little grated lemon rind and/
   or a little nutmeg
salt
freshly milled pepper
1 egg yolk (for glue)

Sift the flour into a bowl. Put the egg and oil into a well in the centre with a little salt and knead into a firm dough. Add more flour if necessary. Leave to relax for 30 minutes while you make the filling.

Cook fresh spinach leaves in a little boiling water for 2 minutes or until they are limp. Press out all the juice you can and chop to a mush. Defrost frozen spinach in a sieve so that excess moisture drains off, squeeze it nearly dry. Beat the egg a little. Mix the spinach, ricotta or other soft cheese, Parmesan, lemon and seasonings together and add most or all of the beaten egg to make a soft filling.

Cut the dough in half and roll and stretch each half into the thinnest possible sheet. This takes a while but is good fun because the dough is amazingly elastic and stretches thinner and thinner. Roll out the other half to as near the same size and shape as possible. Put flat ½ teaspoons of filling (no more) in a grid at 1 in (2½ cm) intervals on one half of the pasta dough. Beat the egg yolk smooth and brush it between the lumps of filling to act as glue for the other sheet of dough. Lay this second sheet on top and press down firmly between

HEARTY CHICKEN CASSEROLE

An all-in-one meal of tender chicken, crispy potatoes and a combination of sophisticated flavours — garlic, rosemary and dry white vermouth.

HEALTH CHECK

- Skinless chicken pieces are low in fat and high in protein
- Dry white vermouth adds flavour without adding extra fat

One-pot Supper

PREPARATION TIME
35 minutes

COOKING TIME
40 minutes

SAMPLE

HEARTY CHICKEN CASSEROLE • Original card from *Delicious Meals Made Easy*

SERVES 6

2 tablespoons vegetable oil

6 skinless chicken pieces, about 100g (4oz) each

3 potatoes, sliced

175ml (6fl oz) hot chicken stock

60ml (2fl oz) dry white vermouth

2 cloves garlic, thinly sliced

1 large onion, thinly sliced

2 rashers rindless streaky bacon

1 teaspoon dried Herbes de Provence or dried rosemary

1 teaspoon poultry seasoning

¼ teaspoon salt

black pepper

4 spring onions, trimmed and finely sliced to garnish

2 tablespoons chopped fresh parsley to garnish

PER SERVING: Kcals *245*/**kJs** *1209* **Sodium** *0.4g* **Fat** *10g* **Fibre** *1g* **Carbohydrate** *12g* **Protein** *25g*

1 Preheat oven to 190°C/375°F/ gas 5. Heat the oil in a large frying pan. Add chicken pieces. Cook for 10 minutes, or until evenly browned on all sides. Transfer chicken to an oven-proof casserole dish.

2 Add potatoe slices to frying pan. Cook for 5 minutes on each side, or until evenly browned. Put into casserole dish. Add the chicken stock and vermouth to the dish.

3 Sprinkle over garlic and onion. Finely chop bacon rashers and scatter on top. Sprinkle over Herbes de Provence or dried rosemary, poultry seasoning, salt and black pepper.

4 Cook in oven for 30–40 minutes, or until the chicken juices run clear when thickest part of chicken is pierced with a skewer and potatoes are tender. Garnish with sliced spring onions and chopped parsley. Serve hot.

MME 07 97/01 ©1996, 1997 IMP BV/IMP Ltd. Delicious Meals Made Easy

Printed in Heanor, England by Heanor Gate Printing Ltd.

PARTY FRUIT PLATTER

An easy, no-cook snack that's ideal for a casual gathering of family or friends. The creamy dip brings out the flavours in the juicy fresh fruits.

- Watermelon is low in calories and fat and provides vitamin C

- Greek-style yoghurt and soft cheese are sources of both protein and calcium

Colour Carnival

PREPARATION TIME
20 minutes plus chilling

PARTY FRUIT PLATTER • Original card from *Delicious Meals Made Easy*

SERVES 6

2 large oranges, peeled

1 peach, stoned and sliced

½ watermelon, scooped into balls

½ cantaloupe melon, peeled and cut into small wedges

½ honeydew melon, peeled and cut into small wedges

225g (8oz) seedless green grapes

mint sprig to decorate

FOR THE DIP

100g (4oz) low fat soft cheese

300ml (½ pint) Greek-style yoghurt

1 teaspoon grated lime rind

2 tablespoons reduced-sugar marmalade

2 teaspoons crystallized ginger, finely chopped

1 teaspoon finely grated lemon rind to decorate

PER SERVING: Kcals *187*/**kJs** *791* **Sodium** *0.06*g **Fat** *6*g **Fibre** *3*g

1 Divide oranges into segments. Arrange orange segments and other prepared fruit on a large serving plate. Garnish with mint. Cover plate with cling film. Chill until required.

2 For the dip, put cheese into a mixing bowl. Beat with an electric mixer or wooden spoon until very soft and fluffy. Beat in yoghurt, lime rind and marmalade until smooth and blended. Stir in the ginger.

3 Spoon dip into bowl. Cover with cling film. Chill for 1 hour. Garnish with lemon rind. Serve with the fruit.

✂ SHORT CUT

To save time, use ready-prepared fruit. Larger super-markets now sell orange and grapefruit segments, mango and papaya slices and pineapple chunks. You can also use peeled and sliced kiwi fruit and hulled strawberries on the platter.

Carbohydrate *28*g **Protein** *8*g

COOK'S TIPS

Use a lemon zester to remove just the citrus rind and not the bitter white pith which lies underneath. You can also use a potato peeler to remove the rind, then cut into strips.

Some oranges have a slightly green skin while being perfectly ripe inside. Prepare the orange segments over a bowl to catch any juices. Add the juices to a salad dressing or fruit salad.

MME 07 97/02 ©1996, 1997 IMP BV/IMP Ltd. Delicious Meals Made Easy

Printed in Heanor, England by Heanor Gate Printing Ltd.

each lump of filling. Cut into separate ravioli, with a wide border so that the filling does not escape, and check that the edges are well glued. Poach in simmering, salted water for 4 to 5 minutes, drain and add to the soup as you serve it.

NOODLES

Use the rolled-out ravioli dough (above) and cut it into ribbons $\frac{1}{4}$ in ($\frac{1}{2}$ cm) wide. Poach these noodles in any thin soup or broth for 3 to 4 minutes before serving.

Enrichments

The addition of cream, sour cream and eggs or egg yolks constitutes such a basic form of enrichment that it is dealt with under Basic Processes on p. 21. Described here are a variety of thick, rich, highly flavoured sauces that can be used to ginger up a simple purée or add panache to a mixed vegetable or fish soup. They can all be made in advance and freeze well, except for aioli, although some texture and depth of flavour are lost.

AIOLI: GARLIC MAYONNAISE

This is used as a final enrichment and liaison (binder) in Mediterranean French fish and vegetable stew-type soups. It should be added in the same way as egg alone (see p. 21). There is no need for lemon or seasoning since the soup will provide them.

1 to 2 egg yolks
2 to 4 cloves garlic, peeled and
    crushed with salt
8 tablespoons fruity olive oil

Beat the egg yolk(s) thoroughly with the crushed garlic until they become a little paler. Add olive oil $\frac{1}{2}$ teaspoon at a time, stirring hard between each addition. You will end up with a thick little mayonnaise. It will keep well, covered in a cool place. (See 'curdling' on pps. 278-9) if in difficulties.

AUBERGINE CAVIAR

1 small or ½ large aubergine
2 cloves garlic, peeled and
crushed with salt
4 to 6 tablespoons olive oil

1 oz (30 g) walnuts or almonds
(optional)
salt
freshly milled pepper

Dice the aubergine and sprinkle with salt, leave in a colander for 30 minutes, then rinse thoroughly; see p. 52 for further details of this process. Fry the crushed garlic in 2 tablespoons of the olive oil for a minute or two. Dry the drained aubergine on kitchen paper, add to the garlic and fry gently for 10 minutes. Grind or crush the nuts to small crumbs. When the aubergine is cooked, remove from the heat and stir in the nut crumbs and the rest of the oil to make a thick paste; alternatively blend the mixture. Season rather highly.

AUBERGINE AND TOMATO

1 small aubergine or ½ large
aubergine
2 large, ripe tomatoes
1 small clove garlic, peeled and
crushed with salt

2 to 4 tablespoons olive oil
pinch of basil or 2 fresh basil
leaves
salt
freshly milled pepper

Prepare the aubergine for cooking as for Aubergine Caviar. Peel and core the tomatoes (see pps. 247-8) and dice them. Take the drained and rinsed aubergines, dice and fry them with the garlic in the oil for 10 minutes, stirring occasionally. When the mixture is soft and nearly cooked, add the basil, seasoning and tomato dice. Cook for a couple of minutes. If you want to keep the mixture for a day or two, cook for 10 minutes longer.

AILLADE

This is the southern French version of the Italian pesto and is the final addition to the soup called Pistou. It can also be added to any mixed vegetable soup of the Mediterranean type.

small handful fresh basil, say 20 leaves at least

2 large, ripe tomatoes

4 tablespoons olive oil

salt

freshly milled pepper

Chop the basil and tomatoes together to form a pulp. Put into a small bowl and drip in the olive oil, stirring hard all the time, to make a thick paste. Season highly. Stir in a ladleful of hot soup to the mixture, then return to the pan, stirring hard. Serve the soup at once.

BACON, PARSLEY AND ONION: LA FRICASSÉE

2 oz (60 g) streaky bacon, green or smoked

1 medium onion

1 small clove garlic, peeled and crushed with salt

2 tablespoons olive oil

1 tablespoon chopped parsley

salt

freshly milled pepper

Cut the bacon into small dice and chop the onion finely. Fry them together with the garlic over a low heat until well cooked and soft. Remove from the heat and stir in the parsley and seasoning.

Variations

1. Use 1 oz (30 g) anchovy fillets, pounded to a paste, instead of bacon.
2. Salami can be substituted for bacon. Add it to the softened garlic and onion.
3. Use 3 tablespoons finely chopped parsley and no meat or fish. Fry the onion and garlic in the oil. Stir in the parsley and fry for another minute.
4. If preferred or more appropriate, any of these enrichments can be cooked with 1 oz (30 g) butter, and another 1 oz butter or 3 to 4 tablespoons thick cream added towards the end of cooking. The parsley can be varied with other fresh herbs as available.

ANCHOVY BUTTER

8-10 anchovy fillets

2 oz (60 g) butter

1 dessertspoon lemon juice

freshly milled black pepper

Chop the anchovy fillets to a slush. Soften the butter in a very warm place such as over a radiator until it is like thick mayonnaise but not melted. Beat the anchovy, lemon juice and quite a lot of pepper into the butter. To serve, either keep the anchovy butter in a warm place and serve it in a bowl with a spoon, or scoop the mixture into a small piece of greaseproof paper. Roll up into an even sausage about $\frac{1}{2}$ inch (1 cm) thick and chill till firm. Cut into slices for serving.

HERB BUTTER

1 tablespoon chopped watercress
　leaves and stalks
1 dessertspoon chopped parsley
1 dessertspoon chopped chives
2 oz (60 g) butter
2 dessertspoons lemon juice

Any combination of fresh green herbs and garlic can be used, but this is a good basic mixture. Soften the butter in a warm place, when it is like thick mayonnaise but not melted, beat in the other ingredients. Serve in the same way as anchovy butter.

RED PEPPER AND ONION

1 small onion
1 small clove garlic, peeled and
　crushed with salt
2 tablespoons olive oil
1 small red pepper
1 tablespoon chopped parsley
salt
freshly milled pepper

Chop the onion and fry it with the garlic in the oil for 5 minutes. Seed and chop the pepper and add it. Fry for another 10 minutes over a gentle heat until the pepper is soft and cooked. Stir in the parsley and seasoning and cook a few minutes more.

Variations

1. Use salami instead of onion, adding it when the pepper is half cooked.
2. Use 2 to 3 large, ripe, peeled tomatoes instead of the red pepper. Cook for only 5 minutes after adding the tomatoes.
3. Use 2 medium onions instead of red pepper and onion.
4. Use 3 to 4 oz (90 to 110 g) diced mushrooms instead of the red pepper. Cook for only 5 minutes after adding the mushrooms.

5. If preferred or more appropriate, any of these enrichments can be cooked in 1 oz (30 g) butter and another 1 oz butter or 3 to 4 tablespoons thick cream added towards the end of cooking. The parsley can be varied with other fresh herbs as available.

PEPERONATA

1 to 2 cloves garlic, peeled and crushed with salt	2 large ripe tomatoes, peeled
	or 2 fresh or dried chilis
1 small onion (optional)	1 teaspoon dried basil *or* 6 fresh
2 to 4 tablespoons fruity olive oil	basil leaves, chopped
1 small red pepper	salt

Fry the crushed garlic and onion in 2 tablespoons of the olive oil. Dice the pepper and add. Fry for another 5 minutes. Dice the tomatoes and chop the chilis, removing the seeds if you are using fresh ones. Add them with the basil and tomatoes. Partly cover the pan and leave to simmer for 20 minutes. Taste and add salt. Add the remaining olive oil if you like.

PESTO

Pine nuts are ludicrously expensive, but do give the right flavour and texture to a pesto. However walnuts make a pleasant substitute, and at a pinch you can use fresh wholemeal breadcrumbs. The basil used *must* be fresh.

2 oz (60 g) pine nuts	salt
2 cloves garlic, peeled and crushed with salt	freshly milled pepper
	4 to 6 tablespoons olive oil
small handful fresh basil or basil and parsley mixed	

Pound or grind the pine nuts to a paste. Chop the basil leaves with the garlic. Mash all three together in a bowl with salt and pepper. Now add the oil by degrees to make a thick paste. Alternatively the nuts, basil and garlic can be ground in a blender or food processor, but the oil should still be added by hand or the result will be too smooth.

43

ROUILLE

This delicious red pepper and garlic sauce is mainly used as a final enrichment and liaison (binder) in Mediterranean fish soups from France, but it is also a treat in hearty vegetable soups such as Minestrone or Pistou.

1 small red pepper	4 tablespoons olive oil
1 to 2 cloves garlic, peeled and crushed with salt	6 tablespoons water
	cayenne
2 slices wholemeal bread	salt

Cut the pepper in half and remove the seeds. Grill the halves slowly all over until the skin is blackened and the flesh quite soft. This is a fiddly job, but don't neglect it, for it makes a great difference to the final flavour. Rub off the blackened skin. Cut up the soft inside of the pepper and put it in a blender with the bread (also cut up), garlic, oil and water. Blend to a smooth paste. Season with salt and cayenne. For a slightly coarser texture, pound all the ingredients together by hand to make a paste, adding the water at the end.

Soup Recipes

Almonds

ALMOND CREAM SOUP

This is an adaptation of a popular eighteenth-century dinner party soup. In her excellent cookery book written in the middle of that century, Hannah Glasse suggested putting a 'French roll' spiked with slivered almonds in the bottom of the tureen and pouring the soup over it. For this reason, she said, the French often called it Hedgehog Soup – *au porc-épic*. She didn't say who, if anyone, got to eat the hedgehog. Don't try to make this soup with blanched almonds, factory white bread and nasty wine, or you will be disappointed. Good-quality almonds in their brown skins are available from most health and whole food shops.

3 shallots *or* 1 very small onion
2 to 3 sticks celery
1 oz (30 g) butter
2 oz (60 g) almonds with skins on
1 medium slice, 1 oz (30 g) wholemeal bread without crusts
¼ teaspoon orange rind *or* 1 teaspoon orange flower water

½ small glass good fruity hock or moselle wine
1 pint (600 ml) good chicken stock
salt
freshly milled pepper
½ pint (300 ml) single cream *or* ¼ pint (150 ml) cream and ¼ pint (150 ml) milk

Peel the onion or shallots and chop them roughly with the celery sticks. Sweat them in the butter in a heavy saucepan over a low heat for 5 minutes, stirring occasionally until they are slightly soft but not brown. Grind the almonds with their skins in a coffee grinder or blender, adding the bread when the almonds are nearly done. Add the breadcrumb and ground almond mixture to the onion and celery and cook gently for a couple of minutes, stirring all the time. Add the wine, a little salt and pepper, the orange rind or orange flower water and the stock. Bring to the boil and simmer very gently for 30 minutes. Blend the soup with the cream until it is a velvety beige with darker flecks. At this point the soup may be stored, well covered, in the fridge overnight.

Reheat gently in a clean pan. Do not let it boil, but when it is hot adjust the seasoning and the consistency by thinning with a little more cream or thickening with another spoonful of fine, fresh crumbs. Serve from a tureen if you can, plain or *au porc-épic*.

Variations

1. Use all milk and cream and leave out the chicken stock.
2. Halve the amount of celery and add the finely chopped green stalks of a ½ bunch of watercress to the onion and celery mixture. Add the chopped watercress leaves when you reheat the soup.
3. Use olive oil instead of butter and 1 small clove of garlic, crushed with a little salt, and a medium red pepper instead of the celery. Use 1½ pints (900 ml) chicken stock or water for the liquid. Add a second slice of crumbed bread, 1 teaspoon chopped parsley and a pinch of saffron (optional), and leave out the cream.

See also:
Aubergine, Red Pepper and Coconut Soup, Variation 1
Purée of Broad Beans with Toasted Almonds
Green Bean and Cashew Nut Cream Soup, Variation 3
Cauliflower and Watercress Soup, Variation 1
Basic Purée of Celeriac, Variation 2
Celery, Almond and Walnut Cream
Chicken: Mulligatawny Soup
Purée of Lettuce Soup with Sour Cream, Variation 3
Garnishes and Accompaniments: almonds, p. 31

Anchovies

See under:
Enrichments: bacon, parsley and onion, Variation 1. p. 41
Anchovy butter, p. 41

Apples

APPLE, RYE AND SOUR CREAM SOUP

If you have boiled a piece of bacon or gammon recently and have $\frac{1}{2}$ pint of the cooking liquid left, this is a very cheap, quick soup. It looks pretty with its garnish of rye bread croûtons and red-rimmed apple slices, and was, to my surprise, much liked by three hearty male guests. It is best eaten the same day.

1 small onion	$\frac{1}{2}$ pint (300 ml) bacon or ham
1 stick celery	stock, smoked for preference
1 oz (30 g) butter *or* 2 table-	$\frac{1}{2}$ pint (300 ml) milk
spoons vegetable oil	5 tablespoons sour cream
3 slices light rye bread without	1 red apple for garnish
crusts	$\frac{1}{2}$ oz (15 g) butter and 1
2 crisp green apples – Coxes,	tablespoon oil for frying the
Worcesters or Granny Smiths	croûtons
$\frac{1}{4}$ teaspoon caraway seeds	freshly milled pepper

Slice the onion and celery and sweat them in the butter or oil in a heavy pan for 6 to 7 minutes. Add one slice of bread, roughly crumbled, and stir it around. Meanwhile peel and core the green apples, chop them roughly and add them with the caraway seeds to the onion, celery and bread mixture. Cook, stirring, for a minute and then add the bacon stock. Cover the pan and bring it to the boil. Simmer for 10 to 15 minutes until the celery is tender. Blend the soup with the milk and sour cream, or put through the medium plate of a food mill. Return to a clean pan. Cut the red apple, unpeeled, into 4 vertically and remove the core. Slice each section thinly into the soup. Put the soup over a low heat and stir it occasionally as it heats. Cut the other 2 slices of bread into small dice and fry them, turning continually, in the butter and oil until crisp (see pps. 27-81). Place on kitchen paper to drain and cool. When the soup is hot, taste it and add fresh pepper; you are unlikely to need salt. When the soup is at simmering point and the apple slices just beginning to soften, serve with a bowlful of the croûtons handed separately.

Variations

1. This soup can be served without blending or sieving, in which case you may like to cut the vegetables, bread and green apples smaller. It then becomes a kind of apple chowder.
2. You can use all ham stock, or a ham stock cube, but take care that the soup does not become too salty. You could also use all milk, in which case watch that it doesn't boil over. It is better to add the minimum necessary to cook the soup to begin with, and the rest later. You may also like to add a little soy sauce to give the soup some zest.
3. Wholemeal bread can be used instead of rye.
4. To make a main course soup, bacon or ham dice can be added.
5. Yogurt can be used instead of cream and the amount of butter or oil used for sweating reduced to 1 teaspoon if you prefer a low calorie or low animal fat soup.

See also:
Cabbage Soup with a Meat Crust, Variation 1
Pheasant and Quince Cream, Variation 2

Apricots

See under:
Mutton, Rice and Apricot Soup

Artichokes

CREAM OF JERUSALEM ARTICHOKE SOUP

Beneath the whiskery, knobbly, misshapen-potato look of Jerusalem artichokes, in the shops just after Christmas, is a flavour every bit as enticing as that of their glamorous globe artichoke taste-alikes, and the price makes them more attractive. The only difficulty is peeling them. It is undoubtedly more nutritious to make the soup with skins and all, but it has rather a grubby tinge. I have suggested a couple of ways round this problem, one in the main recipe and one in Variation 1, but you may prefer to peel them in the ordinary way.

1¼ lb (560 g) cleaned, dewhiskered Jerusalem artichokes *or* 14 oz (400 g) peeled artichokes
1 small onion *or* 6 shallots *or* 1 bunch spring onions
juice of 1 small or ½ large lemon
small pinch of cayenne *or* dash of tabasco
salt
freshly milled pepper
1½ pints (900 ml) water
¼ pint (150 ml) *crème fraîche* (see p. 142 or sour cream

If you are not peeling the artichokes, scrub them very thoroughly with a pan-scourer, changing the water several times, and cut into thick slices. Put the sliced artichokes and the onions, also roughly sliced, with the lemon juice, salt, pepper, and cayenne or tabasco in a stainless steel or enamelled pan, and pour boiling water over them. Boil for 20 minutes or until the artichokes are nicely soft – if you overcook, the fresh flavour will be lost. Blend the soup and then sieve out the skins if you wish, or, better, put it through the medium plate of a food mill, discarding the last 2 tablespoons of skinny mixture in the food mill. Taste the soup and add more salt, lemon or cayenne if required. Reheat in a clean pan and serve with no distractions from the beautiful flavour except a dollop of *crème fraîche* or sour cream in each bowl.

Variations

1. Boil the artichokes whole for 10 minutes in water. Pour away the cooking water and cover with fresh cold water. When they have cooled sufficiently, pinch up a little peel between your thumb and a paring knife, and a little sheet of artichoke skin will come away. It is still a fiddly job. When you have finished, slice the artichokes thickly and boil with the onion as before, but use only 1¼ pints (750 ml) boiling water and cook the soup for 15 minutes or a little less.
2. Use chicken stock (not a cube), vegetable stock (see pps. 263-4) or milk instead of water.
3. This is already quite a low calorie soup, but if you are slimming you can use stock instead of water and leave out the cream.

Asparagus

ASPARAGUS PURÉE WITH CREAM

The Saturday after Derby Day in June is traditionally the last day for cutting English asparagus, by which time the stalks are fat and scaly. This soup is best made with the young, green 'sprue', so start looking out for it in mid-May. Buy the freshest you can find and then invent an occasion worthy of this delicate marvel.

6 shallots *or* 1 bunch spring
  onions
1 to 1½ lb (450 to 675 g) young
  asparagus – you will need the
  larger amount if the sprue has
  whitish-grey ends to the
  stalks, or looks a bit limp
just over 1 pint (600 ml) water
½ oz (15 g) plain flour

1½ oz (40 g) unsalted butter
1 tablespoon lemon juice
salt
freshly milled pepper
¼ pint (150 ml) single or double
  cream
1 tablespoon chopped chives or
  chervil

Slice the peeled and trimmed shallots or spring onions and put in a stainless steel or enamelled pan with the butter. Sweat them gently for a minute or two over a low heat. Trim off and discard any greyish bottoms to the asparagus and, holding all the stems in a tight bunch and starting at the bottom of the stalks, cut them into very thin slices (¼ in or less) until you are left with 2 in (5 cm) asparagus tips. Cut these tips into thicker slices and reserve them. Bring a generous pint of water to the boil and salt it. Add the washed asparagus stalk slices and boil briskly for 5 minutes. Stir the flour into the onion and butter, then add the stalk slices and their cooking water. Add the lemon juice, salt and pepper and simmer, partly covered, for 20 minutes. Put the soup through the fine plate of a food mill, being careful to scrape every last bit down into the mill and from the bottom of the plate after the mixture has been passed through. Alternatively the soup can be blended and then pushed through a sieve with the back of a ladle to discard any tough bits; scrape the bottom of the sieve thoroughly. Put this purée into a clean stainless steel or enamel pan, and add the cream plus a little water if the soup is still too thick. Bring it gently to the boil, throw in the reserved asparagus tips and simmer for exactly 5 minutes. Check the seasoning and serve sprinkled with the chopped herbs.

Variation

To make a soup for slimmers, sweat the shallot or onion dry (without fat), or with only a very little butter; leave out the lemon and use plain yogurt instead of cream.

See also:
Cream of Chicken Soup, Variation 3

Aubergines or Egg Plants

TREATING FOR BITTERNESS

All aubergines and some mature courgettes need this treatment to reduce their bitterness. Slice the vegetables or dice them, according to the needs of the recipe. Put a layer of vegetables in the bottom of a sieve or colander and sprinkle heavily with salt; continue to add alternate layers until all the vegetables are used up. Put the sieve or colander over a bowl and leave to drain for at least 30 minutes. When draining is complete, the vegetables should be quite limp and flabby, with a lot of juice in the bowl. Rinse off the salt in a large bowl of cold water; you may need more than one change of water. Taste a piece to make sure it is not excessively salty before proceeding with the recipe.

Alternatively, the diced or sliced vegetables can be left to soak in plenty of heavily salted water for the same time and then rinsed as above.

AUBERGINE, RED PEPPER AND COCONUT SOUP

The exotic but delicate flavour of an aubergine is easily overwhelmed by accompanying ingredients, as is its subtle texture. Both flavour and texture seem enhanced by a rich and aromatic oiliness such as that of ratatouille or the tomato and aubergine enrichment on p.40. In this soup the basic liquid, made from coconut milk, spices and tomatoes, is simmered, and the diced aubergines and red pepper fried separately and added only shortly before serving. Served fourth in a dinner consisting of five vegetarian soups, it was picked as the favourite by several tasters, though by that time they were all feeling like over-filled hot water bottles.

1 medium aubergine
¼ fresh coconut *or* 3 oz (90 g) desiccated coconut
1 pint (600 ml) water
3½ oz (100 g) canned tomatoes *or* 4 oz (110 g) fresh tomatoes
½ inch (1 cm) slice of peeled

green ginger, grated, *or* ½ teaspoon ground ginger
¼ teaspoon ground chili or cayenne *or* shake of tabasco sauce
1 teaspoon ground coriander
1 medium bright red pepper

2 tablespoons vegetable oil	freshly milled pepper
1 clove garlic, peeled and	fresh coriander leaves or flat
crushed with a little salt	parsley leaves for garnish
salt	(optional)

Cut the aubergine into ½ in (1 cm) dice and stir in 2 teaspoons salt. Leave in a bowl or colander for at least 30 minutes, then rinse and drain as described on p.52. Grate the coconut, if fresh, cover it (or the dessicated coconut) with 1 pint (600 ml) boiling water and leave to soak for 20 minutes. If you are using fresh tomatoes, peel and core them (described on pps.247-8). Chop the pulp, fresh or canned, into a slush. Squeeze the coconut in the water with your hand to extract more of the coconut flavour, then sieve the coconut milk into a heavy pan. Squeeze the milk out of the coconut. The coconut may now be used to obtain a second, lighter, milk or discarded. Add the tomatoes and spices to the coconut milk and bring to the boil. Simmer very gently, partly covered. Put the oil in a frying pan and add the garlic and aubergine. Fry for 5 minutes over quite a high flame until brown and nearly cooked. Slice the red pepper finely, add it to the aubergine and stir. Fry for another minute or two. Add this mixture to the soup and simmer for a minute or two longer. Taste and add salt at this point, if needed. Serve at once, plain or garnished with coriander or flat parsley leaves, or cool and refrigerate overnight.

Variations

1. 1½ oz (40 g) ground unblanched almonds can be used instead of coconut. Add them directly to the pan with the water and spices.
2. The coconut can be left out and the quantity of tomato doubled. The soup will have a more familiar flavour in this variation, but will lose its rich sweetness, so you may like to use more oil, perhaps olive oil.
3. If you are in a real hurry the soup can be made in a single process, frying the aubergines and peppers and then adding the coconut milk, but some of the aubergine flavour and texture will be lost.

See also:
Enrichments: aubergine caviar, p.40; aubergine and tomato, p.40

Avocado

ICED AVOCADO CREAM SOUP

This is not a way of using up over-ripe avocados with stringy black bits lurking in their interiors, or bullet-hard under-ripe ones either. You must use perfect ripe fruit that would be delicious eaten raw. Since this soup neither keeps nor freezes, though it is very simple to make, it is really a luxury for the avocado addict. It must not be made more than a few hours before serving since avocado flesh blackens on contact with the air.

3 medium or two large avocados, ripe enough to yield under the pressure of a gentle thumb
$\frac{3}{4}$ pint (450 ml) cold chicken stock
juice of a small lemon
salt, freshly milled pepper

dash of tabasco or a pinch of cayenne
$\frac{1}{4}$ pint (150 ml) sour or single cream
Garnish:
$\frac{1}{2}$ avocado
1 tablespoon chopped chives

Using a silver or stainless knife, cut the avocados in half vertically and prise out the stone. Scoop all the flesh into the blender jar. Keep the optional $\frac{1}{2}$ avocado for garnish cut-side down on a plate in the fridge until you are ready to serve the soup. Add the chicken stock, tabasco, salt, pepper and lemon to the avocado in the blender and blend. Taste and adjust seasoning, bearing in mind that iced foods need extra seasoning and that the soup will be diluted with cream. Scrape the mousse-like soup into a non-metal container which will fit into, or just under, the freezing compartment of your fridge. If possible, the container should have high sides so the minimum avocado is exposed to the air. Stir the cream smooth and pour it delicately on to the surface of the purée to form an insulating layer. Fold a sheet of greaseproof paper (cling film is not air-tight) to the size of the surface area of the container and rest it just in contact with the cream. This is the second insulating layer, separating the avocado from the blackening air. Chill for 30 min. in the freezer or 1 hour in the fridge. Take out the soup and stir in the cream, leaving a slight ripple if you like. Taste once more and serve in bowls which show off the beautiful colour. If you like, garnish each bowl with very thin peeled slices of the avocado, cut vertically, say three to each bowl and a scatter of chopped chives.

Variations

1. Substitute 4 tablespoons dry white wine, say a chablis or white burgundy for an equal amount of stock and part or all of the lemon juice.
2. Vegetable or mild ham stock can be used instead of chicken.
3. You could add a tiny dusting of allspice, say 3 berries crushed, but don't cover the avocado flavour.

Bacon and Ham

BACON OR HAM STOCK

The meaty smoked ham bone which our parents and grandparents were advised to use for ham stock is now an expensive and much sought after item which you are unlikely to get unless you are a good customer of a delicatessen or an especially enterprising butcher. It is therefore necessary to devise other sources of ham and bacon flavouring. A joint of boiling bacon gives quite good value for money, and, if released from its polythene cooking bag, will make a respectable stock. If you don't want meat for slicing, a bacon hock will make an even better stock. An individually cured piece of ham or bacon, however, will give a far more delicate and interesting flavour. The home-curing of pork is much easier than one would think – see Jane Grigson's excellent *Charcuterie and French Pork Cookery*.

Good-quality all-meat pork sausages, which usually means sausages bought from a continental butcher or delicatessen, will give a pleasant, light ham flavour to the water in which they are boiled. Even a piece of ham skin will give depth of flavour and richness to a split pea or lentil soup.

For 3 pints (1.75 l):

1 piece of ham or bacon weighing at least 2 lb (1 kg) – the meat can be either smoked or green

5 to 6 pints (3 to 3.5 l) cold water

1 medium onion *or* onion trimmings weighing 3 oz (90 g)

2 small carrots weighing 3 to 4 oz (90 to 110 g) together *or* 1 small parsnip or turnip

2 sticks celery *or* an equivalent-sized piece of celeriac

2 fresh parsley stalks

2 big sprigs thyme or marjoram (*or* 2 teaspoons dried)

NB The following spices can be reduced by half if the ham or bacon is individually cured with spices:

2 bay leaves and 2 cloves *or* 10 to 12 allspice or juniper berries
small piece of cinnamon

small piece of nutmeg or mace
15 to 20 peppercorns

Soak the piece of ham or bacon in cold water overnight. Salty stock (and ham stock can be very, very salty) is unpleasant. Next day drain the ham, put it in a large pan and cover with fresh water. Bring very slowly to simmering point and skim off any grey scum that rises. When only white foam is rising (after 10 minutes or so) add the vegetables, spices and herbs. Leave to simmer on top of the stove over a very low heat, so that one bubble breaks the surface every second or so, or put the pan, covered, into a low oven (300°F, 150°C, Gas 2) or cook in a slow cooker. The meat will be ready for using in another dish in about 1½ hours if cooked on top of the stove, in 2 to 3 hours if cooked in the oven, and in 10 hours or so if done in a slow cooker. The more slowly the meat is cooked, the better flavoured will be the stock. Strain the stock, cool and refrigerate, or use at once.

Bacon or ham stock keeps very well because of its high salt content. For storage purposes it can be reduced to a glaze in the same way as chicken stock (see p.118).

See:
Red Bean and Bacon Soup
Beef: Oxtail, Bacon and Vegetable Soup
Smoked Haddock Chowder, Variation 1
French Onion Soup, Variation 4
Split Pea and Bacon Soup
Tripe Chowder, Variation 2
Tripe: Zuppa di Trippa alla Milanese, Variation 3
Vegetables: Garbure
Vegetables: Gonlaschsuppe
Vegetables: Minestrone, Variation 1
Rich Venison Soup with Port
Enrichments: bacon, parsley and onion, p.41

Barley

See under:
Lamb and Mutton: Scotch Broth

Bass

SEA BASS, VERMOUTH AND GARLIC SOUP

Making a soup from a firm-fleshed, delicately flavoured fish which has to be imported from the Mediterranean is downright extravagant. But it can be the centrepiece of the meal, and the quality of flavour is such that you are transported to a table among pines, with the sea lapping a few yards away and the warm night filled with the sound of cicadas. Serve with very fresh, warm French bread and unsalted butter, and young red wine.

1 12 oz (350 g) sea bass (gutted weight)
1¼ pints (750 ml) water
1 sherry glass red or sweet white vermouth
2 sprigs fennel *or* 8 seeds fennel
salt

freshly milled pepper
1 small red pepper, seeded
2 cloves garlic, peeled and crushed with a little salt
6 ripe tomatoes – 8 oz (225 g) after peeling and coring
2 tablespoons fruity olive oil

Put the whole, gutted fish in a large stainless or enamelled pan with the water, vermouth, fennel, salt and pepper. Bring very slowly to simmering point and simmer very gently until just cooked (12 to 15 minutes). Lift out as soon as the fish flesh gives under the gentle pressure of a finger. Leave to cool. Meanwhile grill the halved and seeded pepper until the skin blackens and peels away a bit. Rub off most of this charcoaly skin, but leave a little to get that slight charcoal-grilled flavour. Slice the pepper fairly finely. Peel and core the tomatoes as described on p.247-8, and chop the flesh roughly. Strain the fish cooking liquid into a bowl and rinse out the pan. Put in the olive oil and garlic and fry over a medium heat for 5 minutes. Add the tomatoes and leave to cook for a further 5 minutes over a lower heat. Very carefully remove the flesh from the sea bass in chunks ½ in (1 cm) or so square. Remove all the skin and bones. Add the fish cooking liquid to the tomato mixture and bring to simmering point. Add the bass and red pepper and simmer for 1 minute only, or the delicate texture of the fish will begin to spoil. Check seasoning and add salt, pepper and a touch more vermouth if needed. The soup can be kept overnight in the fridge; however the texture of the bass suffers rather in freezing.

Variations

1. To keep the authentic Mediterranean flavour, bream or red mullet can be used instead of bass. Otherwise any firm-fleshed fish will do.
2. A wineglass of red wine can be used instead of vermouth.
3. It might be interesting to try anis, ouzo, or any other aniseed-flavoured drink instead of both vermouth and fennel; try 2 tablespoons to start with.

Black Beans

See under:
Mung Bean and Black Olive Soup

Broad Beans

BROAD BEAN AND MUSHROOM SOUP

This is a really delicious soup which keeps and freezes well. If there is a glut of broad beans it is worth buying a large quantity and making several batches of the basic bean purée, which can be frozen and used later in any of the ways suggested in the variations.

2 lb (1 kg) broad beans in the pod
1 pint (600 ml) boiling water
1 small onion *or* 6 shallots *or* 1 bunch spring onions
4 oz (110 g) button or cup mushrooms, wiped clean and sliced finely

1 small clove garlic, peeled and crushed with a little salt (optional)
1 oz (30 g) butter or oil
¾ pint (450 ml) milk
¼ teaspoon salt
1 tablespoon fresh chopped basil, savory, chives or parsley

Pod the beans and put them in a stainless or enamelled pan. Pour over the boiling water and add the salt. Boil briskly for 8 minutes or until tender. Put through the medium plate of the food mill, or

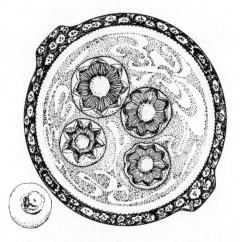

blend. If the beans are old and have tough skins, you may like to sieve out the skins after blending. About $\frac{1}{2}$ pint (300 ml) of thick purée will remain, which is the basic unit for freezing.

Chop or slice the onion finely or coarsely according to whether the soup is for an elegant party or a family lunch. Sweat it with the mushrooms and the garlic, if used, in the butter or oil for 5 minutes, or until soft but not brown. Add the bean purée and the milk. Heat through but do not boil. Taste and adjust seasoning. Stir in the chopped herbs just before serving.

Variations

1. If you have no fresh herbs, use $\frac{1}{4}$ teaspoon dried basil, marjoram or oregano, plus the grated rind of $\frac{1}{4}$ of a small orange or lemon. Add these to the mushroom and onion mixture and sweat them.
2. Instead of the onion and mushroom mixture, use one of these delicious alternative enrichments: aillade (p.40), bacon, parsley and onion (p.41), pesto (p.43).
3. For a low calorie soup, omit the mushroom and onion mixture and wash and finely slice 2 small leeks and cook with the broad beans. Leave a ladleful of the bean and leek mixture unpuréed to give texture to the soup, and add to the purée $\frac{3}{4}$ pint (450 ml) of liquid in the form of light stock or equal quantities of water and tomato juice. For a richer flavour add a clove of garlic and a teaspoon or two of really fruity olive oil.

59

PURÉE OF BROAD BEANS WITH TOASTED ALMONDS

This soup invents a new colour, 'bean green', and has an exquisitely earthy flavour. Since the recipe uses pods as well, it is essential to use young broad beans, which are available at the end of June and in early July. The soup is delicious, quick and easy, keeps well in the fridge and freezes well. It is, in fact, an ace.

2½ lb (1.2 kg) young broad beans
salt
1½ pints(900 ml) boiling water
1 small onion *or* 1 bunch spring
   onions *or* 6 shallots
1 oz (30 g) butter

¼ pint (150 ml) milk
¼ pint (150 ml) single or double
   cream
freshly milled pepper
1½ oz (40 g) flaked almonds
a little oil

Wash the pods thoroughly and cut away any decayed bits or stems. Open up the pods and slide the beans out of their damp, velvet hollows. Cut the pods into 2 inch (5 cm) pieces and put them into a stainless or enamelled pan with ¼ teaspoon salt. Pour the boiling water over the pods and boil them uncovered for 15 minutes or until soft. Meanwhile peel and roughly chop the onion, spring onions or shallots and sweat in the butter for 5 minutes. Add the beans and the milk and simmer for 7 minutes or until just tender. Blend the pods and their cooking water and then push them through a sieve with the back of a ladle or – a quicker method – put them through a food mill using the medium plate. Put this mixture back in the rinsed-out pan and then blend or mill the bean mixture. For a rougher texture you may like to leave a spoonful of beans whole, or to put them through the coarse plate of the food mill. Put the bean mixture in with the pod mixture, add the cream and taste. You will need pepper but not much salt. Put the almond flakes, mixed with a little salt and oil, under the grill and stir and turn them while they toast. Watch them carefully for they burn very easily. Reheat the soup, but do not boil. Serve with the almonds scattered on top.

Variations

1. For a slimmer's soup, use 1 teaspoon butter and substitute chicken stock for both the milk and the cream.

2. Chopped toasted cashews can be substituted for almonds, or the nuts can be left out and chopped chives, parsley or savory used instead.
3. Use 2 tablespoons oil (preferably olive) instead of the butter. Make as in the main recipe, then serve chilled with the hot toasted almonds. Alternatively substitute 2 tablespoons chopped chives as a garnish.

See also:
Green Bean and Cashew Nut Cream Soup, variation 2
Vegetables: Pistou, Variation 3

Dried Beans, Lentils and Peas

CHOOSING AND USING

Dried beans and peas are now immensely popular with young people, and a very good thing too, for pulses have skulked dustily in the backs of cupboards for far too long. Beans are good sources of protein, vitamin B and iron. The protein they contain does not fill all our dietary requirements, but is easily complemented by bread or other grain foods. Being fairly high in fibre and starch, yet fat-free, they are just the kind of food that nowadays we are encouraged to eat. Rose Elliott's *The Bean Book*, published by Fontana in 1979, lists 21 types of beans, peas and lentils, many of which are available in the whole food shops now found in most towns and cities. Pulses are generally much cheaper in these shops than in supermarkets, besides being much more varied, but do not buy too much at once because pulses are at their best in the year after harvesting.

Soaking

Dried beans and chick peas, but not lentils, split peas or the tiny mung beans, need to soak overnight in order to reabsorb water and swell a little before cooking. If the beans are newly harvested and only partly dried out this is not so important, but if fully dried beans are cooked without soaking they will not soften properly and you will spend time and money boiling them for longer than you really need have done. They should be left overnight in plenty of cold water, which is afterwards thrown away and not reused.

If you have forgotten to soak the beans, the same effect can be achieved by putting them in a pan with plenty of cold water (at least four times the volume of the beans) and bringing them very, very slowly to the boil. As soon as boiling point is reached, turn off the heat, cover the pan tightly and leave for 45 minutes. The beans can then be drained and used as if they had been soaked overnight. Salt prevents beans from softening and is therefore always added at the end of a recipe.

Recipes for the various types of dried beans, peas and lentils are listed alphabetically throughout the book under the name of the particular pulse being used.

Dried Mixed Beans

HARIRA

In Morocco, as in other Muslim countries, during the fast of Ramadan no food may be taken between sunrise and sunset. At sunset a cannon goes off and the entire population rushes into homes and restaurants to eat Harira, an extremely filling and sustaining mixture of chick peas, lentils, haricot beans or vermicelli, vegetables and lemon. It is excellent holiday food, needing no sieves or blenders and being made in a single process. It keeps and freezes well. The herbs and lemon juice should be added just before serving.

2 oz (60 g) chick peas
2 oz (60 g) brown lentils
1 heaped teaspoon coriander
½ teaspoon turmeric
1 medium onion
2½ pints (1.5 l) water or lamb stock
1 oz (30 g) vermicelli or small pasta

3 to 4 tomatoes – 6 to 8 oz (175 to 225 g) after peeling and coring
1 large clove garlic, peeled and crushed with a little salt
salt
freshly milled pepper
good handful parsley
juice of ½ to 1 lemon

Soak the chick peas overnight, or use the quicker method described (*see above*). Put the chick peas, lentils, coriander, tumeric and onion, sliced, in a heavy pan and cover with stock or fresh water. Bring to the boil and simmer until the chick peas are soft, which may take as long as 2½ hours. Add more water if necessary. Crush the chick peas against the sides of the pan with the back of a spoon, leaving some of them whole. You should have about 1½ pints (900 ml) of thick soup. Reduce the soup by fast boiling, or add more water as necessary. Add the vermicelli 15 minutes before you serve the soup. Peel the tomatoes (see pps. 247-8) and chop the parsley. Ten minutes before serving add the tomatoes, cut in pieces, the garlic and the lemon juice. Taste and adjust seasoning. The soup should be lemony and garlicky. Stir in the parsley and serve.

Variations

1. Chick peas and lentils are essential to this soup, but the pasta may be replaced by 1 oz (30 g) haricot beans or by 1 tablespoon wholemeal flour mixed into ¼ pint (150 ml) water and left in a warm place for a day or two to go sour and thick. Add this paste 30 minutes before serving.,
2. If you are using lamb stock, add a few tablespoons of diced cooked lamb just before serving.
3. The traditional herb to stir in is not parsley but fresh coriander leaves, which are available at Indian grocers.

Green Beans (French or Runner)

GREEN BEAN AND CASHEW NUT CREAM SOUP

Green beans and nuts, especially cashews and almonds, are one of those heavenly culinary marriages like strawberries and cream. The beans give the soup colour and a delicate flavour and the nuts richness and an interesting texture. British runner and French beans are in the shops from the end of June to the end of August, and they certainly have more flavour than the beautiful, uniform little French beans which are now flown in all the year round. Be careful, though, not to buy those old dark green beans which have strands of steel wool woven into the pods. Early July is the best time to find the perfect bean. The best source of broken cashews is a Chinese grocery shop.

1½ oz (40 g) broken cashews
1 small onion
3 small sticks celery
½ oz (15 g) butter *or* 1 tablespoon oil
1 pint (600 ml) chicken stock
salt
freshly milled pepper

6 oz (175 g) runner or French beans
½ pint (300 ml) boiling water
¼ pint (150 ml) or less milk or single cream
1 tablespoon chopped savory, parsley, chervil or marjoram

Grind the cashews in an electric coffee grinder, or put them in a heavy plastic bag and bash them with the end of a rolling pin. Toast the ground cashews under the grill, stirring frequently and watching them like a hawk for they burn in a second. Chop the onion and the celery into large dice and sweat them in the butter or oil for 5 minutes. Add the nuts, chicken stock, salt and pepper, and simmer gently, half-covered for 15 minutes. Meanwhile top, tail and string the beans and either slice them into little diamonds or put them through a bean slicer and then cut into 1 inch (2.5 cm) lengths. Put them in an enamelled or stainless pan and pour the boiling water over them. Add a pinch of salt and boil briskly for 5 to 7 minutes or until just tender. Strain them and keep the water. Run lots of cold water over the beans to set the colour. Blend the nut and celery mixture, or pass it through the food mill using the medium plate, and put into a clean pan. Add the bean water and some of the milk or cream to make the right consistency. Taste, then add the herbs and the beans. Reheat, simmer for a minute or so, and serve at once. The soup (with the beans in it) will keep beautifully overnight before reheating, but always add the herbs at the last minute.

Variations

1. Although a good chicken stock does give this soup a wonderful richness, vegetable stock or water or all milk will do instead. If you do not have chicken stock, 2 tablespoons lemon or orange juice are a good addition.
2. Four and a half ounces (125 g) broad beans without pods can be used instead of green beans. If you are a perfectionist, remove the skins of the individual beans after boiling them.
3. Use almonds, ground with their skins on, instead of cashews.
4. If you like a thicker soup, increase the nuts to 2 oz (60 g).

See also:
Beef: Meat Ball and Tomato Soup
Green Leaves: Zuppa di Verdura
Vegetables: Minestrone
Vegetables: Pistou

Mung Beans

MUNG BEAN AND BLACK OLIVE SOUP
(See cover photo)

Black bean soup, using more or less these ingredients, is a famous American dish, but the only black beans I have found in Britain tasted like minced egg boxes, so I have substituted mung beans, which are like drab green seed pearls and have a good lentil texture and flavour. If you have a supply of good black beans do try out this recipe with them. Without the garnishes, which should be freshly prepared, the soup keeps and freezes well.

1 small onion	salt
2 sticks celery	freshly milled pepper
3 tablespoons vegetable oil	*Garnish:*
1 small clove garlic, peeled and crushed with a little salt	1 oz (30 g) black olives, stoned and sliced
3 oz (90 g) mung beans	1 tablespoon chopped parsley
½ teaspoon cumin seeds	1 hard-boiled egg, sliced
2 pints (1.2 l) water	¼ pint (150 ml) sour cream
¼ pint (150 ml) fruity white wine	

Put the roughly chopped onion and celery, the oil and garlic in a heavy pan and sweat them over a low heat for 10 minutes, stirring occasionally. Add the mung beans (which don't need soaking) and the cumin seeds, and cook for another minute or two. Add the water and wine, bring to the boil and simmer, half-covered, for an hour or until the beans are soft. Add salt and pepper, then blend or mill the soup. At this point it can be stored in the fridge or frozen.

To serve the soup, add the sliced, stoned olives to it and reheat, simmer for a few minutes, taste and adjust the seasoning. Cut the sliced hard-boiled egg into quarter circles. Serve the soup and hand round separately the egg pieces, parsley and sour cream.

Variations

1. Besides black beans, lentils, split peas or red beans (which must be soaked) can be used in this soup.
2. The black olives used in the garnish do add to the flavour, but if you do not have any cut wedges of lemon instead.
3. A vegetable or meat stock can be used instead of water. Stock from a smoked ham bone would be particularly good.
4. For a hotter soup, use fennel or dill seeds instead of cumin and add a pinch of cayenne or a shake of tabasco.

Red Kidney or Other Red Beans

RED BEAN AND BACON SOUP

This is a very satisfying and nutritious main course soup. It keeps and freezes well, so when you have ham or bacon stock available it is worth making several times the quantity given and freezing some.

1 medium onion
$\frac{1}{2}$ oz (15 g) lard, pork fat or bacon fat
2 oz (60 g) good bacon or lean scraps of ham
2 oz (60 g) garlicky salami
4 oz (110 g) kidney beans, soaked overnight
2 pints (1.2 l) water or unsalty

ham or bacon stock (or half and half)
2 large fresh tomatoes, 4 oz (110 g) when peeled
salt
freshly milled pepper
2 tablespoons chopped parsley or marjoram

Chop the onion into small dice and sweat it in the fat in a heavy pan for 5 or 6 minutes. If you are using uncooked bacon, cut off the rind and bone, and slice the bacon into little strips about $\frac{1}{4}$ in ($\frac{1}{2}$ cm) wide. Add these to the onion mixture and cook for another minute or two. If you are using cooked ham or bacon, cut it and the salami into $\frac{1}{4}$ inch ($\frac{1}{2}$ cm) slices and then into strips about 1 inch (2.5 cms) long. Add them to the onion mixture and turn them over in it, but do not let them frizzle and harden. Drain the water off the beans and add them to the pan. The stock should be spicy with bay, clove etc., but not too salty or the beans will not soften. If your stock is salty, add only 1 pint (600 ml) water to the soup at this stage; if it is not salty, add all the liquid now. Bring the soup to the boil and simmer half-covered for 45 to 60 minutes, until the beans are tender. If the beans are threatening to dry out completely during cooking, add a little more water. When the beans are tender, add any salty stock and cook another 10 minutes. Purée the soup in the blender in a few short bursts, so as to leave some variety of texture, or better still put it through the coarse plate of a food mill. Add the peeled, cored and roughly chopped tomatoes (see pps.247-8). At this point the soup can be stored overnight or longer in the fridge, or cooled and frozen. To serve, reheat in a clean pan. Taste when it is hot and adjust the seasoning. The soup should be thick and comforting. Sprinkle each bowlful with chopped parsley or marjoram.

Variations

1. If you have neither blender nor food mill, squash the beans against the bottom of the pan with the back of a ladle or with a fork until you are satisfied with the consistency. You may also like to cut the ham and salami into larger pieces to suit this country version of the soup.
2. The stock from spiced salt beef makes a very good substitute for bacon stock. A ham stock cube will do if you must, but with good bacon and salami you can make a very good soup using just water.
3. If you are using water, or if your stock is dull, cook the soup with a bay leaf threaded on to a clove. Remove them before blending the soup.
4. Garlic can be added to the soup; and diced carrot, celery or even parsnip used instead of onion or instead of some of the beans. Substitute 2 oz (60 g) vegetable for 1 oz (30 g) beans

See also:
Mung Bean and Black Olive Soup, Variation 1
Beef: Jamaican Red Pea Soup
Tripe: Zuppa di Trippa alla Milanese, Variation 5
Vegetables: Minestrone

White Haricot Beans

BASIC BEAN PURÉE

A purée of white beans makes a pleasant and nutritious soup in itself, and can form the base of a hundred other soups. It freezes admirably, and it is well worth making several times the quantity given and freezing some of it, so that with the last-minute additions of any of the flavourings and enrichments suggested in the variations a whole range of more or less instant but still home-made soups can be produced. If you intend to make a large quantity of this soup, it is worth finding a source of good beans (see p.61), since some supermarket beans are very dull and very expensive.

5 oz (140 g) dried white haricot
  beans, soaked overnight
2½ pints (1.5 l) cold water
6 allspice berries *or* 1 clove plus a
  small piece of nutmeg and a
  small piece of cinnamon stick
8 black peppercorns

salt

If serving plain add:
1½ oz (40 g) butter *or* 3 tablespoons olive oil or 6 tablespoons double cream

Put the drained beans in a large stainless or enamelled pan and add the water and spices, but no salt. Bring the beans to the boil and simmer, half-covered, until tender. This will take about 1½ hours but may be more or less depending on the age of the beans. Allow the mixture to cool a little, then blend it or put it through the food mill. The spices can be removed first or not, as you like. Your preference for a smooth purée or a certain amount of texture will determine whether you use the medium or the coarse plate of the food mill, and whether you blend in short bursts or leave some of the beans unpuréed. Now make the soup up to 1½ pints (900 ml) if it has reduced too much, and add salt to taste. This is the basic bean purée. If you want to serve it plain – and if you have good beans, this is not to be sniffed at – reheat the purée and stir in a little butter, olive oil or thick cream. Bring just to the boil, taste and serve. Otherwise serve with any of the flavourings and enrichments listed below, or cool and store in the fridge, or freeze.

Variations

1. The soup can be made with chicken, beef, vegetable or game stock instead of water. Ham or bacon stock is delicious, but if it is salty it may take the beans longer to soften. It could be safer to cook the beans in less water and add bacon stock when puréeing the soup. In the same way, if you have only, say, ½ pint (300 ml) stock, the beans can be cooked in water and the stock added at the end.
2. The spices may be replaced with a bay leaf, or a couple of sprigs of fresh or 1 teaspoon of dried thyme or marjoram.
3. The simplest additional flavouring is a clove of garlic chopped with the leaves from 2 to 3 sprigs of parsley, or 8 to 10 fresh basil leaves, and fried for a minute in 3 tablespoons oil or 1½ oz (40 g) butter.
4. Good enrichments such as pesto (p.43), peperonata (p.43), aubergine caviar (p.40), cut mushrooms, salami and pepper, anchovy, tomato, bacon and onion and so on can be fried up in a minute or two and added to the basic purée just before serving.
5. If you intend to freeze the purée, you may prefer to make it in a more condensed form which takes up less space and can be diluted after defrosting. If so, reduce the cooking water by fast boiling when the beans are just about cooked, or cook them without a lid on the pan. If you are blending the soup you will need more liquid than if milling it. This method should give you ¾ pint (450 ml) batches for freezing, to which an equal amount of water or stock should be added when reheating.
6. Chopped herbs or tender green leaves and cream or sour cream also make lovely additions. See the following recipe, for Haricot Bean and Watercress Soup.

See also:
Tripe: Zuppa di Trippa alla Milanese
Vegetables: Pistou

HARICOT BEAN AND WATERCRESS SOUP

White beans and watercress do not sound an alluring combination, but in this French bourgeois recipe they form an elegant pale green cream with a delicate, peppery flavour. The soup also provides a surprisingly large amount of protein, calcium, vitamins A, B and C and iron. New season's beans from Soissons in France will be a revelation compared with any old year's crop of haricots 'from more than one country of origin'.

4 oz (110 g) white haricot beans, soaked overnight
1 bunch watercress (see notes on watercress, p.273)
2 pints (1.2 l) water
freshly milled pepper
1½ oz (40 g) butter

1 small onion
1 clove garlic, peeled and crushed with a little salt
1 pint (600 ml) milk
a little salt
about 6 tablespoons of single cream

Boil the soaked beans in the water with some pepper, but no salt, until tender; if the beans are this year's crop they will take 45 to 60 minutes to cook, if older up to 1½ hours. Melt the butter in a heavy stainless or enamelled pan. Slice the onion and sweat it with the garlic in the butter for 5 minutes or so. Stir the mixture occasionally and keep the pan covered in between. Keeping the watercress in a tight bunch, wash it, discarding any faded or yellow leaves. Chop the stalks roughly. Then chop the leaves for a garnish, finely or coarsely according to your taste, and keep them on one side. Take the pan off the heat and add the watercress stalks and the milk to the butter and onion mixture. Strain the beans, keeping some of the cooking liquid, and add them to the soup. Now blend the soup, then put it through a sieve, pressing with the back of a ladle, into a clean pan; this removes any fibrous pieces of stalk. Alternatively, if you enjoy a soup with texture, put the soup through the medium plate of a food mill, which will purée and sieve simultaneously. Add bean liquid until the soup is the right consistency. Up to this point the soup can be prepared in advance. Heat the soup and add salt at this point only, also more pepper if needed. Add the watercress leaves and cream and serve at once, before the fresh flavour and colour deteriorate.

Variations

1. Chicken, bacon or ham, or vegetable stock may be used instead of milk.
2. Half a small lettuce, or a good handful of sorrel, young beet leaves or nettle tops, or fresh green herbs such as parsley, savory, lemon balm or basil can be used instead of watercress. Add the scrappy bits to the butter and onion mixture and slice or chop the best

parts for the garnish.
3. Sour cream or *crème fraîche* (see p.142) can be used instead of fresh cream.

Beef

CHOOSING AND USING

The revolution in the role of women has had a few unfortunate consequences, one of them being the relative unavailability of mature bits of meat and marrow bone. When simmered together, these produce a depth of flavour which the meat of a young beast can't begin to match. Shin of beef from an older animal can often be bought in West Indian or Pakistani (Afro-Muslim) butchers, and shin of beef and marrow bones from bullocks, which will do well enough, can be supplied by most butchers if you telephone in advance. The butchery departments of supermarkets, too, are generally obliging. Don't start looking the day you want to make the soup, however, since many butchers only go to market once a week and get rid of all their bones to the bone man the same day. The shin (or leg) of beef will be very dark red and entirely lean. It is the best cut for stock because of its cheapness, leanness, hearty flavour and jellying quality. If you can't get it, any lean cheap cut will do. If you want to use the piece of beef for cutting, silverside or brisket will give you an attractive display piece of boiled beef plus some quite good stock. The stock can be made without bones, but if so is sadly lacking in flavour. Don't be fobbed off with whole marrow bones, for the marrow itself must be exposed to the boiling water; the bones must be at least cracked or, ideally, sawn into 3 inch (7.5 cm) lengths.

Since getting the ingredients may take a little organization it is worth making as large a quantity as you can fit on your stove, reducing the excess to a glaze (see Beef Stock and Broth) and keeping it in the fridge or freezer for future use as delicious home-made stock cubes. Bought beef stock cubes and beef extract are wonderfully convenient and seem to have a more authentic flavour than do chicken stock cubes, but home-made ones taste much better. Why not combine convenience and flavour?

If your beef stock was made without bones, you may like to add a little meat extract or a stock cube, but don't overdo it or your creation will taste like a canteen lunch.

71

BEEF STOCK AND BROTH

Many people tell me that no one will make a stock these days, let alone a beef stock with bones. But a home-made beef broth is not only cheap compared with any other way of eating beef, it is also extremely easy and will be much appreciated by those hearty old-fashioned eaters among your friends. You also have the bonus of another meal or two of hot boiled beef with spicy tomato sauce, or cold beef with garlic mayonnaise.

The stock takes 30 minutes or less to prepare but 5 to 6 hours to cook, plus another hour or two if you are making beef glaze, so choose a day when you do not need to go out much and make as much as you have pots for.

For about 3 pints (1.75 l) beef stock:
1½ lb (675 g) shin of beef or other muscular cut, in a piece
2 lb (1 kg) beef marrow bones, cut into 3 in (7.5 cm) lengths
2 small onions *or* the peelings, tops and tails from 4 to 6 onions
2 small carrots *or* the peelings, tops and tails from 4 to 6 carrots
2 sticks celery *or* the trimmings from 4 to 6 sticks
5 pints (3 l) cold water
10 peppercorns
1 bay leaf with a clove stuck into it
2 sprigs *or* 1 flat teaspoon dried thyme or marjoram
2 thin, short strips orange peel

Preheat the oven to 425°F (220°C, Gas 7) and put the bones and meat in a roasting tin. When the oven is hot, put in the tray and roast for 15 minutes in the hottest part of the oven. Take it out, turn the meat and bones over, and roast for a further 10 minutes. Meanwhile wash the vegetables and slice them roughly. Put the browned bones and meat in a large, heavy pan and cover with cold water. Put the pan over a low heat and bring it to the boil as slowly as possible. Let it boil for 10 minutes or so while you skim off all the greyish scum that rises. When only white foam is left, add the vegetables, herbs, spices and orange peel, but no salt. Turn the heat as low as possible, or use a stove mat to reduce the temperature so that one bubble breaks the surface every second or so. Leave it to cook for at least 3 hours. If the meat is brought quickly to the boil and then boiled fast, it will become hard and the stock cloudy. If you have an Aga type of oven, the meat and stock can be cooked overnight in the cooker oven; the new electric slow cookers also give good results.

Meat

When the beef is thoroughly tender, lift it out, cool and serve cold, sliced, with a dressing like mustard vinaigrette or avocado mayonnaise or serve hot with potatoes, carrots and onions boiled separately.

First Stock and Broth

Strain off the beef stock, but do not press the juice out of the vegetables or the stock will cloud. The first stock becomes broth when the excess fat is removed from the surface and salt and other seasoning are added. If you couldn't get beef bones, ginger it up with a little beef stock cube or meat essence, and use for recipes in which beef is the main ingredient, including consommé. When the first stock is cold it will jelly and a layer of fat will form on the surface, which acts as a preservative by insulating the stock against the air and should not be removed until you use the stock. The stock can be stored in the fridge in this way for several days, but by turning it into a glaze (see below) it can be stored in less space and for much longer.

Second Stock

A second stock can be made by covering the bones with fresh cold water and adding some more vegetables. It will be weaker and cloudy, and should be used to give body to bean or vegetable soups.

Meat Glaze and Stock Cubes

To make a glaze you will need at least 3 pints (1.75 l) of good stock. Put it in a clean, heavy pan and reduce it over a fairly high heat until only ½ pint (300 ml) remains. Now you must stand over it, for in the last stages of reduction it can easily burn and all your hard work will go to waste. Go on reducing the stock until you have perhaps ¼ pint (150 ml) or less and the liquid is dark brown and bubbling thickly like toffee. Pour it into egg cups or ice cube moulds. It is so thick that there will be a residue in the pan which should be used for gravy or in the second stock. The meat glaze will cool to a hard jelly. To store, dunk the bottoms of the moulds in very hot water, ease out the lumps of glaze and put in plastic bags. They can be kept for weeks in the fridge and for months in a freezer. It is obviously sensible to make as much glaze as possible at once. You will find your personal stock cubes have a depth of flavour and a body far superior to those of any bought stock cube or meat extract.

BIG BEEF BROTH

The main recipe is for 3 pints (1.75 l), double the usual quantity, in order that several different vegetables can be used. It works perfectly well in smaller quantities using fewer vegetables (see Variation 2), but you may find the large amount worth making as it keeps and freezes very well. The vegetables can be varied according to season and taste, but in any case this is a real one-pot meal, containing plenty of protein and vitamin A and some B and C.

8 oz (225 g) cooked boneless shin of beef (cooked with the stock; see p.72)
soy sauce
1 small onion
1 medium potato
1 medium carrot
2 oz (60 g) fresh runner or frozen

cut green beans
2 small courgettes
3 pints (1.75 l) good beef stock
1 clove garlic, peeled and crushed with a little salt (optional)
salt
freshly milled pepper

Cut the beef into cubes, removing all skin and gristle. Sprinkle it with soy sauce. Cut the onion, potato, carrot, beans and courgettes to the same size. Put the beef stock in a large pan over a low heat. Add the carrot, onion and garlic and some salt and pepper. Bring to the boil and simmer for 10 minutes. Add the potato and simmer a further 10 minutes. Add the courgettes and beans and simmer for 5 minutes. If you intend to serve the soup immediately, add the beef; otherwise add it when the soup is cold. Taste the soup and add more salt, pepper and soy sauce as required. At this point the soup can be cooled and refrigerated overnight, or longer in cool weather, or frozen. In any case it tastes better if made a few hours in advance and reheated just before serving.

Variations

1. If the ingredients for a proper beef stock are not available, cook 12 oz (350 g) shin of beef, cut across the leg and including the bone, in 4 pints (2.3 l) water to which have been added 2 beef stock cubes or 3 teaspoons beef extract, plus peelings from 2 to 3 onions and 2 to 3 carrots, 1 bay leaf, 2 sprigs of thyme or marjoram and a few peppercorns. When the beef is cooked lift it out, strain and skim the stock, make up to 2 pints (1.2 l) with water and proceed with the main recipe.
2. For a less robust soup, use only root vegetables and 3 to 4 oz)90 to 110 g) cooked shin of beef, and stir in 2 tablespoons chopped parsley just before serving.
3. Parsnip or turnip can be used instead of carrot; celery, cabbage or mushrooms instead of courgettes; peas, broccoli or canned sweetcorn instead of beans.
4. The amount of beef can be halved and replaced with more potato or other vegetables, or with beef balls (p.33), liver balls p.34) or suet dumplings (p.32).

CONSOMMÉ

At the turn of the century, when Escoffier cooked for King Edward VII, consommé cleared the palate after the *hors d'oeuvres muscovite* before our gluttonous forefathers got down to demolishing the next eight courses. Nowadays beginning a meal with a clear amber liquid, which takes only seconds to consume having taken hours to cook, seems an extravagance of both time and money. But a perfectly clear, perfectly flavoured consommé is a very satisfying achievement, and if you are already making beef broth it takes very little more time. It can be served plain, garnished in a hundred ways, or cold and jellied which is a most delicious appetizer in hot weather.

2 pints (1.2 l) good beef broth (see p.72)
2 egg whites
8 oz (225 g) lean raw shin of beef, minced or ground in a food processor
2 tablespoons madeira
salt
freshly milled pepper
any of the garnishes suggested in the variations
You will also need:
a large clean cloth, boiled for 10 minutes in plenty of plain water to get rid of any detergent or grease

Remove as much fat as possible from the beef broth. This is an easy operation if the broth is cold, since the fat becomes white and hard and can be lifted off. If the stock is warm, the grease must be delicately scooped off with a metal spoon and the last traces removed by drawing sheets of kitchen paper lightly across the surface of the soup. When only tiny beads of fat remain, pour the broth into a large, heavy pan. Mix the white of egg with the lean minced beef and then whisk both into the beef broth. Put the mixture over a low heat and bring to the boil, whisking constantly. A lot of thick, grey scum will form, which is the egg white cooking and collecting all the particles in the broth. When the mixture boils move the pan so that only one side is over the heat and leave it to boil gently for 10 minutes. Meanwhile put the boiled cloth in a large sieve over a bowl. Pour the mixture slowly into the cloth. When most of the liquid has drained through, pick up the corners of the cloth and draw them together to encourage a little more liquid through. Do not squeeze the cloth, though, or the consommé will cloud. You will now have about 1½ pints (900 ml) of clear consommé. Feed the mince and egg mixture to a dog or cat. Put the consommé back in a very clean pan, add the madeira and reheat. Taste when hot and add salt and pepper if necessary. Serve quite plain in pretty soup cups, or with any of the garnishes suggested below. The consommé will keep well for several days.

Variations

1. Cool the consommé and refrigerate in a non-metal container. It will form a jelly. Break the jelly up with a fork and pile into pretty cups. Serve as cold as possible, plain or topped with chopped chives and *crème fraîche* (see p.142).
2. Madeira is the best addition to a consommé, but any spirit, dry sherry or port can be used instead.

Garnishes:

3. A garnish for consommé must be very small and very elegantly cut; it is much better to serve consommé plain than to fill it with great lumps of floating vegetable. The great Victorian and Edwardian cookery writers give dozens of suggestions for consommé garnishes.
(i) Roll 4 lettuce leaves into a cigar shape and cut across into the thinnest possible slivers. Boil in ½ pint (300 ml) water for 3 minutes. Drain, and cover with cold water. Drain and add to the consommé 1 minute before serving.

(ii) Peel, core and seed 2 scarlet tomatoes (see p.247). Dice the flesh into $\frac{1}{4}$ in ($\frac{1}{2}$ cm) pieces. Add to the consommé 1 minute before serving.

(iii) Slice 8 button mushrooms into very thin, even slices. Sauté for 1 minute in a very little oil. Add to the consommé just before serving.

(iv) Peel a small, sweet orange, removing all pith and pips. Peel the skin off each individual segment, and then cut the flesh into tiny dice. Add to the consommé just before serving.

(v) Drop about 24 fresh tarragon leaves, separated into individual leaves, into a little boiling water. Boil for 1 minute. Drain and cover with cold water. Add to the soup after draining just before serving.

(vi) Use croûtons (p.27), omelette shreds (p.30), or noodles (p.37), but use only half the quantity given and cut them very finely.

(vii) Julienne carrots and vermicelli.

POT AU FEU

In these days of expensive fuel, small families and limited storage space the Pot au Feu is no longer a convenience, but it is pleasant on occasion to prepare a dish with a long and famous history. If there are visitors staying a Pot au Feu will provide a beef broth and the basis for at least one more soup, plus a main course and extra beef for cold meals and sandwiches. It is easier to serve the hot beef main course first, and the broth on the following day. Any remaining broth can be reduced to a glaze (see pps.73-4) for long-term storage. The silverside listed in the ingredients keeps its shape well, makes good-quality stock and does not get too dry. The veal and oxtail, both optional, will give added body and flavour. Serve with slices of French bread baked hard in the oven and then reheated.

To make 4 to 5 pints (2.3 to 3 l) beef broth, of which 1½ pints (900 ml) is garnished for serving:

1 lb (450 g) chicken giblets	2 parsley stalks
6 inch (15 cm) section of marrow bone, both ends removed	10 peppercorns
	2 medium leeks, trimmed
1 knuckle of veal and/or 1 oxtail (both optional)	2 carrots, peeled
	1 onion, cut in 4 but not peeled
3 lb (1.35 kg) silverside, in a piece	1 small turnip
6 pints (3.5 l) water	1 stick celery
2 bay leaves	salt
1 sprig thyme or marjoram	slices of pre-baked French bread

The steamer/stockpot described on p.16 comes in particularly handy for this soup, but any large, heavy pan, with high, straight sides if possible, will do.

Put the chicken giblets, marrow bone and veal knuckle and oxtail, if you are using them, in the bottom of the pan. Place the beef, tied into a nice shape if you like, on top, cover with the water and bring to the boil as slowly as possible. As it begins to boil, greyish scum will rise to the surface. Skim it all off very thoroughly. When only white foam is rising, add the seasonings, vegetables and salt. Turn the heat as low as possible and simmer, partly covered, for 3 to 4 hours. This is also very successful done in a slow oven (300°F, 150°C, Gas 2) for 4 to 5 hours. When the beef is very tender, lift it out and serve it with separately cooked vegetables and a little of the stock for gravy.

Strain the stock, keeping the oxtail and the leeks and carrots in a bowl with a little of the broth. A second, weaker, stock may be made with the giblets, veal and marrow bone. Leave the main stock overnight, and next day lift off the hardened fat and use it for frying, etc. Measure $1\frac{1}{2}$ pints (900 ml) of the stock into a pan and heat it, and put the pre-baked bread slices in the oven to heat. Dice the leeks and carrots. When the stock is hot taste it and adjust the seasoning. Add the leek and carrot dice, simmer for a minute and serve with the hot baked bread. The rest of the stock and the oxtail can be used for other soups.

Variations

1. The marrow bone can be tied up in some cheese cloth or a very clean piece of old tea towel and put in the pan 45 minutes before the end of cooking. Untie the cloth, scoop out the marrow and spread it on the baked bread slices before they are heated.
2. Two soft, ripe, red tomatoes, cut in quarters, can be added to the stock with the other vegetables to give it a good colour.
3. Instead of the traditional garnish of overcooked leek and carrot, fresh rings of leek and dice of carrot can be cooked in the broth, or the broth can be served with $1\frac{1}{2}$ oz (40 g) cooked rice or small pasta and garnished with a chiffonade made from 6 lettuce leaves sliced very finely (see p.31).
4. For a special occasion, cook with the beef a chicken stuffed with minced pork and herbs instead of the chicken giblets.

JAMAICAN RED PEA SOUP

This recipe and the Pepperpot Soup on p.84-5 are the standard cheap lunch in Jamaica. They are both quite simple combinations of beef and vegetables which make a good main course dish and can be varied endlessly. Either will blow your head off. This is a tamed European version which lacks the fat, gristle and fire of the original but still has plenty of character. Since the soup has many ingredients, it is best made in large quantities: this recipe makes 3 pints (1.75 l) or a little more. It keeps well for several days and freezes very well indeed, so it is worth making in even larger quantities and adding a greater variety of vegetables (see Variation 2). The soup has a pungent, rich flavour which most people like at once, and it makes an easy, filling dish for an informal party.

For 3 pints (1.75 l):
4 oz (110 g) salt belly of pork or streaky bacon
3 or 4 dried or fresh chilis
2 sprigs thyme
2 to 4 cloves garlic
2 medium onions
4 oz (110 g) red kidney beans, or red peas from a West Indian grocer
12 oz (350 g) shin of beef with the bone, cut in 2 thin steaks
3 pints (1. 75 l) cold water
½ fresh coconut *or* 6 oz (175 g) desiccated coconut
1 lb (450 g) altogether of various West Indian vegetables such as yellow or white yam, sweet potato, coco etc., or use European root vegetables
salt
freshly milled pepper

Cut away the rind and bone from the salt pork or bacon and cut the meat into dice or strips. Crush, chop or grind the chilis, thyme and garlic to rough dice or a fine pulp according to your taste and guests. If you are using fresh chilis, remove their stalks and seeds before chopping. Wash your hands thoroughly after this process, or wear rubber gloves, since chili in the eyes or mouth is very unpleasant. Slice the onions. Put the soaked beans, the beef slices, salt pork or bacon, onions and seasoning (but no salt or pepper at this stage) in a large, heavy pan and pour the cold water over them. Bring to the boil and skim off any greyish scum. Lower the heat to a gentle simmer with a bubble breaking the surface every second or so, and partly cover the pan. Cook for 1½ to 2 hours, until the beans and the beef are really soft.

Meanwhile make the coconut milk by grating the fresh coconut

meat, pouring 1 pint (600 ml) boiling water over it (or over the desiccated coconut) and leaving it to cool. Peel the yam, sweet potato or other vegetables and cut into small cubes. Yam discolours very fast after peeling so do it last. Squeeze and stir the coconut in the cooling water until the maximum amount of flavour has been dissolved, then sieve the milk into the bean and meat mixture. Cut up the cooked beef into cubes, removing all fat, bone and gristle, and put it back in the soup. Add the cubed vegetables and, if the soup is too thick (though it should be like a stew), add a little water. Reheat the soup and simmer until the vegetable cubes are tender. Taste, and add salt and pepper as required. Serve, store or freeze.

Variations

1. This soup is traditionally made with half and half salt and fresh beef. Caribbean salt beef is very definitely an acquired taste, and you may like to use ordinary salt brisket or silverside plus the fresh shin of beef. Use at least 8 oz (225 g) of each and leave out the pork or bacon.
2. If you are making the soup in double quantity or more, a larger variety of vegetables can be used, including green banana or plantain, red or green pepper, pumpkin, courgette, potato or any starchy vegetable.
3. This recipe makes a pungent soup, but still mild compared with the real Jamaican version. You can of course add more or less chili and garlic as you like.

MEAT BALL AND TOMATO SOUP

Meat balls can, of course, be added to more or less any chunky vegetable soup, such as Vegetable Broth, Minestrone and Pistou, and to plain Beef Broth. This version is made with water, tomatoes and other vegetables, and because it keeps and freezes well it is worth making a large quantity. It was a great success with a group of rather conservative and apprehensive soup tasters. Ordinary mince is too fatty for this recipe. Choose a piece of chuck, clod or flank and ask the butcher to mince it twice, or buy best dark red mince.

For 3 pints (1.75 l):
12 oz (350 g) lean stewing beef, minced twice
1 small egg
1 teaspoon dill weed *or* 8 dill seeds
salt
freshly milled pepper
4 tomatoes
1 small onion
2 small carrots
2 small sticks celery

1 to 2 cloves garlic, peeled
6 oz (175 g) runner beans *or* a 4 oz (110 g) packet frozen beans
2 rashers smoked streaky bacon (optional)
1 oz (30 g) beef dripping or butter
extra dill weed or fresh or dried basil
$3\frac{1}{4}$ pints (1.9 l) water
$\frac{1}{4}$ pint (150 ml) sour cream

If your meat is only once minced, it would be wise to pound it in a pestle and mortar, or grind it in a mincer or food processor, otherwise the meat balls may be rather hard and lumpy. Put the meat in a bowl and mix well with the egg, dill or dill seed, and some salt and pepper. Roll little pieces between your palms to make 24 balls in all, and leave them in a cool place. Skin the tomatoes (see p.247-8) and cut away the hard piece of core just under the stalk. Roughly chop the flesh and put flesh and juice into a bowl. Slice the onions, carrots, celery, garlic and beans and the rinded and boned rashers of bacon. Put all these except the beans with the butter or dripping in a large, heavy pan and fry for 10 minutes over a brisk heat until they are brownish and sizzling. Add the tomato pulp, more dill or basil (say 1 teaspoon), salt and pepper and the water. Bring to the boil and simmer for 15 minutes. Add the beans and simmer a further 5 minutes. Add the meat balls and leave the pan half-covered on a very low heat, so that a bubble breaks the surface every second or so. Cook for 15 minutes. Feel a meat ball – it should be springy but not hard. Taste the soup and add more salt, pepper and dill as you like. At this point the soup can be cooled and stored overnight or longer in the fridge, or frozen. Reheat and simmer gently for 5 minutes. Serve topped with sour cream.

Variations

1. Use any of the other meat or liver dumpling recipes on pp. 33-34 instead of this one, making sure that you have 12 to 14 oz (350 to 400 g) of ingredients.
2. For a starter soup, the quantity of meat ball mixture can be halved and the amount of vegetables increased by about 8 oz (225 g).
3. Alternative vegetables can include sliced courgettes, cauliflower sprigs, French beans, parsnip and turnip in small quantities, and so on. The green vegetable can be replaced with 1 medium diced potato, or 2 oz (60 g) small pasta or broken spaghetti.
4. If the butter or dripping and bacon are left out and the vegetables sweated dry or in 1 teaspoon good fruity olive oil, the soup will be both low calorie and low in animal fat. Serve without the sour cream.

OXTAIL, BACON AND VEGETABLE SOUP

Surprisingly oxtail is, after tomato, Heinz's best-selling soup in Britain. Obviously we haven't lost our taste for richly flavoured, deep brown oxtail, though we are not keen to make it at home. Unless you are sufficiently uninhibited to suck the bones (see Variation 2), the soup has to be made in two stages, the bones and fat being removed after the first. But not too much work is involved and the resulting soup is rich, thick and delicious. If you think it takes too much time for a single meal, either make extra and freeze the surplus, or use Variation 1 and make an oxtail stew and broth from the same ingredients.

For 3 pints (1.75 l):
Stage 1
1 lb (450 g) oxtail, divided into
    sections
6 to 8 oz (about 200 g) piece of
    boiling bacon
4 pints (2.3 l) water

1 bay leaf
3 cloves
2 sprigs thyme or marjoram
salt
freshly milled pepper
trimmings from the vegetables
    below

Stage 2
1 oz (30 g) butter or lard *or* 2
  tablespoons oil
1 medium onion

1 medium carrot
2 small sticks celery
1 heaped tablespoon white or
  wholemeal flour

Put the oxtail and boiling bacon in a heavy, large pan and add the water. Bring to the boil and skim off the grey scum as it rises. When only white foam remains add the spices, herbs, vegetable trimmings and a little salt. Lower the heat until a bubble breaks the surface only every second or so, and cover the pan. Leave to simmer for $2\frac{1}{2}$ to 3 hours until oxtail and bacon are both quite tender. Lift out the meat and put on one side to cool. Strain the stock into a tall glass jug if you have one (so you can see where the fat ends) and spoon off most or all of the fat according to taste. You should have about $2\frac{1}{2}$ pints (1.5 l) of stock. If it is more convenient this part of the cooking can be done the day before, hence the two-stage list of ingredients.

Chop the vegetables. Clean the pan and add the butter or oil and vegetables. Put the pan on a medium heat and brown the vegetables for 15 minutes, stirring occasionally. Lower the heat, add the flour and continue cooking until the flour too is nut brown. Do not let it burn or the flavour may be spoilt. Meanwhile, remove the oxtail meat from the fat and bones and cut it and the bacon into $\frac{1}{2}$ in (1 cm) pieces. Add the stock to the browned roux by degrees, stirring thoroughly between each addition, until you have a thin, smooth soup. Bring to the boil and simmer for 15 minutes, uncovered. Taste and add more salt and pepper if needed. Add the meats. At this point the soup can be cooled and stored overnight or longer, or frozen. Serve with well-flavoured whole grain bread and real ale or country cider.

Variations

1. Cook the meats as in the main recipe, adding another 8 oz (225 g) oxtail if you wish. Leave the vegetables in larger pieces and use only 1 pint (600 ml) stock to make the gravy. This is oxtail stew. Use the other $1\frac{1}{2}$ pints (900 ml) stock the following day in any of the ways suggested for Beef Broth; alternatively thicken it with another roux of 1 oz (30 g) fat and 1 heaped tablespoon flour, season it with a little cayenne and serve as a thick brown soup.
2. If you do not have a small piece of boiling bacon, use 4 to 6 rashers of bacon. Chop them and fry them with the vegetables instead of using fat. Butchers sometimes sell bacon scraps which

would do well, and of course a bacon or ham bone with a bit of meat on it would be ideal.

3. Oxtail is enhanced by the addition of a tablespoon of madeira before the final simmering. Don't add too much or you'll have madeira soup.
4. Parsnip or turnip can be used instead of celery, and, to make a real meal, a plain boiled potato can be served in each bowlful.

PEPPERPOT SOUP

If you can only afford the roast beef of Old England on special occasions, here is an Old Jamaican way of getting the flavour and nourishment of beef at an everyday price. This is a main course soup and I have given double the usual quantities in the recipe because it would be fiddly to buy the ingredients in very small amounts; in addition, the soup keeps and freezes very well. It can be varied according to your taste and the season (if you don't live near a West Indian community, see Variation 3), but the original combination is particularly nutritious.

For 3 pints (1.75 l):
1 lb (450 g) shin of beef, cut in slices across the bone, *or* 12 oz (350 g) lean boneless stewing beef and 1 marrow bone, cracked by the butcher, *or* 12 oz (350 g) shin of beef, cut across the bone, and 4 oz (110 g) salt pork or streaky bacon
3 pints (1.75 l) cold water
2 fresh or dried chilis
2 to 4 cloves garlic, peeled

1 large bunch spring onions
scrape of nutmeg *or* 4 to 6 allspice berries
salt
1 lb (450 g) fresh spinach *or* about 6 oz (175 g) frozen leaf spinach
6 to 8 okra (ladies' fingers; see Variation 2)
8 oz (225 g) yellow yam
8 oz (225 g) coco or pumpkin or green banana
freshly milled pepper

Put all the meat (and marrow bone) if you are using one into a large, heavy, stainless or enamelled pan. Cover with the water and bring very slowly to the boil. Meanwhile discard the seeds in the chilis, unless you want the soup to be fiery hot, and chop the rest finely with the garlic. Peel and trim the spring onions and chop into ½ inch (1 cm) pieces, keeping the bulbs and stalks separate. When the beef stock boils, skim off the scum as it rises. When only white foam is rising, add the spring onion bulbs, garlic, chilis and a good scrape of nutmeg or the allspice berries, crushed or ground, and a little salt. Simmer the stock, half-covered, for 2 hours or until the meat is well cooked. Lift out the meat (and marrow bone) and leave it to cool a little. Wash the fresh spinach very thoroughly in several changes of water and remove the central spine from each leaf (see Green Leaves: p.169) if it seems tough. Roll several spinach leaves at a time into enormous cigars and cut across into 1 inch (2.5 cm) strips. Discard the okra stalks and cut the okra into ½ inch (1 cm) pieces. Add the spinach and okra to the beef broth. Do not cover the pot from now on, or the spinach may bleach to an ugly yellow. Leave the spinach and okra to simmer gently for 20 minutes while you peel the yam and coco or other vegetable; yam should be used immediately after peeling, as it gets slimy and discoloured very quickly. Cut these vegetables into ½ inch (1 cm) cubes, add them to the soup and simmer for another 15 minutes. Cut away all the bone, skin, fat and gristle from the meat and add the lean to the soup in small cubes, along with the spring onion tops. When using a marrow bone, if you can, scoop out the marrow and add that too. If the surface of the soup is oily, lift off the excess with a metal spoon. Now taste the soup and add salt and pepper to the degree of heat you enjoy. Serve, or cool and store overnight, which matures the soup and improves its flavour.

Variations

1. In a real Caribbean Pepperpot, callalou, a spinach-like vegetable obtainable in Britain in tins from West Indian grocers, is used instead of spinach, and the meat is added in chunks. As with Bouillabaisse, you are left to do battle with the bones as they appear in your bowl. Personally I don't care for this, but you may well be made of sterner stuff and enjoy sucking the bones in the traditional way.
2. Okra is a small, green, pointed vegetable with rather a slimy consistency. It can well be replaced by chunks of courgette, green bean or broccoli.
3. The Caribbean vegetables can be replaced by European root vegetables such as potato, carrot, parsnip, or celery.
4. One pound (450 g) oxtail makes an excellent substitute for shin or stewing beef.

WEDDING SOUP: BEEF AND TOMATO BROTH WITH PARMESAN BALLS

Though this recipe has emigrated and came to me from Columbus, Ohio, the original wedding was obviously Italian. It is very suitable for such an occasion, since it is successful in large quantities, simple and yet luxurious. The flavour is improved if the soup is made the day before, and the green vegetables and Parmesan balls added just before serving. The tomatoes can perfectly well be the ones that are sold cheaply because they have gone a little soft. You may wish to combine making this soup with cooking some boiled beef; if so, simply buy a bigger piece of shin.

For 3 pints (1.75 l):
2 lb (1 kg) beef marrow bones, cut in 3 to 4 inch (8 to 10 cm) lengths
5 pints (3 l) cold water
8 oz (225 g) shin of beef, cut in slices across the bone
1 medium leek
10 peppercorns
1 to 2 cloves garlic, peeled and crushed with a little salt
about 12 fresh basil leaves *or* 1 heaped teaspoon dried basil
freshly milled black pepper
12 oz (350 g) ripe, red tomatoes
1 oz (30 g) Parmesan, freshly grated if possible
2 egg yolks *or* 1 whole egg
salt

Put the oven on high and place the bones in a roasting dish. Brown them on the top shelf of the oven for 20 minutes on one side and 15 minutes on the other. Put them in a large, heavy pan. Swill out the roasting dish with some of the water and pour the swillings into the pan. Add the rest of the water and the shin of beef, which should be covered by the water. Wash and trim the leek, and add the trimmings and the peppercorns to the pan. Bring to the boil, and skim off any grey scum that rises. Simmer for 3 to 4 hours or until the beef is tender. Lift it out and leave to cool. Strain the stock, preferably into a tall glass jug. There will be a lot of marrow fat on top: skim some of it off and keep it in the fridge for making sauté potatoes, etc. Leave between 2 and 6 tablespoons of the fat, according to taste.

Take a clean pan and measure 2 pints (1.2 l) stock into it. (The marrow bones can be used to make a second, weaker stock.) Add the garlic and the basil, chopped or rubbed small, and some pepper and bring to the boil. Meanwhile slice the leek very finely and peel the tomatoes (see p.247). Remove the tomato cores and cut the flesh into about 8 pieces. Separate the leek rings and wash well to make sure there is no sand or grit left between them. Add the leek and tomato to the stock and leave to simmer gently for 10 to 15 minutes. Remove all bone, fat and gristle from the cooked beef and cut the meat into $\frac{1}{2}$ inch (1 cm) cubes. Grate the Parmesan, and mix well with the egg yolks; a whole egg will make looser, more omelette-like cheese balls. Taste the soup and add salt, pepper or basil as required; it should be rather highly seasoned. Turn the heat down very low and add the cubes of beef. Let the soup come back to simmering point, then drop in $\frac{1}{2}$ teaspoons of the egg and Parmesan mixture all over the surface of the soup. Leave for 2 to 3 minutes until the little balls are just firm, and serve.

Variations

1. For an everyday soup, you can reduce or omit the beef cubes and substitute another vegetable such as 5 oz (140 g) finely sliced white cabbage, or courgettes. It would best be made with the marrow bones and a piece of beef to be used for another meal. However a very tasty soup can be made with just the bones and a little beef extract or a stock cube for extra colour and flavour.
2. The stock can be flavoured while cooking with celery, carrot and onion peelings, a bay leaf, thyme and a clove or two, plus a little piece of thinly pared orange rind.
3. The quantites given make quite a stew-like main course soup. For a lighter starter soup, the quantities of leek and beef can be cut by a third.
4. If all the marrow fat is carefully removed (easiest when cold), the cheese balls omitted, and 3 oz (90 g) finely chopped courgettes or cabbage added, the soup will be very nutritious but quite low in calories.

See also:
Cabbage Soup with a Meat Crust

Beetroot

BORSCHT WITH MUSHROOMS AND SOUR CREAM

Offering this Russian Borscht to a Jewish friend might be tactless since, with its smoked ham and stock and sour cream garnish, it breaks two Jewish dietary laws at once, however this makes a good party soup, for it can be cooked in advance and is filling, pretty and delicious. If the stock is mild use more stock and less water than the quantities given below.

For 3 pints (1.75 l) – 4 pints (2.3 l) when garnishes are added:

1 lb (450 g) raw beetroot
1 small onion
1 to 2 cloves garlic, peeled and crushed with a little salt
2 pints (1.2 l) water
½ pint (300 ml) good bitter beer
1 pint (600 ml) smoked ham or bacon stock (see p.55-6)
3 to 4 tablespoons lemon juice or wine vinegar
freshly milled pepper
dill (optional)
salt
sugar to taste
3 to 4 oz (90 to 110 g) shredded green cabbage
4 oz (110 g) mushrooms, cut in quarters
4 tablespoons chopped parsley
½ pint (300 ml) sour cream
1 small, floury potato per person

Peel and grate the beetroot and onion and put them with the garlic, water, beer and stock in a large, heavy pan. Bring to the boil and cook for 30 to 40 minutes, until the vegetables are a slush and the soup is a dramatic ruby red. Make the flavour equally dramatic with lemon or vinegar and pepper, plus dill, salt and sugar if you like. You should have about 2½ pints (1.5 l). If you have more, reduce by fast boiling; if less, add more water or stock. The soup can be prepared to this point the day before. Twenty minutes before serving, assemble the shredded cabbage, quartered mushrooms, chopped parsley and sour cream, and boil the appropriate number of potatoes in water. Bring the soup back to the boil and add the cabbage and mushrooms. Simmer for 5 minutes. Taste the soup and adjust seasoning. Drain the potatoes and place one in each bowl of Borscht. Add plenty of sour cream and chopped parsley.

Variations

1. Unsmoked bacon or ham stock, vegetable stock or beef stock can be used instead of smoked ham stock.
2. Cooked beetroot can be used instead of raw, in which case reduce the amount of water or stock by ½ pint (300 ml) and cook for only 15 minutes. Do not buy the cooked beetroot flavoured with dreadful non-brewed condiment (artificial vinegar), and lots of sugar.
3. Serve with the traditional accompaniment, the little Russian pasties called piroshkis (see p.29).

JEWISH BORSCHT

In order not to mix meat with milk, practising Jews thicken their beetroot with eggs. The Polish Jewish friend who gave me this recipe says that, though it is sometimes eaten hot with a boiled potato in the middle, she mostly remembers it served as an iced drink with the meal. Hot or cold, the soup must achieve a fine balance of sweet and salt, sharp and smooth.

12 oz (350 g) raw beetroot	1 potato per person (optional)
1 medium onion	2 whole eggs *or* 3 egg yolks
1 medium carrot	juice of ½ or 1 lemon
2 pints (1.2 l) beef or chicken	salt
stock	sugar to taste

Coarsely grate the vegetables. Put them in a pan with the stock, bring to the boil, cover and simmer for 30 minutes. Strain the clear juice through a fine sieve, pressing the pulp gently (don't use a food mill).

You should now have about 1 pint (600 ml) of clear liquid of an amazing cyclamen colour. If you have much less, make up the amount with water. If you are going to add potatoes, boil them in water. Reheat the Borscht in a clean pan and beat the eggs or egg yolks in a small bowl with the lemon juice until slightly fluffy; if whole eggs are used the final appearance of the Borscht will be a little flaky and less elegant than if yolks only are used. When the soup boils, add salt and sugar to taste and beat a ladleful of liquid into the egg mixture. Remove the soup from the heat and strain the egg mixture back into the soup, beating as you do so. Taste again and add more lemon if you like. Serve immediately, either plain or with a boiled potato in each bowl. Alternatively allow the soup to get thoroughly chilled, taste again (chilled food always needs more seasoning) and serve plain in pretty glass dishes. The wonderful deep rose colour needs no additional attraction.

Variation

Water or vegetable stock can be used instead of meat stock.

Beet

For leaves see under:
Purée of Lettuce with Sour Cream, Variation 2
Spinach: Crème Florentine, Variation 3

Bilberries or Blaeberries

See under:
Iced Plum Soup with Sour Cream, Variation 4

Blackberries

See under:
Iced Plum Soup with Sour Cream, Variation 4
Iced Raspberry Yogurt Soup

Potage Bonne Femme

See under:
Potatoes

Borscht

See under:
Beetroot

Bouillabaisse

There is no recipe for Bouillabaisse in this book because the classic version needs many different Mediterranean fish which are not available in Britain. Fish Stew with Garlic, Tomatoes and Olive Oil (p.158) achieves a similar result.

Bread

See under:
Apple, Rye and Sour Cream Soup
Hare Soup with Madeira and Bread Balls
French Onion Soup
Tomatoes: Gazpacho
Garnishes and Accompaniments: croûtons, p.27; hot herb bread, p.28; bread and herb balls, p.28

Sea Bream

See under:
Sea Bass, Vermouth and Garlic Soup, Variation 1

Broccoli

See under:
Cauliflower Cheese Soup, Variation 4

Cabbage

CHOOSING AND USING

Cabbages can be green, red or white. Except for spring cabbage, in which the head has not yet fully formed, a head of cabbage should be tight and heavy for its size, with a bloom on the inner leaves. Avoid cabbages with wilting, faded outer leaves, blackened or slimy bits where the stalk has been cut, and brown or black smudges on the leaves. If you buy half a large cabbage, rather than a whole small one, you get a full view of the cabbage's inner state. It should be clear in colour, with no faded or brown parts.

Spring cabbage and spring greens have not much head and therefore few of the tender inner leaves which are good for soup-making. Use inner leaves only, and use them as soon as possible after purchase. Summer cabbage has a good head of tender green leaves. It reduces a lot during cooking and should not be cut in very small pieces or cooked for long.

Winter cabbages, such as Drumhead, Savoy, Christmas Cabbage and January King, are an excellent vegetable. Again pick the ones with a firm, clearly coloured head. Winter cabbages will reduce more in cooking than red or white cabbage, but not as much as summer cabbage.

White cabbage is now grown in Britain – it used to be called Dutch white cabbage and was all imported. It is available nearly all year round, but may go brown in the centre in hot weather. Since it reduces less than green cabbage during cooking it is more economical, and you need only two-thirds the amount of white cabbage as summer cabbage in a recipe.

Red cabbage has an even coarser texture and is mostly used for long, slow cooking or pickling. If you are using it for any of the recipes in this book (Cabbage Soup with a Meat Crust would be suitable) cook it at least 15 minutes longer than the time stated in the recipe.

HUNGARIAN CABBAGE SOUP

The appalling sadism exercised on cabbage in the name of mass catering often prejudices people against this delicate and highly nutritious vegetable for years after they have left their last educational institution. If you still doubt the potential deliciousness of cabbage, this recipe will instantly convert you. It is quick, easy and cheap, and can at a pinch be made with a ham or beef stock cube or extract, though a good pork or bacon stock (see p.55-6) will give a much more subtle, sensuous flavour. Variation 1 transforms the soup from an elegant little starter into a main course soup which, if eaten with wholemeal bread, will provide useful amounts of protein, vitamins A, B, C and D, iron and fibre.

1 piece of young green or white cabbage weighing 8 to 11 oz (225 to 310 g) after trimming – use smaller weight for white, larger one for green
1 large onion
1 oz (30 g) butter or 2 tablespoons oil
$\frac{1}{2}$ teaspoon caraway seeds
1 dessertspoon paprika
$\frac{1}{4}$ pint (150 ml) sour cream
1$\frac{1}{2}$ pints (900 ml) good beef, ham or pork stock
salt
freshly milled pepper
1 tablespoon chopped parsley

If you are using white cabbage shred it finely; if you have green, cut it in $\frac{1}{2}$ inch (1 cm) squares. Chop the onion finely. Melt the butter in a heavy stainless or enamelled pan and sweat the onion in it over a low heat for 10 minutes. Stir occasionally and cover the pan in between stirs. Meanwhile crush the caraway seeds in a mortar if you have one, otherwise leave whole, and mix with the paprika into the sour cream. When the onion is soft and translucent, but not brown, add the stock and a little salt, if necessary, and pepper. Add the cabbage when the stock has come to the boil, and boil briskly for about 4 minutes, until the cabbage is cooked but still slightly crisp. Stir in the chopped parsley. Taste and adjust the seasoning. Serve immediately with a dollop of the sour cream mixture on top.

Variations

1. Use 1 lb (450 g) green cabbage or 12 oz (350 g) white cabbage, cut into small squares if green and shredded fairly fine if white; 8 oz (225 g) pork sausage (British will do, but pure meat would do better): $2\frac{1}{2}$ pints (1.5 l) rich pork or bacon stock, 1 large potato, 1 clove garlic, peeled and crushed with salt; 1 bay leaf; 2 tablespoons or more chopped parsley; and seasoning. Cut the sausages into slices or twist the skins at 1 in (2 cm) intervals to make mini-sausages, and fry them in a stainless or enamelled pan for a few minutes until they are brown. Add the stock and seasoning (no salt for a bacon stock) and the potato, cut into large dice. Cook for 15 minutes. Add the cabbage and simmer for 5 minutes more. Stir in the parsley, taste, and adjust seasoning. Serve as it is or with a lot of sour cream. This version makes 3 pints (1.75 l) and can successfully be halved.
2. In either the main recipe or Variation 1, 3 to 4 oz (90 to 110 g) mushrooms, sliced or quartered, can be substituted for an equal amount of cabbage or onion or all the potato.

MAJORCAN SOUP

Recipes for this soup and for Variation 2 of Carrot and Coriander Soup were offered to me more often than any others while I was preparing this book. It is interesting that they are both vegetarian, and it would not have been the case, I think, even five years ago. This soup has a lovely fresh flavour and is certain to be popular. However the flavour and texture of the cabbage suffer with keeping and the soup certainly will not freeze.

1 very small onion or leek
1 medium bright red pepper or $\frac{1}{2}$ red and $\frac{1}{2}$ green pepper
8 oz (225 g) green cabbage or 6 oz (175 g) white cabbage – both weights after trimming
2 tablespoons fruity olive oil
4 juicy red tomatoes – 8 oz (225 g) after peeling
1 to 2 cloves garlic, peeled and crushed with a little salt

$1\frac{1}{4}$ pints (750 ml) water
salt
freshly milled pepper
8 to 10 fresh basil leaves or 1 teaspoon dried basil or 2 sprigs fresh marjoram
Garnish (for non-slimmers only):
2 slices wholemeal bread
a little crushed garlic
2 to 3 tablespoons olive oil

Slice the onion or leek, pepper and cabbage very finely, preferably in an electric slicer/shredder. Put the oil in a stainless or enamelled pan. Add the garlic and leek or onion and fry over a medium heat for 5 minutes, stirring most of the time. The onion should be semi-cooked but not brown. Add the red or red and green pepper and stir-fry for another minute or two. Skin the tomatoes (see p.247-8), core and chop roughly. Add to the pan and stir-fry for another few minutes. Now add the water, seasoning and herbs.

Meanwhile make the garnish, if you want one, by smearing the bread with crushed garlic, cutting it into dice, and frying till brown and crisp in the olive oil

When the water boils, simmer the soup for 10 minutes, then add the cabbage. White cabbage will take 5 to 10 minutes to cook, green cabbage only a minute or so. Taste the soup and adjust the seasoning. Serve at once, either plain or with the garlic croûtons.

Variations

1. A small glass of red wine or the juice of a small lemon can be added to the soup to give it more zap.
2. Replace 2 oz (60 g) of the cabbage with 2 sticks celery; slice them and add with the onion.
3. Courgettes can be used instead of cabbage. Use 8 oz (225 g) – about 7 oz (200 g) after trimming. Cut them in $\frac{1}{4}$ inch ($\frac{1}{2}$ cm) slices or dice them, and put in a bowl with 2 teaspoons salt. Leave for 20 minutes, then rinse very thoroughly to remove both the bitter juice and the salt. Proceed with the main recipe and add the courgettes 3 to 5 minutes before serving the soup.

CABBAGE SOUP WITH A MEAT CRUST

A food processor makes the preparation of this unusual and sustaining main course soup very swift and easy. If kept waiting the cabbage acquires a canteen flavour and the meat crust tends to sink to the bottom, so it is best served immediately, though all the preparation can be done in advance. It can be made with butcher's mince and chopped bacon, but if you only have these ingredients they would taste better turned into a cabbage and meat ball soup (see p.33) for the Meat Ball recipe).

For 3 pints (1.75 l):

8 oz (225 g) lean stewing beef, in a piece
4 oz (110 g) smoked bacon
½ teaspoon dill seed
salt
freshly milled pepper
12 oz (350 g) white or red cabbage *or* 1 lb (450 g) green cabbage

1 clove garlic, peeled and crushed with a little salt
1 oz (30 g) butter *or* 2 tablespoons olive oil
1 tablespoon paprika
1¾ pints (1 l) water
1 tablespoon flour
2 tablespoons wholemeal breadcrumbs

Cut the beef and bacon into small cubes and put them with the dill seed in the food processor. Grind to a fine pulp. Stir in a little salt and pepper. Slice the cabbage very finely and put it with the garlic and butter or oil in a stainless or enamelled pan which will fit under your grill. Sweat the cabbage for a minute or two over a high heat, stirring often, until it begins to wilt. Stir in the paprika and cook for another minute. Add the water and a little salt, and bring to the boil. Meanwhile sprinkle the flour on a board and pat or roll the meat mixture into a circle the same diameter as the pan. When the soup begins to boil, reduce the heat and delicately place the meat circle on top of the soup. Simmer for 15 minutes, uncovered. The meat will rise to the surface as it cooks and form a crust. Taste the broth without disturbing the crust too much, add more salt and pepper and stir it in gently below the crust. Light the grill and sprinkle the crumbs on top of the crust. Brown the crust under the grill and serve immediately.

Variations

1. Use 8 oz (225 g) cabbage plus a small onion and a small eating apple, both peeled and chopped.
2. All beef, or fresh pork can be used instead of bacon.
3. Fennel, caraway or cumin seeds can be used instead of dill.
4. Garnish with yogurt or sour cream and chopped fresh dill weed or flat parsley.

See also:
Vegetables: Garbure

Carrots

CARROT AND CORIANDER SOUP

Carrot soup doesn't sound very glamorous, but this one was a favourite at John Tovey's Miller Howe, the Lake District hotel which has become world-famous for its food. I learned how to make it from one of his former assistants with whom I cooked in Sidney. The soup is cheap, quick and very simple, but elegant in both appearance and flavour. You will need to purée the soup in a blender or put it twice through the fine plate of a food mill to achieve the correct homogeneous texture. Excellent hot, it is also delicious chilled. It is important to use fresh young carrots.

1 oz (30 g) butter
1 medium onion
5 medium carrots (8 oz 225 g,
  after peeling)
1 teaspoon coriander
¼ teaspoon freshly milled black
  pepper
salt

1 small carrot for garnish
  (optional)
½ pint (300 ml) milk
½ pint (300 ml) plain yogurt
¼ pint (150 ml) water or
  light vegetable, ham or
  chicken stock

Take a heavy pan with a tight-fitting lid and melt the butter over a low heat. Peel and slice the onion and carrot and add with the coriander and pepper. Put a lid on the pan and sweat the mixture gently for 12 minutes, shaking the pan frequently and making sure that the contents do not stick or colour. Add the stock or water and continue cooking for a further 10 minutes or until the carrots are thoroughly soft, but not over-cooked or the delicate flavour may be destroyed. If you are using the extra carrot for garnish, cut it into small dice, or, more elegantly, julienne strips (see p.31), and simmer for 5 minutes in a little boiling water. Drain and reserve. Blend the soup with the milk or put it twice through the fine plate of a food mill, using the milk as a chaser. Remember to scrape the bottom of the mill, or your soup may be thin. Stir in the yogurt. At this point the soup may be stored in the fridge overnight, but do not store it longer than this for it is really at its best freshly made. Reheat in a clean pan, but do not allow it to boil or the yogurt may curdle. Taste the soup when it is hot and add more pepper, coriander and a little salt if you like. Add the carrot garnish a minute before serving. Use contrasting coloured bowls to set off the colour of the soup, but do not be tempted to garnish with parsley to create an attractive visual contrast because it would be too strong a flavour.

Fried crumbs or croûtons are a pleasant accompaniment, either plain or with coriander (adapt the recipe for curry croûtons on p.28).

Variations

1. Use all milk for a richer soup, but when it first comes to the boil with the carrots and onion make sure it does not boil over.
2. Use $\frac{1}{2}$ flat teaspoon curry powder instead of the coriander.
3. If you find the soup too carroty, substitute potato for 2 to 3 oz (60 to 90 g) of the carrot.
4. Use sour cream instead of yogurt. When I first met this soup it was made with equal parts of chicken stock and single cream and served topped with whipped cream. You may or may not consider this excessive.
5. If you are serving the soup iced, make it a little thinner and add a squeeze of lemon or orange. Adjust the seasoning after chilling.

CARROT AND LEMON SOUP

If you have a reasonably fast hand with a potato peeler this soup can move from paper bag to table in 25 minutes flat. It is pretty, low calorie and full of vitamins A and C. It will keep overnight but isn't worth freezing.

1 small leek	crushed with a little salt
12 oz (350 g) carrots	1¼ pints (750 ml) water
1 small lemon	salt
2 tablespoons olive oil *or* 1 oz	freshly milled pepper
(30 g) butter	cayenne (optional)
1 small clove garlic, peeled and	2 tablespoons chopped parsley

Slice the leek finely and put it into a large bowlful of cold water. Peel the carrots and grate them coarsely. Grate the lemon rind. Put the oil or butter in a heavy pan over a low heat. Scoop the leek slices up in a sieve and shake off the water; put them with the crushed garlic and carrots into the pan and sweat, covered, for 5 minutes, stirring occasionally. Add the water and lemon rind and bring to the boil. Boil gently for 10 minutes. Taste and add salt, pepper, cayenne and the lemon juice, strained through a sieve. Stir in the parsley and serve.

Variations

1. Vegetable, chicken or beef stock can be used instead of water, but don't spoil the flavour with a stock cube.
2. A small orange can be used instead of lemon, but grate only a third of the rind.

See also:
Potatoes: Potage Bonne Femme. Many other recipes contain carrot, but in such small quantities that they are not worth mentioning.

Cashew Nuts

See under:
Purée of Broad Beans with Toasted Almonds, Variation 2
Green Bean and Cashew Nut Cream Soup

Cauliflower

CAULIFLOWER CHEESE SOUP

The basic recipe is for a filling main course soup. It is very easy and quick and could, I suppose, be made with a packet of white sauce mix, though it seems a confidence trick to market a product which can be made with basic ingredients almost as quickly and far more cheaply. If you would like a lighter, smoother version as an appetizer, use Variation 1. The other variations alter the spices and the richness and are all delicious. In fact there are only two ways to ruin this soup (apart from burning it): one is to omit blanching the cauliflower, leaving it with a rank flavour; and the other is to keep it any length of time, for it acquires an unpleasant school canteen flavour.

1 small, firm white cauliflower weighing about 12 oz (350 g)

2 pints (1.2 l) water or more, for blanching the cauliflower

1½ oz (40 g) butter *or* 3 tablespoons oil

1 rounded tablespoon wholemeal or plain white flour

1 pint (600 ml) milk

salt

freshly milled pepper

grated nutmeg

½ teaspoon English or Dijon mustard

3 to 4 oz (90 to 110 g) grated cheese – half and half Stilton and Cheddar is good, or see p.109 for more cheese combinations

Cut away the coarse parts of the stalk and leaves of the cauliflower and discard them. Remove the florets. The easiest way to do this is to lay the cauliflower face-down on a board and dig a large, sharp knife slantwise into the centre, about ½ (1 cm) in from where the florets begin. Cut right round the stem of the cauliflower, with the point of the knife remaining in the heart of the cauliflower, so that you are removing a conical section of stalk and leaves. Break up the florets. Roughly chop any tender bits of stalk and leaves. If you are blenderless, put the trimmed cauliflower on a large board, and, using a heavy knife, chop it into ¼ in pieces. Boil the blanching water, add a little salt and the cauliflower pieces, and boil uncovered for 8 to 10 minutes – only 5 minutes if the florets are very small and you have chopped the rest finely – until it is just tender. Drain off the water.

Meanwhile melt the butter or oil in a stainless or enamelled pan. Add the flour and cook, stirring, for a minute over a low heat. Pour in half the milk, little by little, stirring each addition to smoothness before pouring in the next. You will now have a thick white sauce. Season it with salt, pepper and a little nutmeg (an easy spice to overdo) and leave the sauce to cook over a very low heat, preferably on a heat-absorbent mat. Put the cauliflower and remaining milk in the blender, and blend, in a few one-second bursts, to a rough purée. Stir this mixture into the sauce and bring back to simmering point. If you are not using a blender, make the sauce with all the milk and add the cauliflower. Add the mustard and taste the soup. At this point the soup can be cooled as rapidly as possible and stored overnight in the fridge. When ready to serve, put the hot or just reheated soup into an ovenproof casserole or bowl, sprinkle with the grated cheese and brown quickly under a hot grill. Serve immediately.

Variations

1. For a lighter, smoother soup, use only 1 flat dessertspoon flour and 1 oz (30 g) fat or 2 tablespoons oil, and blend or mill the cauliflower to a finer texture. Finish as above.
2. The fat and flour can be replaced by 4 crustless slices of toasted wholemeal bread. Put the unthickened soup in bowls or a casserole and float on top slices of toast thickly covered with grated cheese. Grill until brown and bubbling and serve immediately.
3. For a rich, elegant soup, substitute $\frac{1}{4}$ pint (150 ml) *crème fraîche* (see p.142) or single cream for a quarter of the milk. Make the soup as in Variation 1, but instead of grilling the cheese serve it in the form of cheese croûtons (see p.28).
4. Fresh or frozen broccoli spears – 8 oz (225 g) – can be used instead of cauliflower. Follow the instructions on the packet for blanching frozen broccoli, but under-cook it slightly. Cook fresh broccoli for 7 to 8 minutes. Flavour with 1 teaspoon grated lemon or orange rind instead of mustard.

CAULIFLOWER AND WATERCRESS SOUP

Do not omit to blanch the cauliflower or the delicate flavour of this soup will be ruined. Variation 3, which uses egg yolk instead of flour to thicken the soup, has a more subtle texture than the main recipe, but needs calm nerves and your full attention for a minute before serving.

1 small, white, tight cauliflower –
  8 oz (225 g) after trimming
$\frac{1}{2}$ pint (300 ml) boiling water
1 oz (30 g) butter
1 small onion *or* 6 shallots
1 flat dessertspoon flour
$1\frac{1}{4}$ pints (750 ml) milk *or* half and

half milk and light vegetable
  stock *or* light chicken stock
$\frac{1}{2}$ bunch fresh watercress
salt
freshly milled pepper

Remove the florets (see p.100), break them up and put them in a pan. Pour the boiling water over them, and boil uncovered for 3 minutes. Drain the water off and rinse the cauliflower in cold water. Melt the butter in a heavy stainless or enamelled pan. Slice the onion, add it, let it sweat gently for 2 or 3 minutes, and then add the flour. Stir it thoroughly into the butter and onions and let the roux cook for a minute. Add a little of the milk or stock and stir until the mixture is smooth. Then add a little more liquid, and so on, until you have a smooth, very thin sauce. Chop the watercress stalks finely, reserving the leaves, and add the stalks. Season lightly and simmer, half-covered, for 15 minutes. Add the florets and simmer for a further 7 to 10 minutes or until the cauliflower is just tender. Allow to cool for a few minutes, then blend or put through the food mill, using the fine plate. If you have no blender or food mill, do not attempt to push the cauliflower through a sieve – it is a thankless task. Put the florets on a large board and chop them finely with a big knife, then proceed with the recipe. At this point the soup may be stored till the next day. Reheat in a clean, stainless or enamelled pan with the watercress leaves, left whole or chopped as you prefer. When the soup is hot, taste it and add more seasoning if necessary. Serve in dark coloured bowls.

Variations

1. Instead of the flour use 1 oz (30 g) ground almonds, plus another 1 oz (30 g) flaked toasted almonds as a garnish.
2. The soup can be made without watercress. Add extra pepper or a $\frac{1}{4}$ teaspoon curry powder or garam masala, and garnish with chopped parsley.
3. For a richer, more elegant thickening, omit the flour. When the soup is ready to serve, beat 3 egg yolks in a bowl. Thickening with egg is a slightly tricky process: follow the detailed instructions on p.21, and serve the soup immediately it has thickened.

Celeriac

BASIC PURÉE OF CELERIAC

For many of the soups in this book stainless or enamelled pans are recommended ['You're telling me,' said my father.]; for a few, including this one, they are essential. If it is made in an uncoated aluminium pan it will acquire an unpleasant metallic flavour which tingles at the back of the palate, and an unhealthy grey colour instead of a creamy one. In the right pan you can make a beautiful soup with a delicate celery flavour. The basic purée is delicious served as it is, but can be dressed up for a special occasion. The ultimate gourmet version appears in Variation 1.

1 lb (450 g) celeriac	freshly milled pepper
1 pint (600 ml) water	salt
1 small clove garlic, peeled and crushed with a little salt	1½ oz (40 g) butter *or* 4 to 5 tablespoons thick cream
2 thin strips lemon rind	2 tablespoons chopped chives

Peel the celeriac either with a stout potato peeler or a sharp knife – it often has to be peeled quite deeply to remove all the blackened cracks. Cut it into ¼ in thick slices. If you do not intend to cook it immediately, cover the slices with cold water and add a squeeze of lemon or 1 teaspoon vinegar to preserve the creamy colour. Put the slices in a stainless or enamelled pan and add the water, garlic, lemon peel and pepper. Bring to the boil, cover and simmer for 15 minutes. Check that the celeriac is tender and then blend or mill it with its liquid. If you prefer a little texture to the purée, use the medium plate of the food mill or use the blender in short bursts of a second or so, checking the consistency after each burst until you are satisfied. Test the seasoning and add more salt and pepper as needed. At this point the purée can be cooled and stored overnight or frozen, though it is delicious served at once.

Reheat the purée in a clean pan (still stainless or enamelled) with the cream or butter. Check the seasoning once more when the soup is very hot, and serve sprinkled with the chopped chives. You may, however, prefer some of the more glamorous variations given below.

Variations

1. The celeriac can be cooked in milk, mildly flavoured vegetable stock, or mild chicken, beef or ham stock. Most delicious of all, it can be made with duck or goose stock. If you are lucky enough to be able to make this version, serve it plain and don't waste this delicate marvel on heavy smokers or drunks.
2. Serve with any of the croûtons on pp. 27-8, or with toasted almonds.
3. For a low calorie garnish, blend 3 oz (90 g) cottage or curd cheese with a little milk until smooth. Season and stir in 2 tablespoons chopped chives. Serve a dollop on each bowl of soup.

CHINESE CELERIAC AND CHESTNUT SOUP

This is an elegant yet simple soup whose only difficulty lies in obtaining the dried chestnuts, green ginger and good beef stock. You can of course use fresh chestnuts and canned consommé or beef broth, but if you are reduced to using a stock cube it is better to try Variation 1. For information on chestnuts, see Chestnut: Choosing and Using (p.111-12).

2 oz (60 g) dried chestnuts, soaked overnight *or* 8 oz (225 g) fresh chestnuts
1 pint (600 ml) water
1 small head of celeriac – 7 oz (200 g) when peeled
6 spring onions
1½ pints (900 ml) good beef stock or broth

½ in (1 cm) piece of green ginger, peeled
1 clove garlic, peeled and crushed with a little salt
1 tablespoon thin soy sauce
2 tablespoons medium sherry
freshly milled pepper
salt

If you forget to soak the dried chestnuts, cover them with cold water in a small pan, bring them to the boil, then cover the pan, turn off the heat and leave for 40 minutes. If you are using fresh chestnuts, slit the shell with a sharp knife from top to bottom on the curved side, and bake them in a medium hot oven (350°F, 189°C, Gas 4) for 20 minutes. Leave them to cool for a few minutes. While they are still as hot as you can bear, peel off both skins, being sure to get off all the inner one, which is very bitter. Peeling fresh chestnuts is a fiddly and irritating job, while a pound of dried chestnuts from a Chinese supermarket is relatively cheap and lasts for ages.

Boil the chestnuts in the water for 20 minutes or so until they are tender. Drain off the water and leave the chestnuts to cool. Peel the celeriac and slice it thinly. Keep it fresh in a bowl of cold water with a little lemon juice or vinegar added if you are not making the soup all in one process. Cut the slices into elegant little diamonds or double-size matchsticks. Peel the spring onions and cut them into ½ inch (1 cm) pieces, keeping the white and the green parts separate. Grate the green ginger or cut it into minute dice. When the chestnuts are cool remove any lingering pieces of dark brown inner skin and cut them in quarters. The soup can be prepared in advance to this point.

Twenty minutes before serving, put the beef stock in a stainless or enamelled pan and add the green ginger, garlic, soy sauce, sherry and some pepper. Bring to the boil. Add the white part of the spring onions and the celeriac and boil briskly for 5 minutes, then add the chestnuts and cook for a further 5 minutes on a low heat. A minute before serving add the green part of the onions and taste the soup. The celeriac should be crisp but just tender. Add more soy sauce or a little salt if you like. Serve in bowls that show off this delicate brown and green soup.

Variations

1. If you have no beef stock, make an equally delicious celeriac and chestnut chowder by using milk instead. The procedure is just the same, except that the whole thing can be made in advance, since chowders are traditionally well cooked, with the vegetables slushy rather than crisp. If you want to cook it just before serving, it takes 30 to 35 minutes.
2. Beef is the best stock for this soup, but a well-flavoured chicken or vegetable broth can be substituted.

Celery

CELERY, ALMOND AND WALNUT CREAM

Unlike root celery (celeriac), stalk celery does not contain starch and is mostly fibre and water. This makes it very useful to slimmers but less useful for soups, for unless the celery is left semi-raw and crunchy another ingredient must be added to give the soup body. In this recipe, nuts and cream are the ingredients which give richness and substance. If you are not a nut fan, see Variation 1 for a flour-thickened cream of celery soup.

1 head of celery – 1 lb (450 g) after trimming	salt
1 oz (30 g) butter	1½ oz (40 g) shelled almonds and walnuts, mixed
1 small clove garlic, peeled and crushed with a little salt	¼ pint (150 ml) milk
¾ pint (450 ml) chicken stock	2 tablespoons dry sherry
	¼ pint (150 ml) single cream

Trim off the base of the celery head and any yellowish leaves, and wash the stalks thoroughly, removing any brown parts. Chop the stalks into $\frac{1}{2}$ inch (1 cm) slices and put them in a really heavy-bottomed pan with a tight-fitting lid. Add the butter and garlic and sweat over a low heat for 30 minutes, stirring occasionally. Take care that the celery doesn't catch – a stove mat is useful. The celery will become limp and watery. Add the stock and a little salt and simmer for a further 10 minutes. Then put the mixture through a food mill, using the coarse or medium plate so as to get rid of the stringy bits but retain some texture. If you do not have a food mill, blend and then sieve the mixture.

Meanwhile wash and dry the pan and grind or pound the nuts to a coarse or fine powder, depending on your taste, and whether or not your family or guests have false teeth. Put the nuts in the pan and toast them a little over a low heat, stirring continuously and ignoring all distractions: telephone, front door, armed intruders. After 2 minutes or so, when the nuts are hot and smelling delicious, add the celery mixture, milk, sherry and cream. Reheat the soup. Taste it when hot and add more salt if necessary; I don't think pepper is an asset to this recipe. The soup is best made a few hours in advance, to allow the flavours to blend. It freezes well, but you may like to substitute a flat dessertspoon of flour for $\frac{1}{2}$ oz of the nuts to guard against the soup curdling when it is reheated. Add the flour to the celery mixture just before adding the stock.

Variations

1. For a cream soup, use $1\frac{1}{2}$ oz (40 g) butter to sweat the celery. Add 1 oz (30 g) flour, stir it in thoroughly, and then add the broth little by little, stirring as you go. Simmer with the stock for 15 minutes, then proceed with the main recipe. As a garnish $\frac{1}{2}$ to 1 oz (15 to 30 g) flaked almonds may be toasted carefully under the grill and sprinkled on top of the finished soup.
2. Vegetable stock or more milk can be used instead of chicken stock.
3. The soup can be made without cream just with the stock and extra milk, and then garnished with whipped or sour cream or *crème fraîche* (see p. 142).

CELERY AND TARRAGON MOUSSELINE SOUP

Potato and egg yolks thicken and enrich this soup, which makes it much cheaper than Celery, Almond and Walnut Cream though no less tempting and elegant. If you want to keep it overnight, do not add the egg yolks until you are reheating it.

1 small head of celery – 7 oz (200 g) after trimming
1 small potato
1 small leek
1½ oz (40 g) butter
6 to 8 fresh tarragon leaves *or* ½ teaspoon dried tarragon

1¼ pints (750 ml) chicken or vegetable stock
salt
freshly milled pepper
2 egg yolks
2 teaspoons lemon juice

Pick out the best-looking celery stalk and cut into tiny dice for garnish. Chop the rest of the celery roughly. Cut the potato into large cubes and the leek into rings. Leave the leek rings to soak in plenty of cold water for 10 minutes so that any grit will drop out from between the rings. Melt the butter in a heavy-bottomed stainless or enamelled pan and add the celery, leek and potato. Cover the pan and sweat gently for 5 minutes, stirring occasionally to make sure that the vegetables don't stick. Add the tarragon and stock and a little salt and boil gently for 15 to 20 minutes or until the vegetables are soft. Blend the mixture thoroughly. If the celery is stringy, you may need to sieve the soup after blending. Push it through the sieve with the back of a ladle. At this point the soup may be cooled and refrigerated until the following day.

Return the soup to the rinsed-out pan. You should have just under 1½ pints (900 ml). If you have much more, heat the soup and reduce by boiling for a few minutes; if too little, add water or stock. When the soup has come back to the boil, add the celery garnish and salt and pepper to taste. Beat the egg yolks and the lemon juice in a bowl, then add a ladleful of hot soup, whisking as you do so. Take the soup off the heat and add the egg mixture to it, whisking all the time. The soup will thicken slightly. Taste again and serve at once.

Variations

1. A small fennel bulb can be substituted for the celery, and the tarragon omitted. This makes a lovely soup.
2. For a low calorie, low animal fat version, use 1 teaspoon fruity olive oil instead of the butter. Sweat the vegetables over a very low heat, stirring regularly. Omit the lemon juice and use 5 tablespoons plain yogurt instead of the egg yolks, added in the same way.

See also:
Purée of Cucumber and Fennel, Variation 3
Purée of Duck and Celery

Cheese

CHOOSING AND USING

Cheese is really just salted and preserved milk. Cheese-making was already an established craft in Roman times, and some kind of cheese and some kind of soup must have been eaten together when man still lived in caves. Most cheese contains a lot of fat and so is not good for slimmers or those watching their animal fat intake, but it is a high-quality protein food containing all eight essential amino-acids necessary for human cell regeneration, and it has good levels of vitamin A and calcium. It is an excellent accompaniment to grain, bean and vegetable soups because these are generally low in fat and have incomplete protein but good levels of vitamins B, C and E. As an ingredient cheese also gives body and richness of flavour to these soups. It is not so good, however, in sweet vegetable soups such as Borscht, or in recipes using very delicately flavoured green vegetables such as lettuce. For these soups, eggs perform the same function more discreetly. In meat and fish soups the protein in cheese is superfluous, but used as a garnish like the Parmesan balls in Wedding Soup (under Beef) provides a luxurious final fillip.

Cheese for adding to soup should dissolve well and be strongly flavoured, since it will be much diluted by the soup, especially by a thick one. Parmesan is, of course, the king of soup cheeses. The little drums of ready-grated Parmesan are expensive and contain cheese of poor quality. A chunk of Parmesan keeps for ages, works out cheaper, and takes only moments to grate fresh each time it is needed. The difference in depth of flavour is very marked. Apart from Parmesan, the other classic foreign cheese for cooking is Gruyère, with Emmenthal for second-best. Gruyère melts beautifully and has a milder but still very distinct flavour. For everyday use, a sharp Lancashire or Cheddar cheese works very well, or for a gentler effect Leicester or Caerphilly. Powerfully flavoured blue cheese like Stilton can be added to a simple celery or chicken base, but the soup will inevitably become Stilton soup since the other flavours will be overwhelmed.

Cheese should always be grated for soup. It can be added either in large quantities, as in the following recipe, or by the spoonful to complement other flavours. It can be heaped on toasted bread and grilled on top of the soup (see French Onion Soup). It can be cooked in little ravioli (p.36) or croûtons (p.28). Or it can simply be put on the table in a bowl, to be sprinkled on the soup as desired.

Cottage and curd cheeses have all the other nutrients of full fat cheese but most of their fat has been removed. They are therefore very useful to slimmers. The main recipe for Vichyssoise and several of the slimmers' variations on soups (see list on p.286-7) have cottage or curd cheese blended into them.

Cheese should be stored covered, but not airtight, in a cool place. For this purpose, a fridge is a poor substitute for an old-fashioned larder. Grated cheese can be stored in a sealed plastic bag in the fridge for a day or two, but it rapidly becomes hard and loses its flavour.

FONTINA, EGG AND MILK SOUP

Fontina is a semi-soft Italian cheese with a distinctive flavour. It is available in Italian delicatessens, but if you cannot get it Gruyère or any of the English cheeses mentioned above can replace it. This recipe came from a friend in Turin, where the food is rich and refined, influenced as much by France and Switzerland as by the rest of Italy. It is an extremely simple soup, but has subtlety of texture and flavour; it should be eaten at once.

2 large eggs
a little over 1 pint (600 ml) milk

4 to 5 oz (125 to 150 g) Fontina, grated
freshly milled pepper

This soup takes less than 5 minutes to make and cannot be kept hot, so make sure that people are seated at the table before you begin. Break the eggs into a basin and whisk them smooth. Put the milk and grated cheese in a heavy pan and heat, stirring continuously. When it begins to steam, whisk a ladleful into the egg mixture, then pour the egg mixture into the soup, whisking all the time. If the soup does not thicken a little when the eggs are added, go on whisking and heating gently until it does so, keeping an eye open for the least sign of curdling or boiling. Remove from the heat. Add pepper, taste, and serve immediately with hot bread or toast.

Variations

1. As a precaution against curdling, 1 heaped teaspoon white flour can be whisked with the eggs to stabilize the mixture a little.
2. Chicken stock can be used instead of milk: 1 pint (600 ml) plus 5 tablespoons fruity white wine or cider makes a good combination.
3. The amount of cheese can be decreased by 2 oz (60 g), and the same quantity of thinly sliced mushrooms or finely chopped or minced celery cooked with the milk for 3 minutes before the cheese is added. Make sure the soup has gone off the boil before you start adding the egg mixture.
4. Two tablespoons finely chopped parsley or chives can be stirred into the soup as you serve it.

See under:
Beef: Wedding Soup
Cauliflower Cheese Soup
Basic Purée of Celeriac, Variation 3
Chicken Noodle Soup, Variation 4
French Onion Soup
Vegetables: Minestrone
Garnishes and Accompaniments: Parmesan balls, p.30

Morello Cherries

See under:
Iced Plum Soup with Sour Cream, Variation 3

Chestnuts

CHOOSING AND USING

Fresh or Dried

Edible chestnuts come from the Spanish chestnut tree. These trees do grow in Britain, though they are less common than the horse chestnut tree which produces conkers, but the chestnuts are usually too small to be worth picking and marketing. The fresh chestnuts sold in Britain between November and January come from Spain and Italy. Naturally fresh chestnuts have the best flavour and texture, but dried and canned chestnuts are much quicker to use. Dried ones come from France and China, canned ones from France. The canned purée is very expensive and, though the flavour is good, the lovely meal texture is lost. French dried chestnuts, too, are very expensive and difficult to obtain, but the Chinese dried variety are available by the pound in Chinese grocers. Though the flavour is coarser and sweeter than that of fresh chestnuts, they work out cheaper. It is a good example of the dottiness of the present world food economy that chestnuts which have first been processed and then shipped thousands of miles work out considerably cheaper than unprocessed chestnuts which travel only a few hundred miles.

Eight ounces (225 g) fresh chestnuts yield 4 to 5 oz (110 to 140 g) chestnut meat after removing both shell and inner skin; 1½ oz (40 g) dried chestnuts yield, after soaking, 3 oz (90 g). No more than this quantity of dried chestnuts should be used in 1½ pints (900 ml) soup, or the coarse, sweet flavour will be overpowering. Dried chestnuts are best used in recipes with a strong meaty or gamey stock, and fresh ones kept for a delicate cream soup. The dried variety need to be soaked overnight; alternatively they can be covered with water, brought to the boil, then left covered with the heat off for 45 minutes before using. If you intend to use fresh chestnuts, allow 10 to 15 minutes' peeling time per 8 oz (225 g).

Peeling

There are two methods of peeling chestnuts: both begin by making a slit from tip to base of the rounded side of the chestnut with a sharp-pointed knife. Then either roast the chestnuts at 350°F (170°C, Gas 3) or boil them for 15 to 20 minutes in water. If you have boiled them, turn off the heat, remove the chestnuts one by one, and peel off the shell, which will now be soft. The inner skin can be peeled away in strips with a small, sharp knife. If roasting them, put the slit chestnuts for 30 minutes on a baking tray on the top shelf of an oven preheated to 325°F (170°C, Gas 3). Then turn off the oven, remove the chestnuts (one by one) and peel them. This is the method for those with a gambler's temperament, for sometimes both shell and inner skin peel sweetly away together, leaving the pale yellow chestnut perfectly whole, while others will break up or hang on to their inner skins for dear life. The inner skin must then be chipped or rubbed away with maddening slowness. It is essential to remove all the inner skin, or the delicate sweetness will be ruined by a bitter tree-bark flavour.

Either way will leave you with burnt thumbs, because the shells only remain pliable while the chestnut is rather too hot to handle. The burns will be slightly worse if you use the oven method, but the texture of the chestnuts will be more floury and tempting in compensation.

CHESTNUT, BACON AND CABBAGE SOUP

Strictly speaking, cabbage is the main ingredient of this soup, because nearly half the weight of the chestnuts is in their shells. However the sweet, floury chestnut flavour pervades the soup so heavily that the cabbage is reduced to a mere walk-on-part. This is a lovely soup for a nasty winter night. If you use dried chestnuts it is also very quick and simple.

6 oz (175 g) fresh chestnuts *or*
   1½ oz (40 g) Chinese dried
   chestnuts, soaked overnight
1 small onion
1 small carrot

3 rashers streaky bacon
1 chunk of green cabbage – 4 oz
   (110 g) after trimming
1½ pints (900 ml) water
salt

112

freshly milled pepper
2 tablespoons chopped parsley or marjoram

Peel fresh chestnuts, if you are using them (see p.112). If you have forgotten to soak dried chestnuts overnight, also see p.111. Cut the prepared chestnuts into quarters, slice the onion and carrot, cut the bacon rashers into ½ inch (1 cm) squares and slice the cabbage into very fine strips 1 inch (2.5 cm) or so long. Fry the bacon, carrot and onion together in a heavy pan over a low heat for 10 minutes or until all the items are slightly crisp and faintly brown. Add the chestnuts and water, a little salt and pepper. Cover the pan and simmer for 15 minutes for fresh chestnuts, 30 minutes for dried ones, or until the chestnuts are well cooked and just beginning to disintegrate. At this point the soup can be cooled and stored or frozen. Add the cabbage and simmer the soup, uncovered, for another 5 minutes. Taste the soup and add more seasoning as needed. Stir in the chopped parsley and serve.

Variations

1. Bacon or vegetable stock can be used instead of water, but make sure that the stock and bacon together don't make the soup too salty.
2. Provided that it is still fresh-flavoured, leftover chestnut stuffing can be used in this soup.
3. Cooked bacon, gammon or ham can be used instead of streaky bacon, in which case fry the onion and carrot in 1 oz (30 g) butter, lard or ham fat, chop the bacon or ham into dice or small strips, and add with the cabbage.

CHESTNUT AND MILK SOUP

Apart from the task of peeling the chestnuts this soup is as easy as easy as falling off a log. If you only have dried or canned chestnuts, try another recipe, since it is the delicate flavour and texture of fresh chestnuts that give this soup its charm.

8 oz (225 g) fresh chestnuts – 4 to
    5 oz (110 to 140 g) after
    peeling
1 medium onion
1 medium carrot

1 large stick celery
1 oz (30 g) butter
1 pint (600 ml) milk
salt
freshly milled pepper

Peel the chestnuts (see p.112) and cut into quarters. Slice the onion, carrot and celery as finely as possible and put them with the butter in a heavy pan. Sweat them for a few minutes without browning them. Add the chestnuts, milk and seasonings. Simmer for 10 minutes or until the chestnuts are tender and the vegetables just cooked. Check the seasoning and serve at once.

Variations

1. For a richer soup, substitute $\frac{1}{4}$ pint (150 ml) cream for an equal quantity of milk.
2. Serve the soup garnished with 2 to 3 tablespoons chopped parsley, grated Gruyère or the mild Italian cheese called Fontina.
3. Half a bay leaf, a strip of lemon or orange rind or a little nutmeg may be added as extra seasoning, but don't get carried away, the charm of this soup lies in its nursery simplicity.

See also:
Vegetables: Garbure, Variation 2
Chinese Celeriac and Chestnut Soup
Chicken and Chestnut Soup
Tripe: Zuppa di Trippa alla Milanese, Variation 5
Devilled Turkey Soup, Variation 4

Chick Peas

See under:
Mixed Dried Beans: Harira

Chicken

CHOOSING AND USING

During the affluent sixties and seventies two-year-old hens, which had finished their enslaved egg production and were sinewy but tasty, became increasingly difficult to find. Let us hope that, during the recession of the eighties, there will again be a market for them and they will become widely available. A six-month-old roaster, however tender, just does not give the same depth of flavour to a stock or broth. The best source for finding boiling fowls at present are markets, specialist poultry shops and Afro-Muslim butchers, which sell tougher and older cuts of meat which often have more flavour but which many people nowadays foolishly despise.

Having tracked down a source of boiling hens, it is worth buying two or three at a time if you have a really large cooking pan and some space in your freezer for cooked chicken meat and cubes of condensed frozen stock. Very little more work is involved in preparing several chickens than in dealing with just one, and your efforts will be rewarded with several economical chicken main courses and many pints of good chicken stock for future use. Choose hens with a fleshy, well-plucked breast, and weighing $3\frac{1}{2}$ to 4 lb (about 2 kg). If the butcher is gutting the hen for you, make sure he includes the unlaid eggs if you like them (see below), the gizzard, neck, heart, feet and especially the liver, which he may try to slip into a bucket at his feet for later sale by the pound. All these innards were weighed when the price was calculated and belong to you. If a boiling hen is not available ask your butcher to save about $1\frac{1}{2}$ lb (675 g) chicken giblets, which will produce quite a good stock though not as well-flavoured as that made from a boiling hen. If you would like to make more stock, buy extra giblets with your hen.

Gutting

If the butcher will not gut the bird, or if you prefer to do it yourself, get him to remove the head and feet with a chopper, but to put the feet in the parcel. Spread out a few sheets of newspaper inside your kitchen waste bin. Take a small, pointed knife and make a slit in the chicken skin from the parson's nose up towards the breastbone, and 2 to 3 inches (5-7 cms) long. Hold the chicken over the newspaper and plunge your hand into the chicken through the slit. You may well find a huge egg blocking your path. If so, pull it out and keep it. Ignoring the smell, grasp a handful of the whitish entrails and shoot them into the waste bin. The worst is now over. Gently pull out the rest of the eggs. There may be five or so, attached near the spine and diminishing in size to a tiny button of an embryo egg near the heart. Pull out the gizzard – a walnut-sized lump with bits of fat sticking to it. Pull off the fat and discard it. Slit the gizzard open and scoop out the bits of grit inside it into the waste bin. Pull out the liver and cut away the round, green bead of the gall bladder plus any bits of the liver that are stained yellow or greenish. Lastly pull out the heart. Now wash all the bits, including the feet and the inside of the bird, pulling away any remaining lumps of fat adhering to the walls of the cavity. Pull off any little bits of feather or ends of quills. Wash the eggs and store them, covered with cold water, in the fridge. They can be served poached in a soup such as Chicken and Chestnut Soup, or used in scrambled egg, custards etc. Wrap up the entrails in the newspaper and put them straight in the dustbin, since they get pretty smelly in a warm kitchen. You are now ready to produce one major main course and two soups from one cheap boiling hen.

CHICKEN STOCK AND BROTH

Making a separate stock to be used as the base of a soup is not practical in these days of small, busy families, but bought chicken stock cubes taste almost exclusively of salt and monosodium glutamate. Here is a compromise: a chicken stock with good flavour and body, made in one operation with an old boiling hen, the meat of which can be used for a pie, salad or fricassée. If you have freezer space and a 14 to 16 pint(9-10 l) pan, it is economical in time, fuel and energy to cook three hens at a time, plus extra raw giblets if available. Freeze the extra portions of cooked chicken in some of the stock. These can form the basis of future quick meals, while the rest of the stock is reduced and reduced until it becomes a thick glaze, which will keep for weeks in the fridge and months in the freezer. However, for those who don't have large pans, families or freezers, here is a recipe for a single hen. The principle is the same for turkey broth.

1 boiling hen weighing $3\frac{1}{2}$ to 4 lb (about 2 kg) or larger, with its feet, gizzard, heart, liver and neck (see p.115) and/or $1\frac{1}{2}$ lb (675 g) chicken giblets and some feet (2 to 4) if possible
1 medium onion
2 sticks celery or 3 oz (90 g) celery trimmings
1 carrot, trimmed and scrubbed
1 clove garlic

1 bay leaf
$\frac{1}{4}$ small, ripe lemon or 2 table-spoons wine vinegar
1 sprig thyme or marjoram or $\frac{1}{2}$ teaspoon dried thyme or marjoram
2 sprigs or 3 stalks of parsley
freshly milled pepper or 8 to 10 peppercorns
salt

Gut and wash the hen, if it has not already been done, according to the instructions on p.115. Put all the giblets in a heavy pan of at least 7 pints' (4 l) capacity. Peel the onion and chop it roughly, along with the celery and carrot, and put these vegetables on top of the giblets. Lay the hen on its side on top and cover the whole lot with cold water. Put the pan, uncovered, on the lowest possible heat and bring to the boil, taking if possible 45 to 60 minutes in the process. This very slow heating makes the bird tender and the stock well-flavoured and clear.

When the stock begins to simmer (a bubble should only break the surface every second or so), take a bowl and a large metal spoon and skim off all the greyish lumps of scum as they surface. This takes about 10 minutes but does give a very clear stock. Now add the chopped garlic, the bay leaf, the lemon or vinegar, thyme or marjoram, parsley, some pepper or peppercorns and a little salt, and leave the bird to simmer for 2 to 3 hours until it is really tender. The most beautiful clear stock is made by covering the pan after the scum has been removed and putting it in a very slow oven for several hours or overnight. On the other hand the bird can be pressure cooked for speed and economy, although both the flavour and the appearance of the stock will be rather muddy. When the bird is tender, lift it out and leave it to cool, or use it immediately for a main dish. You now have a pan containing several pints of chicken stock which can be used in different ways.

First Stock and Broth

Without stirring up the giblets in the bottom of the pan, ladle off most of the stock and put it through a sieve into a non-metal container. As it cools, a layer of fat will form on the surface, which will keep the stock fresh in the fridge; remove it just before use. This is the first and best stock, which when properly seasoned becomes Chicken Broth, to be enjoyed on its own or with any of the additions suggested on the following pages. It is also very nice eaten chilled and jellied in which case add more seasoning and break up the jellied broth into pretty cups. This first stock should always be used in recipes in which the chicken flavour is intended to predominate. If you would like to clarify it, see (p.75) Beef Consommé, but omit the beef!

Second Stock

Cover the giblets with cold water again, and add the bones from the boiling hen when the flesh has been removed. Add fresh vegetables (another onion, another carrot, and 2 sticks celery, if you like), bring this second stock to the boil and skim off any scum. Simmer for 2 hours, then strain off the whitish-looking stock and throw away the bones, giblets and vegetables. This second stock can be used for any recipe in which chicken is not the main flavour.

Chicken Glaze

Provided you have at least 4 pints (2.3 l), either of these stocks can be reduced to a glaze for long-term, compact storage. Put the stock in a clean, heavy pan, bring to the boil and boil steadily, uncovered, for 1 to 2 hours until the stock has reduced to about a tenth of its original volume. Reduce the heat. At this stage it is necessary to watch it, for it can catch and burn easily. Have ready some egg cups or a metal ice tray and make sure they are very clean. When the stock has reduced to the thickness of cream and looks like pale toffee, bubbling slowly and thickly, pour it into your containers and allow them to get cold. They will set like jelly cubes and can be turned out of their containers into plastic bags and frozen; alternatively they can be kept in the little containers, covered with an extra layer of melted butter or chicken fat, then with some foil or other suitable covering, and stored in the fridge for several weeks – your own delicious, home-made chicken stock cubes.

CHICKEN AND CHESTNUT SOUP

This soup takes a couple of hours to prepare and longer to cook, but there will be enough cooked chicken left for a large fricassée or salad. It can be presented as a thin purée, or as an almost-stew with big chunks of chicken and chestnut in it (see Variation 1). Eaten the day it is made, each flavour lies separate on the palate, with the chestnuts predominating, but if it is kept in the fridge overnight the flavours blend and mature to an exquisite subtlety. The soup is so rich if made with a chicken that any cream would be gilding the lily, and even fresh chopped herbs are unnecessary. The best way to present it would be in a pretty old tureen, with the little golden eggs bobbing on the surface.

For 3 pints (1.75 l):

a boiling hen with its giblets and feet – see Variation 2 if a fowl is not available
about 5 pints (3 l) water
2 bay leaves
10 peppercorns

2 medium onions
2 sticks celery
8 oz (225 g) fresh chestnut *or* 2 oz (60 g) dried chestnuts
salt
freshly milled pepper

If your boiling fowl has not been gutted, follow the directions on p.115-16 and reserve the unlaid eggs, covered in cold water, in the fridge. Wash the hen and the giblets and put them, giblets first, in a stockpot or other large pan. Add the water, bring to simmering point and skim off the scum as it rises. When only white foam is rising, add the bay leaves and peppercorns and the onion and celery trimmings and cook very gently for 2 to 3 hours, with a bubble breaking the surface only every second or so, until the chicken is tender but not falling off the bones. Meanwhile prepare the dried or fresh chestnuts as described on p.111 and chop the onion and celery. Lift out the fowl and leave to cool. Take another large, heavy pan and cook the onion, celery and chestnuts in ½ pint (300 ml) fatty stock for 30 minutes keeping tightly covered or until the chestnuts are tender. Lift out 4 nice chestnuts and reserve them for garnish. Purée the vegetable and chestnut mixture in the blender, adding more strained stock if necessary, or put the mixture through the medium plate of the food mill. Pour this soup base into the clean pan and add more of the strained stock, to make it up to 2 pints (1.2 l). Chop a breast or leg of the chicken into small dice, removing all skin and gristle, and add to the soup. Roughly chop the extra chestnuts and add them too. The soup can be made in advance to this point. When reheating, check the seasoning and serve, do not let it boil, or the texture of the diced meat will deteriorate.

Variations

1. Use 12 oz (350 g) fresh chestnuts or 3 oz (90 g) dried; purée half of them and cut the rest in large pieces. Take one third of the chicken meat and cut it into chestnut-sized pieces. Poach the unlaid eggs in the soup for 2 minutes before serving. This is now a substantial and even more dramatic main course soup.
2. A boiling fowl has an excellent flavour and is very good value for money, but if you can't get one use 1½ lb (675 g) chicken giblets (many butchers now sell these) including one pair of feet, and one

119

good-sized chicken portion, plus 2 oz (60 g) butter or ¼ pint (150 ml) cream. Make the stock with the giblets and feet and cook for 2½ hours, then add the chicken piece and cook for another 30 minutes or until cooked. Proceed as in the main recipe, softening the celery and onion in stock and butter or cream.

3. Some of the stock can be replaced by milk if necessary, but there is no point attempting this dish without at least 1 pint (600 ml) really well-flavoured chicken stock.

CHICKEN, EGG AND LEMON SOUP

To Greeks, Turks and some Arabs, this soup or some version of it is standard fare. Probably the most familiar version, which in Greece is called Avgolemono, is given in Variation 1. The main recipe contains spinach instead of the traditional rice and is high in protein, iron and vitamin C. It is a delicately thickened, refreshing summer soup which, given good chicken stock or your own chicken glaze (see p.118) can be made in 20 minutes or so. For a low calorie (though not low cholesterol) soup, see Variation 2.

8 oz (225 g) fresh spinach *or* 4 oz (110 g) frozen leaf spinach
1 stick celery
1 carrot
1 oz (30 g) butter
1 teaspoon flour (optional)
1½ pints (900 ml) rich chicken stock *or* 1 to 2 lumps of chicken glaze (6 to 8 table-spoons) plus water to make up

1½ pints (900 ml)
salt
freshly milled pepper
½ teaspoon dill weed *or* ¼ tea-spoon dill seeds
1 dessertspoon chopped parsley
juice of ½ to 2 lemons, according to taste and the juiciness of the lemons
2 large or 3 medium egg yolks

Defrost frozen leaf spinach or wash fresh spinach thoroughly in several changes of water. Pull the fresh spinach leaves off the central rib and discard it (see p.168). Roll the fresh leaves into a fat cigar shape and cut across into thin slivers ¼ inch (½ cm) wide. Cut the defrosted spinach in the same way. Chop the celery and carrot into ¼ inch (½ cm) dice. Put the butter in a heavy stainless or enamelled pan and melt it over a low heat; add the celery and carrot and cook gently for 5 minutes. Stir in the flour and cook for a minute. Pour in the chicken broth and bring to simmering point. Add salt, pepper, dill and parsley. From this point the soup cannot easily be kept waiting, so begin to get people seated at the table.

120

Add the spinach to the soup and immediately squeeze about 2 tablespoons lemon juice on to the egg yolks in a small bowl. Whisk for a minute until the mixture is smooth and a little bubbly. Now add a ladleful of soup and whisk again. Remove the soup from the heat and transfer the whisk to the pan. Pour in the egg mixture, whisking all the time. The soup will become lemon-coloured and slightly thick (for more details of this process see p.21). Taste and add more salt, pepper or lemon, without returning the soup to the heat, and serve at once.

Variations

1. Leave out the celery, carrot and spinach and add 1 oz (30 g) long grain white rice. You may include the butter or not, depending on your taste and the richness of the stock. Simply simmer the rice in the seasoned stock, half-covered, for 12 minutes or until it is just tender. Meanwhile mix the yolks with the lemon and, if you are nervous of it curdling (see p.21), a flat teaspoon flour. When the rice is cooked add the yolks as in the main recipe and serve immediately.
2. For a low calorie soup, leave out the butter and flour, or use just 1 teaspoon butter in which to sweat the carrot and celery.
3. The essential ingredients of this soup are good chicken broth, egg yolks and lemon juice. The spinach, however, can be varied with watercress or sorrel, the carrot and celery with spring onion and garlic or bulb fennel, and the rice with barley or small pasta.
4. To make this already nutritious soup into a more satisfying main course, add 3 to 4 oz (90 to 110 g) diced cooked chicken.

CHICKEN NOODLE SOUP

After hamburgers and ice cream, Chicken Noodle Soup is one of the most universal features of North American food. As with Cream of Chicken, it is only the canned and dried versions which are widely known, and the robust and satisfying character of the home-made variety is quite a revelation. It should be made with chicken stock or glaze and some cooked chicken if you have it, or a small raw chicken joint (see Variation 1). It keeps and freezes well.

1½ pints (900 ml) chicken stock
1 small clove garlic, peeled and
    crushed with a little salt

½ teaspoon dried *or* 1 sprig fresh
    marjoram or oregano
salt

freshly milled pepper
1½ oz (40 g) vermicelli, broken
  spaghetti, or alphabet or
  other small pasta or, ideally,
  make the noodles on p.37

5 spring onions, peeled and
  trimmed
3 to 4 oz (90 to 110 g) cooked
  chicken

If using dried pasta, put the chicken stock in a large pan with the garlic, marjoram and a little salt and pepper. Bring to the boil and add the pasta. Stir well and boil gently for 12 minutes or until the pasta is nearly tender. Meanwhile cut the spring onions into ½ inch (1 cm) lengths and the cooked chicken into small dice. When the pasta is nearly ready, add the onion and chicken and simmer for a further 2 minutes. Check the seasoning, and either serve or cool and refrigerate.

Variations

1. Put a chicken joint weighing about 8 oz (225 g) in the pan with the chicken stock and seasonings. Simmer, tightly covered, for 20 minutes, or until the chicken is just cooked. Lift it out and let it cool. Meanwhile begin to cook the pasta, having first added water to make up the stock to 1½ pints (900 ml) again if it has reduced. Cut the chicken meat off the bone and dice it. Proceed with the main recipe.
2. You can use half chicken and half chicken livers, sautéed in a very little butter for 2 minutes and then diced.
3. Reduce the pasta by a third and add 2 tablespoons cooked green peas, or 2 oz (60 g) mushrooms, sliced and sautéed for a minute in a little butter. A combination of 1 oz (30 g) dried pasta, 2 oz (60 g) sautéed chicken livers, 2 tablespoons cooked green peas and 1 oz (30 g) sautéed, sliced mushrooms is particularly delicious.
4. The Parmesan balls on p.30 are delicious in this soup. Grated Parmesan can be sprinkled on top of any version of the soup.

CHICKEN, PUMPKIN AND PEANUT BUTTER SOUP

Don't be put off by this odd combination of ingredients, for although the soup comes from West Africa, this adaptation is just exotic enough to make a good exhibitionist start or centrepiece to the meal, and has a rich, spicy and very chickeny flavour. It keeps and freezes very well, and if you already have some cooked chicken and stock is very simple. Before you read on, see pps.116-18 for notes on chicken stock and broth.

2 medium onions
2 small sticks celery
12 oz (350 g) slice pumpkin
1 small fresh or dried chili, seeded
1 to 2 cloves garlic, peeled and crushed with salt
8 allspice berries or $\frac{1}{4}$ teaspoon each cinnamon, clove and ginger
salt
freshly milled pepper
1$\frac{1}{2}$ pints (900 ml) good chicken stock

1 heaped tablespoon peanut butter
the meat from half a breast or half a leg of the chicken or boiling hen

For garnish:
1 small onion
1 small red pepper, seeded
1 dessertspoon oil
1 tablespoon roughly chopped parsley

Roughly chop the onion, celery and pumpkin flesh and put in a heavy pan. Add the chili, garlic, spices, a little salt and pepper and the chicken stock. Bring to the boil and simmer for 30 minutes, or until the vegetables are soft. Remove from the heat. Stir in the peanut butter and, having allowed the soup to cool for a few minutes, blend it, or put it through the coarse or medium plate of the food mill. Return the soup to a clean pan, or to a non-metal container if you want to store it overnight. Dice the cooked chicken into neat cubes and add to the soup. When you want to serve it, reheat gently and taste when hot, adding more salt, pepper and spices to your taste. Do not let it boil.

Start the garnish when you are ready to reheat the soup. Slice the onion and pepper into very fine rings, as near paper-thin as you can manage. Heat the oil in a small pan and sauté the onion and pepper over a high heat, stirring continuously for a couple of minutes. Add the parsley and stir again. Remove from the heat and season with salt and pepper. Serve the soup in a tureen or bowls, decorated with the hot, crisp pepper mixture.

Variations

1. If you don't have a boiling hen, follow the directions on pps.116-18 for alternative methods of making stock. There is no point in using a stock cube for a recipe whose main flavour is chicken.
2. For a main course soup use two or three times the amount of chicken, cut in larger pieces, and, if you like, leave the vegetables in the soup base unblended or sieved, in which case make sure to use smooth peanut butter.

123

CHINESE CHICKEN SOUP

In smart Chinese restaurants soup is sometimes served from a charcoal brazier with a curious moat around its chest. The moat is filled with chicken broth, to which beautifully sliced vegetables and meats are then added. Five minutes later this colourful concoction, containing all kinds of interesting flavours and textures, is ladled into your bowl. If you enjoy a little flamboyance you may like to do the same thing with a fondue set in front of your admiring guests; in any case get them seated before adding the bits to the boiling broth, since preserving the crisp freshness of the vegetables is the whole point of the exercise. The main recipe and its variations by no means exhaust the possibilities of this type of soup, and Chinese cookery books or a visit to a Chinese supermarket will suggest many more ideas.

3 to 4 oz (90 to 110 g) cooked
    lean ham, pork or chicken
2 tablespoons dry sherry
½ bunch spring onions – 1 oz
    (30 g) peeled and trimmed
2 to 3 sticks celery
1½ pints (900 ml) good chicken
    stock (see pps. 116-18)

2 oz (60 g) white cabbage *or* 4 oz
    (110 g) Chinese cabbage
salt
freshly milled pepper
a ½ inch (1 cm) piece of fresh
    ginger, peeled and grated
1 to 2 tablespoons thin soy sauce

Cut the meat into thin slices not more than ¼ inch (½ cm) thick. Divide these slices into matchsticks and pour the sherry over them. Cut the spring onions, celery and cabbage or Chinese cabbage into small, neat slices, on the diagonal so that the maximum surface area of the vegetables is exposed. Bring the chicken stock to the boil in a large pan and season it rather highly with salt, pepper, the grated ginger and soy sauce. Let the broth come to a good rolling boil and make sure that everyone is seated at the table. Add the celery and after 2 minutes the cabbage or Chinese cabbage and spring onion. After another 2 minutes add the meat and its marinade. Serve after one more minute's cooking.

Variations

1. Use 1 oz (30 g) Chinese dried prawns, soaked for 2 hours in enough sherry, soy sauce and cold water to cover them. Cook them for 20 minutes in the broth, then carry on with the main recipe. Instead of the meat, add 3 oz (90 g) cooked prawns or shrimps a minute before serving.
2. Fresh or tinned bean sprouts, bamboo shoots or water chestnuts can be used instead of celery (but add these at the last moment); so can carrots, celeriac or cucumber.
3. The soup can be thickened with 1 tablespoon rice flour, arrowroot or cornflour dissolved in 4 tablespoons cold water and whisked into the soup a minute before serving.
4. A few tablespoons of whole canned sweetcorn may be added to the thickened soup instead of the cabbage.

COCK-A-LEEKIE

No doubt this soup originated as a method of tenderizing some ancient Scottish cockerel, thin and stringy from years of servicing his harem, but cockerels cannot be bought in a butcher's and a boiling hen does very well. If you want to make a large-scale main course soup starting with a raw hen, see Variation 1. The main recipe assumes that you have some good chicken stock or chicken glaze (see p.118) and some leftover cooked chicken or a raw chicken joint.

3 medium leeks
8 prunes, soaked for an hour or two
3 to 4 oz (90 to 110 g) cooked chicken meat *or* 8 oz (225 g) raw chicken joint

1½ pints (900 ml) home-made chicken stock
¼ pint (150 ml) double cream
salt
freshly milled pepper

Trim and peel the leeks, slice them into $\frac{1}{2}$ inch (1 cm) rounds and leave to soak in plenty of cold water (see p.183). Stone the prunes and cut them in quarters. If you are using raw chicken, put it to simmer very slowly for 30 minutes with the chicken stock in a stainless or enamelled pan with a tight lid. When cooked, remove from the broth and put to cool. Cut the cooling joint or the cooked chicken meat into $\frac{1}{2}$ inch (1 cm) squares. Add the leeks and prunes to the stock and cook gently for 15 minutes. Pour in the cream and season to taste. Add the chicken meat and simmer for a minute or two. The soup can either be served immediately or cooled, refrigerated and served the following day.

Variations

1. For a main course soup for 8 to 10 people, choose a boiling hen weighing $3\frac{1}{2}$ to 4 lb (about 2 kg). Cook it as described in the recipe for Chicken Stock, with leek peelings instead of onions. When cooked, lift it out and cool. Strain 4 pints (2.3 l) chicken stock into a very large pan and put over a low heat. Add 3 oz (90 g) brown rice now, or use white rice and add only 15 minutes before the end of the cooking time. Add 2 lb (1 kg) leeks in thick slices. Simmer for 30 minutes while you cut the meat off and put it into the soup in large pieces with 24 stoned and halved prunes. Add seasoning. Check that the rice is cooked, and serve.
2. The prunes can be left out and more leek or a small diced potato substituted.

CREAM OF CHICKEN LIVER AND MADEIRA

Most large supermarkets now sell 8 oz cartons of frozen chicken livers, which are generally well cleaned and not expensive. With 4 oz (110 g) of these and a slug a madeira, a delicious kind of liquid chicken liver pâté can be made in no time, especially since the liver and madeira flavours are so strong that a stock cube can be used, if necessary, without its presence being apparent. The soup is best eaten at once.

4 oz (110 g) chicken livers
1 small onion
1 oz (30 g) butter
1 tablespoon flour
1 pint (600 ml) chicken stock
salt

freshly milled pepper
2 tablespoons madeira
a few tablespoons double or sour
  cream
2 tablespoons chopped parsley

Check the chicken livers carefully and cut away any green or yellow bits. Slice the onion quite finely. Melt the butter in a heavy pan. Put in the onion and sweat gently over a low heat for 5 minutes. Add the livers and stir round for another minute. Now add the flour, stir it in thoroughly, and cook it for a minute. Add the chicken stock little by little, stirring in each addition before making the next. Bring the soup to the boil. Season with salt and pepper and simmer for 3 minutes only. Put the soup through the fine plate of a food mill, or blend and then sieve it to get rid of any little stringy bits in the liver. Reheat in a clean pan with the madeira. Do not boil. Taste when hot, adding more seasoning if necessary. Serve at once, with a little thick cream swirled into each portion and parsley sprinkled on top.

Variations

1. Port, dry sherry or brandy can be used instead of madeira.
2. Curried or herb croûtons would be a suitable garnish (see p.28).
3. Duck, goose or turkey livers make an excellent substitute for chicken livers.

CREAM OF CHICKEN SOUP

Some young Canadians who tasted this soup remarked that they had never eaten fresh Cream of Chicken Soup before. Since canned Cream of Chicken is one of the best-selling soups in the English-speaking world, it is sad to think of all those millions of people going to their graves without tasting their favourite soup at its best. Given some cooked meat and stock from a boiling hen (see the recipe for Chicken Broth on pps.116-17), the soup is very simple and quick to make. It keeps and freezes well and is also delicious iced, as in Variation 1.

1 oz (30 g) butter *or* 2 tablespoons oil
1 tablespoon white flour
1½ pints (900 ml) good chicken
  stock
salt
freshly milled pepper

juice of ½ lemon
¼ pint (150 ml) double cream
3 heaped tablespoons, 2 oz
  (60 g), cooked meat from a
  boiling hen or chicken, cut in
  slivers

Melt the butter in a heavy pan over a low heat. Stir in the flour and
cook for a minute, stirring all the time. When this roux is sizzling and
a light beige colour, add the chicken stock little by little, stirring each
addition to smoothness before putting in more stock. Add salt,
pepper and lemon juice and leave the soup to simmer for 15 minutes.
At this point the soup can be cooled and stored overnight or longer
in the fridge. It also freezes well, and is a very good base for a great
range of additions and garnishes. Reheat in a clean pan with the
cream and slivers of cooked chicken. Check the seasoning when very
hot and serve just before it boils, otherwise the cream may curdle and
the meat may go stringy.

Variations

1. Make the soup as above and chill thoroughly in the freezing
   compartment of the fridge or the coldest part of the main
   compartment. Taste when very cold and add more lemon juice,
   salt and pepper as needed. If you like a little zap add a touch of
   chili or tabasco, but don't mask the lovely chicken flavour. Serve
   either with the slivers of chicken meat or with 3 to 4 tablespoons
   cooked shrimps or prawns and chopped chives to garnish.
2. For an exhibitionist iced version, make the soup as in Variation 1.
   Softly whip the cream and season it with salt, pepper, lemon and
   chopped chives, reserving a few chives. When the soup is iced it
   should jelly a little. Break up the jelly, heap it in pretty cups, cover
   with the whipped cream and garnish with the reserved chives.
3. Instead of slivers of chicken meat add 3 heaped tablespoons
   asparagus tips, blanched in boiling water for 5 to 7 minutes – try
   also tomatoes – skinned, seeded, cored and chopped (see
   pps.247-8) – or cooked small pasta or cooked rice, green peas or
   watercress leaves, or anything else that is fresh and lightly
   flavoured, from avocado slices to wild sorrel leaves.
4. For an even richer but also very nutritious soup, substitute for half

the cream 2 egg yolks beaten with a little lemon. Beat a little hot soup into the yolks. Transfer the whisk to the pan and whisk in the yolk and lemon mixture. The soup will thicken very slightly. Serve immediately, without boiling. (For more details of the egg thickening process see p.21.) For a less rich soup substitute $\frac{1}{4}$ pint (150 ml) plain yogurt for the cream and lemon. Add it in the same way as the egg yolks above.

MULLIGATAWNY SOUP

The British still love spicy and curried food, so it is odd that this Anglo-Indian soup has gone so completely out of fashion. The word means pepperwater, and presumably the original Mulligatawny was, like this recipe, a broth containing hot and aromatic spices. However the excellent and/encyclopædic *Constance Spry Cookery Book* gives three recipes – for broth, for thin gravy soup (called Potage Pondicherry) and for a thick soup. Mulligatawny can be made with proprietary curry powder, but the taste will be much less distinctive.

2 tablespoons brown or white rice
$\frac{1}{2}$ pint (300 ml) water
1 clove
pinch of turmeric
salt
$\frac{1}{2}$ teaspoon cumin – seeds for preference
6 peppercorns

1 small dried chili
6 cardamom pods
1 oz (30 g) unblanched almonds and 1 oz (30 g) fresh coconut meat *or* $2\frac{1}{2}$ oz (75 g) unblanched almonds
$1\frac{1}{2}$ pints (900 ml) good chicken broth

Put the rice to boil in the water with the clove, turmeric and a little salt. Grind the other spices, almonds and coconut, if using, in a good processor, coffee grinder, blender or mincer. If you are using a blender it may be necessary to add a ladleful of the broth to help it to blend, but it is better if you can avoid this. Put the nuts and spices into a heavy pan over a low heat and cook them dry for a couple of minutes, stirring all the time since they burn easily. This process brings out their aroma. Add the chicken broth and a little more salt. Bring to the boil and simmer, half-covered, for 10 minutes. When the rice is cooked, but before it starts to get soggy and sticky, stir it into the soup. Taste, adjust the seasoning and serve. If you are making the soup for the next day, keep the rice separate until you reheat the soup.

Variations

1. This soup can be made equally well with beef, mutton or any other well-flavoured clear meat or vegetable broth.
2. As an appetizer, the soup can be made without the rice, or as a main course soup with double the quantity of rice with 3 to 4 oz (90 to 110 g) cooked chicken added just before serving.
3. For a less peppery soup, omit the chili. The other spices can be varied according to the contents of your spice jars, but the cardamom pods, though extravagant, do add authenticity which it would be sad to lose.
4. If the soup is to be more than an appetizer, a small bowl of plain yogurt or sour cream, with coriander or parsley leaves stirred in, would be a popular addition.

See also:
Beef: Pot au Feu, Variation 4
Purée of Duck and Celery, Variation 1
Duck and Cucumber Soup, Variation 1
Green Pea and Ham Soup, Variation 2

Chicken Livers

See under:
Chicken Noodle Soup, Variations 2 and 3
Cream of Chicken Liver and Madeira

Chinese Cabbage or Celery Cabbage

See under:
Chinese Chicken Soup

Clams

See under:
Mussels: Cream of Mussel Soup, Variation 2
Shellfish Cream

Cock-a-Leekie

See under:
Chicken

Coconut

See under:
Aubergine, Red Pepper and Coconut Soup
Beef: Jamaican Red Pea Soup
Chicken: Mulligatawny Soup

Conger Eel

See under:
Atlantic Fish Stew

Consommé

See under:
Beef

131

Coriander

See under:
Carrot and Coriander Soup

Corn on the Cob

SWEETCORN CHOWDER

Corn on the cob comes into the shops around September, and during that month I have tried again and again to make a chowder with fresh corn in which the nutty sweetness of the corn was preserved. Each time the corn was tough and tasted dull. The only successful occasion was when some leftover chowder had been frozen, defrosted and reheated: it was tender and delicious. Since I can hardly suggest that you first make fresh chowder and then freeze and defrost it before eating, I regretfully suggest that, unless you grow your own corn and can pick it young and tender, you use canned corn.

132

1 small onion
1 small green pepper
1 medium potato
7 oz (200 g) canned corn – whole
   kernel, or creamed 5 oz
   (140 g) raw corn kernels sliced
   from 2 medium ears of corn
1 oz (30 g) butter

1 small clove garlic, peeled and
   crushed with a little salt
1 pint (600 ml) milk
about ¼ pint (150 ml) water
salt
soy sauce
freshly milled pepper

Slice the onion and pepper and cut the potato in cubes. If you are using fresh corn, slice down the sides of the ears with a sharp knife and the kernels will zip off in a most satisfying manner. Melt the butter in a heavy-bottomed pan and add the garlic, onion and pepper. Sweat gently for 5 minutes but do not allow them to brown. Add the corn, if canned, potato, milk and half the water and bring to the boil. If you are using fresh corn, blend half with the milk and add with the potato. Add the rest only 3 minutes before serving the soup. Add some salt and a couple of shakes of soy sauce and simmer gently for 15 minutes or until the potato cubes are cooked. Pour in more water if the soup has reduced too much. Taste and add plenty of pepper and more soy sauce to counter-balance the sweetness. Serve at once, or cool and store overnight, or freeze.

Variations

1. Two rashers of streaky bacon, rinded and boned and cut into ½ inch (1 cm) pieces, may be substituted for both green pepper and butter. You may like to garnish this version with chopped parsley or chives.
2. Up to ½ pint (300 ml) single cream may replace ½ pint of the milk; or a garnish of sour cream, either plain or mixed with fresh parsley, chives, watercress, sorrel or mustard and cress, may be served.
3. Sliced cup or button mushrooms or celery sticks – 2 to 3 oz (60 to 90 g) – can be substituted for the green pepper.
4. If soy sauce is not available, use Worcester sauce or add a pinch of cayenne or dash of tabasco.

See also:
Smoked Haddock Chowder, Variation 3
Turkey Chowder

Courgette

COURGETTE CHOWDER

During the late summer, courgettes can be bought very cheaply and work out just as cheap as they seem, since wastage is so little. They can be quickly transformed into a pretty pale green purée of pleasant consistency – the only trouble is that it tastes of absolutely nothing. If, therefore, you have loads of courgettes, you may consider making a purée (Variation 1) and serving it with cheese croûtons (see p.28), peperonata (p.43) or other enrichment to give it a bit of zazz. Otherwise the courgette retains its character much better in the main recipe.

¾ lb (350 g) courgettes, small for preference	1 oz (30 g) butter
1 small onion	1 pint (600 ml) milk
1 medium carrot	1 tablespoon parsley, marjoram or basil, chopped
4 red ripe tomatoes, 6 oz (175 g) after peeling and coring	salt and fresh pepper

Peel the onion and carrot and dice into ½ inch (1 cm) pieces. Top and tail the courgettes. Cut them in quarters lengthways and then in ½ inch (1 cm) slices. Sweat the onion and carrot in the butter in a heavy non-aluminium pan for 5 minutes, stirring occasionally. Add the courgettes and sweat them too, stirring a couple of times and covering the pan in between stirs. When the courgettes have got rather limp (5-7 minutes) add the milk and bring it to the boil, while you watch. Simmer the soup with a little salt for 10 minutes. Peel and core the tomatoes (see pps.247-8 for details) and cut them into ½ inch (1 cm) pieces. Add the tomatoes to the soup and blend one third of it. Stir the blended part back into the rest, add the parsley, taste and add more salt and fresh pepper. Serve.

Variations

1. 1 small onion, 1 lb (450 g) courgettes, 1 oz (30 g) butter, ½ pint (300 ml) milk, chopped parsley, salt and pepper. Follow the main

recipe but blend all the mixture to a pale green purée. Enrich as suggested in the introduction. The purée keeps and freezes well.

2. ½ teaspoon grated lemon rind and a bay leaf make pleasant additions to the chowder.

3. Potato or runner beans can be substituted for part of the courgettes and celery for the carrot.

Courgettes

See under:
Cabbage: Majorcan Soup, Variation 3
Vegetables: Minestrone
Vegetables: Pistou

Crab

CHOOSING AND USING

Crabs, like lobsters, are in season from April to November. Given that the shell weighs far more than the meat, crabs are definitely in the luxury price range, though not in the astronomical lobster bracket. Cock crabs are more expensive than hens (sometimes a third more, sometimes double the price) because they have more claw meat – the prized white meat as opposed to the flabbier brown body meat. A large cock crab is therefore the best buy for a main dish, but a hen crab will do very well for soup.

Because their delicate flesh deteriorates so quickly after death, crabs are generally brought alive from seaside to shop. It is a good plan to buy your crab alive, but live crabs are not so readily available as live lobsters because crabs must be killed in a particular way. If dispatched by boiling or with a knife, a crab suffers severely from shock and often 'shoots its claws' (sheds it claw shells) so that the white meat becomes tinged with blood. It needs to be gently suffocated in lukewarm fresh water for an hour or two. If you prefer not to involve yourself in these grisly doings, buy your crab ready cooked. A cooked crab must be bought in a reputable shop with a fast turnover, where the crabs really *are* cooked daily – everyone will *tell* you that they are cooked daily. Get the fishmonger to break open the crab so that you can smell it in front of him – it should have a fresh seaside smell. Reject categorically a crab that was previously opened or has a stale or even slightly unpleasant smell.

A 1½ lb (675 g) hen crab is suitable for all the soups that follow. You must make the soup the same day that you buy your cooked crab, but it is perfectly all right to eat the following day, since shellfish soups all improve with keeping. You can buy a live crab the day before you need it, and keep it overnight in a large, heavy plastic or paper bag with air holes, in the bottom of the fridge. Three hours before you want to cook it, suffocate it as described above. When it is quite dead, drop it into simmering salted water in a large stainless or enamelled pan, and simmer very gently for about 30 minutes. Lift it out and cool it as rapidly as possible, particularly in hot weather. When the crab is cool, twist off the claws and feelers. Put your thumb and first finger in the pair of feeler holes just below the eyes, and pull the underpart of the shell out and away from them. With a bit of a tug it will come clean away. Inside this undershell are the grey-green triangular gills. Discard them, along with the eyes and the gristly bits around and behind them. Everything else is edible. If you have bought a cooked crab, the fishmonger will already have done this part.

Scoop all the pinkish-brown body meat from inside the main shell and a few scraps from the underbelly. Put this brown meat in a covered container in the fridge. Now give each section of the claws a gentle biff with a small hammer, being careful not to drive fragments of shell into the white claw meat. Ease the white meat out of the claws, keeping it as whole as possible and perhaps using a skewer to reach the last corners. Do not forget to remove the piece of cartilage in the centre of the main claw meat. Put the pieces of white meat and the feelers in another covered container in the fridge. You will have only about 3½ oz (100 g) meat in all.

CRAB GUMBO

A gumbo is a Creole meat or shellfish stew. The essential ingredient is okra – the five-sided pointed green pods sometimes called ladies' fingers. The okra, which can now be bought quite cheaply in West Indian or African vegetable shops, have a curious viscous, not to say gummy consistency which provides a little thickening for the soup. If you can't find okra or can't stand them, Variation 1 is still excellent. If the crab is the difficulty, see Variation 2. A gumbo is at its best just made, but keeps and freezes quite well.

This recipe makes 3 pints (1.75 litres.)

the meat from a fresh crab
2 pints (1.2l) white fish stock (see p. 157)
2 rashers streaky bacon (smoked for preference)
2 tablespoons oil
a small onion or $\frac{1}{2}$ bunch of spring onions
1 large clove of garlic, peeled and chopped
$\frac{1}{2}$ lb (225 g) fresh small okra
$\frac{1}{2}$ green pepper
3 large very ripe tomatoes
2 pinches of cayenne or 1 small green chili, seeded and chopped
a bay leaf and a pinch of thyme
salt

Rind, bone and cut the bacon into small pieces. Peel and chop the onion roughly. Fry the bacon, onion and garlic in the oil, in a large stainless or enamelled pan for 5-7 minutes browning them a little. Cut the tops off the okra (the tails too if dried up) and slice into $\frac{1}{2}$ inch (1 cm) pieces. Chop the seeded green pepper roughly and add it with the cayenne or chopped chili to the bacon mixture and fry another 3-5 minutes. Add the okra, the fish stock, bay leaf and thyme and bring to the boil. Simmer for 10 minutes. Meanwhile peel the tomatoes (see pps.247-8) take out the cores and cut into rough chunks. Have the crab meat ready in $\frac{1}{2}$ inch (1 cm) pieces. Try a piece of okra, it should be just soft – older larger specimens take longer to cook. Adjust the seasoning to a good rich spiciness and assemble your eaters. Just before serving add the crab and tomato. Stir for a minute without re-boiling and serve.

Variations

1. 4 oz (110 g) each of fresh spinach and sliced runner or French beans can be used instead of the okra. Add in the same way.
2. $\frac{1}{2}$ lb (225 g) prawns or shrimps in the shell can be used instead of crab. Make a stock with the shells and 1 lb (450 g) white fish heads and bones, then proceed with the main recipe. Alternatively any good white fish will make a lovely gumbo, use rather more about 6 oz (175 g) of filleted fish, skinned and cut into pieces, and a white fish stock (see p.157). Cook the fish pieces for 3-4 minutes.

137

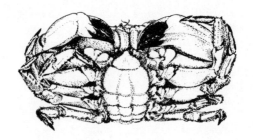

CRAB AND MUSHROOM CHOWDER

Although this chowder takes more time than Smoked Haddock Chowder, it is still quite simple, especially if you start with a cooked crab. With the mastery of this recipe alone you will make your reputation as a soup cook, for it is absolutely delicious. Please begin by reading the instructions on choosing, cooking and extracting the meat from crabs on pps.135-6. No variations to the main recipe are given because it really is a perfect one. If you have only canned crab, don't use this recipe but follow the one for Shellfish Cream.

1 small onion *or* 6 shallots
1 large stick celery and ¼ fennel
 bulb *or* 2 large sticks celery
1 oz (30 g) butter
¾ pint (450 ml) white fish stock
 (see p.157)
the brown meat, white meat and
 feelers from a cooked hen
 crab weighing 1½ lb (675 g) –
 about 3½ oz (100 g) crab meat
¾ pint (450 ml) creamy milk or
 single cream

1 large or 2 small potatoes –
 Edwards or Reds
4 oz (110 g) mushrooms (flat for
 flavour, button for delicate
 colour)
salt
freshly milled pepper
pinch of nutmeg
pinch of cayenne
4 fennel seeds – if you are not
 using bulb fennel

Slice the onions or shallots, celery and fennel bulb and sweat them in the butter in a heavy stainless or enamelled pan for 6 to 8 minutes, until they are slightly soft but not brown. Add the fish stock and simmer for 15 minutes.

Meanwhile wash the crab feelers, break off the tiny claws and discard them. Chop the rest of the feelers into little pieces and pound them in a pestle and mortar, or blend them with some of the milk or cream, or grind them in a good processor or mincer. If you have ground the feelers dry, either blend them with some of the milk or cream and the brown crab meat, or, if you have no blender, heat the pounded feelers in some of the milk and simmer for 10 minutes, pounding the brown meat meantime. Add the brown meat to the simmering milk for 1 minute only and then strain or mill the mixture (use a fine-meshed strainer) into the cooked fish stock and vegetable mixture.

Strain the blended mixture in the same way, pressing through as much of the mixture as possible with the back of a ladle. Swish out the blender jar, food mill, sieve or other equipment with the remaining milk or cream and add it to the main soup. Dice the potatoes – small for a dinner party, larger for a family lunch – and add them to the soup with a little pepper, nutmeg, cayenne and fennel seeds if you are using them. Simmer for 10 minutes or more, until the potatoes are nearly cooked. Add the diced mushrooms and simmer for a further 3 minutes. At this point the soup may be cooled and stored in the fridge; in fact it improves with keeping. Reheat in a clean stainless or enamelled pan with the diced white meat added. Adjust the seasoning when the soup is hot, but do not boil it or the crab meat will become stringy. Serve simply in bowls which set off its rose-beige and cream colours.

CRAB AND RED PEPPER BISQUE

The idea for this combination of flavours comes from George Lassalle's excellent book, *The Adventurous Fish Cook*, and both the flavour and the colour are warm and rich. If you prefer a more standard bisque, try Variation 1.

1 hen crab weighing bout 1½ lb (675 g), cooked and prepared according to the instructions on p.136

1 small onion *or* 6 shallots

2 large sticks celery

1 small, brilliantly red pepper

1½ oz (40 g) butter *or* 3 table-spoons good olive oil

1 small clove garlic, peeled and crushed with a little salt

3 tablespoons reasonable-quality brandy

1 pint (600 ml) white fish stock (see p.157)

1 oz (30 g) long grain rice

salt

freshly milled pepper

cayenne

¼ pint (150 ml) single cream

lemon juice

If your crab has some scarlet roe inside and you want to make coral butter:

the crab roe	salt
2 oz (60 g) butter – unsalted is best	freshly milled pepper
	cayenne
a little lemon juice	

Wash the crab feelers, break off the little claws and discard them. Chop the rest of the feelers fairly small and pound them in a pestle and mortar, or grind them in a good processor or mincer. Slice the onion, celery and red pepper finely and sweat with the butter or oil and garlic for 8 to 10 minutes in a heavy enamelled or stainless pan, stirring occasionally and taking care that the vegetables do not brown. Add the ground-up feelers and the brown crab meat and heat them through for a minute. Then pour the brandy over them. When you have taken the bottle away, touch a lighted match to the contents of the pan; shake the pan as the alcohol burns so that the flavour reaches every part of the contents. Add $\frac{3}{4}$ pint (450 ml) of the fish stock and the rice, with a little salt, pepper and cayenne. Simmer very gently for 15 minutes. Let the mixture cool a little and then blend thoroughly. Pass the soup through a fine-meshed sieve, pressing the last bits of crab and vegetable through with the back of a ladle, or put it through the fine plate of a food mill. In either case, swill out the blender jar with the rest of the fish stock and scrape any particles from the bottom of the sieve or mill. Do not use a wide-meshed sieve or coarse plate in the food mill, or unpleasant little chunks of crab shell will be left in the bisque. The soup can be stored in the fridge overnight at this point, and the flavours will blend and mature if kept for 24 hours before eating.

When you want to serve the soup, cut the white meat, together with the roe, if you have it and are not making coral butter, into small dice; put them and the soup into a clean stainless or enamelled pan. Add the cream and reheat the bisque gently over a low heat. When it is hot, but not boiling, adjust the seasoning with salt, pepper, cayenne and a squeeze of lemon juice if you like. Serve at once with thin slices of wholemeal bread spread with coral, anchovy or herb butter (see pps.41-2 for the last two).

Coral Butter

Mash the cooked crab roe in a small bowl with the softened butter, a squeeze of lemon and rather a lot of seasoning. A fork is the best implement for the job, and a blender or processor will only waste the butter, which will stick to all the different surfaces. When the butter is thoroughly mixed, either keep it at room temperature for spreading on bread later, or wrap it in butter paper or greaseproof paper, form it into a little log and refrigerate. Slice the log into circles and float one on top of each bowl of bisque when you serve it.

Variations

1. For a more traditional Crab Bisque, use the onion or shallot plus 3 oz (90 g) each celery and bulb fennel, and substitute a small glass of dry white wine for $\frac{1}{4}$ pint (150 ml) of the fish stock.
2. You can of course use just water, or water and dry white wine or vermouth (say 3 parts water to 1 part wine and 5 parts water to 1 part vermouth) instead of the fish stock.
3. You can leave out the ground-up feelers, but if so you must use stock, not water, or your bisque will be insipid.
4. If you are reducing your animal fat intake, use extra fish stock instead of cream, add the crab coral to the soup and serve with rouille (p.44).

See also:
Shellfish Cream

Crab Apples

See under:
Pheasant and Quince Cream, Variation 2

Cream

CHOOSING AND USING

The British love creamy soups but are apparently content to be tempted by commercially manufactured and restaurant-made soups called Cream-of-Everything-under-the-Sun, in which actual cream is conspicuous only by its absence.

Cream is still a relatively cheap luxury and is easily available in several forms. Its fat is saturated, which makes it unattractive to the cholesterol-conscious, but the fat content is only a small fraction of that of butter, and it is therefore probably the safest form of animal fat. Double cream has a fat content of 13.6 per cent and costs only half as much again as single cream, which has a fat content of 5.1 per cent, so it is better value to buy double cream and either use less of it or thin it to single consistency with an equal quantity of milk.

Commercially produced sour cream is very pleasant and useful, but has an unsubtle flavour compared with home-made sour cream, confusingly called *crème fraîche* by the French, who invented it. It also works out cheaper than commercial sour cream, though you do need a little of this as a starter for the *crème fraîche*.

Crème Fraîche

$\frac{1}{4}$ pint (150 ml) single cream
1 tablespoon bought sour cream

Mix the creams together thoroughly in a small bowl. Cover and leave overnight in a warm place. The *crème fraîche* will be ready for use in about 8 hours in a warm place or about 24 hours in a cold one; it will then be semi-set like bought sour cream, and have a delicate fresh-sour flavour.

CRÈME VICHYSSOISE

Classic Vichyssoise is made from leeks, potatoes and cream, but since leeks are not available in British shops during the summer here is an equally glamorous and delicious alternative that can be made all the year round. The traditional recipe is given as Variation 1 of Leek and Potato Soup. You will need to make this soup 4 to 5 hours before you eat it, to ensure that it is thoroughly chilled and to allow the potato base to relax to a proper consistency – immediately after blending it is like wallpaper paste. Chill in the fridge freezer which will only take 30 minutes, or in a cold part of the fridge which may take 4 hours. Stir in the salad stuff about 1 hour before serving. Serve with very thin slices of wholemeal bread and dry white wine.

1 smallish potato
3 shallots *or* 5 spring onions
pinch of mace or nutmeg
salt
freshly milled pepper
½ pint (300 ml) milk
5 oz (140 g) cream cheese or
    cottage cheese
¼ pint (150 ml) single cream
4 tablespoons dry white wine

2 oz (60 g) chunk of unpeeled
    cucumber
3 crisp inside lettuce leaves
¼ bunch of watercress *or* ½ punnet
    mustard and cress
2 tablespoons chopped parsley
1 tablespoon chopped fresh
    basil, marjoram, mint or
    chives

Peel the potato and slice into a saucepan. Peel or trim and roughly slice the shallots or spring onions and add with the mace or nutmeg, a little salt, pepper and milk. Simmer this soup base for 10 to 15 minutes, until the potatoes are soft. Blend the mixture with the cream cheese or cottage cheese, the cream and the wine. You can make this base the day before you use it.

An hour before serving, grate the unpeeled cucumber rather coarsely. Roll the lettuce leaves into a cigar shape and cut across into ¼ inch (½ cm) slices. Discard any yellow or hairy bits of watercress and chop coarsely, or snip the mustard and cress off its bed with scissors, and chop the parsley and basil – not too finely. Stir in all these and leave the soup to mature and chill for a further 45 minutes before tasting and adjusting the seasoning.

Variations

1. If you prefer the soup hot, use double the quantity of potato, and all cream, or cream and milk mixed, instead of cream cheese or cottage cheese.
2. For slimmers, use chicken or vegetable stock or low fat milk powder and water instead of milk, and plain yogurt instead of cream, in which case use only 2 tablespoons wine or a squeeze of lemon juice.
3. You can vary the green stuff, but the cucumber and cress are important. Use strongly flavoured herbs such as mint, lovage, lemon balm etc. very sparingly.
4. If you use Variation 2 but not for slimming reasons, you may like to serve it in pretty glass bowls, topped with a whirl of cream whipped with lemon juice, and scattered with chopped chives, freshly milled pepper and/or paprika.

Cucumber

CHOOSING AND USING

The smooth-skinned cucumbers weighing about 1¼ lb (560 g) that are commonly sold in Britain are grown under glass; they have tender skin and seeds and a sweet flavour. The British like their cucumbers straight, therefore 'bent cues', especially if you happen to need a whole box, are worth looking out for since they are cheaper. They are in no way corrupt – merely curly.

Cucumbers grown out of doors are generally coarser. They have tough skin and seeds and often a bitter flavour which must be removed by soaking the slices of cucumber in very salty water for 30 minutes before proceeding with the recipe. You can remove the skin and seeds before cooking or sieve them out afterwards. Outdoor ridge cucumbers, which are short and fat with ridges running lengthways under the skin, are sold in early autumn for cooking and pickling and need the same treatment as outdoor cucumbers.

ICED CUCUMBER AND YOGURT SOUP

This is a quick, easy and elegant soup, closely related to the yogurt and cucumber salad served with kebabs in Greek and Turkish restaurants. Variation 1, with walnuts and mint, shifts the setting from the Mediterranean to the Black Sea.

1 small onion *or* 4 to 6 shallots *or* 1 bunch spring onions
2 tablespoons olive oil, virgin if possible
1 large clove garlic, peeled and crushed with a little salt
½ teaspoon cumin
1 medium glasshouse cucumber *or* 2 garden or ridge cucumbers (see above for skinning and seeding), to make 1 lb

(450 g) cucumber flesh
¼ pint (150 ml) plain yogurt
2 tablespoons chopped parsley – uncurled is better
salt
freshly milled pepper
juice of ½ lemon (optional)
pinch of cayenne
¼ pint (150 ml) *crème fraîche* (see p. 142) or sour cream

Peel and slice the onion or shallots and sweat them in the oil with the garlic and cumin for 7 to 8 minutes. Scrape this mixture into the blender jar; blend in short bursts to start with. When the first pieces of cucumber have formed a purée, add more until all is blended. Pour into a non-metal container, preferably one that fits into the freezing compartment of the fridge. Stir in the yogurt, parsley, salt, pepper, lemon juice and cayenne. Chill the soup very thoroughly, either in the freezer, which may only take 30 minutes, or in a cold part of the fridge, which may take 4 hours. Adjust the seasoning when the soup is very cold, and serve with dollops of *crème fraîche* or sour cream.

Variations

1. Use a slightly smaller cucumber – say 13 oz (375 g) – and leave out the cumin and the parsley. Add 2 tablespoons chopped mint to the soup instead of the parsley and 2 oz (60 g) fresh chopped walnuts just before serving.
2. For a low calorie version use only 1 teaspoon olive oil to sweat the onion and garlic, or sweat them dry, and leave out the sour cream or *crème fraîche*.
3. Use less cucumber – 12 oz (350 g) – and more yogurt – $\frac{1}{2}$ pint (300 ml). Blend half the cucumber and grate the rest, which should be stirred in with the yogurt and parsley. This gives the soup a pleasant variety of texture.

PURÉE OF CUCUMBER AND FENNEL

Boiled cucumber served hot used to be a common dish, but cooking cucumbers went out of fashion during the nineteenth century and now seems an outlandish and foreign idea. After cooking, cucumber retains its cool and delicate flavour, which, combined with the aniseed flavour of fennel, makes a lovely beginning to a summer dinner, especially if you happen to have some duck stock (see Variation 1). Lovage, a celery-flavoured herb popular in the sixteenth and seventeenth centuries, goes particularly well with cucumber.

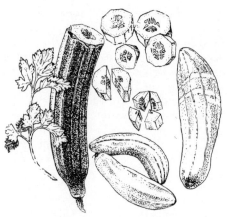

| 1 medium glasshouse cucumber
   or 2 garden or ridge cucum-
   bers (see p.144 for skinning
   and seeding), to make 1 lb
   (450 g) cucumber flesh
1 medium onion *or* 6 shallots *or* 1
   bunch spring onions
½ medium fennel bulb, 4 oz
   (110 g) after peeling and | trimming
1 tablespoon chopped parsley or
   lovage
1½ oz (40 g) butter
1 pint (600 ml) good chicken
   stock
salt
freshly milled pepper
pinch of cayenne (optional) |

Reserve 1 inch (2.5 cm) of the cucumber for slicing into matchsticks for garnish. Do this just before serving. Peel the onion or shallots, or trim the spring onions, and chop roughly. Trim the fennel and discard one layer if the outside is dried-up or very dirty. Otherwise just scrub it and cut it into smallish slices. Cut the rest of the cucumber, with or without skin according to the type of cucumber, into ½ inch (1 cm) slices and finely chop the parsley or lovage. Melt the butter in a heavy enamelled or stainless pan and sweat the onion and fennel for 7 or 8 minutes, stirring occasionally and not allowing them to colour. Add the cucumber slices and pour over the chicken stock. Add salt and pepper and a pinch of cayenne if you like and bring to the boil. Cover the pan and simmer for about 40 minutes, or until the cucumber is soft. Blend the soup or put it through the medium plate of a food mill. It can be made ahead to this point and stored overnight or frozen. Return the soup to a clean stainless or enamelled pan and add the cucumber strips and the herbs. Reheat and adjust the seasoning when hot. Simmer for a minute and serve either plain or with herb croûtons (p.28).

Variations

1. If you are lucky enough to have some duck or goose stock (see p.148), it will lift this soup to great gastronomic heights. These stocks have a rich, full flavour which complements the cucumber and fennel beautifully.
2. Add to the soup while it cooks a thin strip of orange or lemon rind – about $\frac{1}{2}$ x 1 in (1 x 2 cm).
3. If you can't find bulb fennel, you can make a good soup with 4 oz (110 g) celery and $\frac{1}{4}$ teaspoon fennel seeds added with the onion; if you can't find fennel seed, use $\frac{3}{4}$ teaspoon dill seed, which has the same kind of flavour but is much less strong.
4. This soup has an elegantly thin texture; if you prefer a thicker soup, mix 1 tablespoon potato flour, cornflour or arrowroot with 3 tablespoons cold water in a small bowl. When the cucumber is almost cooked add a ladleful of soup to the thickening mixture and stir to a smooth paste. Whisk it back into the soup and cook for 5 minutes.

See also:
Duck and Cucumber Soup

Currants: Redcurrants and Blackcurrants

See under:
Iced Plum Soup with Sour Cream, Variation 4

Duck

CHOOSING AND USING

Ducks and geese are not only more expensive than chickens and turkeys in the first place, but have less meat and more fat and bone: ducks and geese have barrel rib cages, while chickens and turkeys have concave chest bones with plenty of flesh on them. A duck is therefore a luxury, though it offers the bonus of beautiful duck stock and plenty of pure white fat for roasting and frying other dishes. If you are going to be extravagant you may as well go the whole duck and pay the extra for a fresh one. Frozen ones are flabby and can be tough, while a fresh duck roasts to a wonderful, juicy crispness.

Choose a cream-coloured, firm bird with no hint of green or wetness anywhere on its skin. It should have no smell to speak of. Make sure the butcher gives you all the giblets, and does not first include them in the price to you, then clean out the bird and resell the giblets to someone else. You should have the feet, heart, liver (which is large, firm and delicious), neck and crop (with the grit cleaned out). From a 7 lb (3 kg) duck, weighed before cleaning, you should get a good meal of roast or braised duck for 4 to 5, plus one of the following soups, plus 3 to 4 oz (90 to 110 g) duck fat.

DUCK STOCK

For several years I was chef of a restaurant where fresh duck in some form was on the menu every day. In those luxurious days duck stock was always available for soups and vegetable dishes, and pure white duck fat could be used for basting roasts and grilled meats. Duck stock has a rich and powerful flavour which blends exceptionally well with fresh, sweet vegetables such as Jerusalem artichokes, celeriac, beetroot, onions and celery. Apart from tender green vegetables, whose flavour it might overwhelm, there is hardly any savoury dish that duck stock will not enhance, and but for the expense I would have recommended it for many of the soups in this book. Goose stock is made in the same way and has the same properties, which is why a piece of preserved goose or duck is traditionally added by the French to many of their famous soups, such as Garbure (pps.268-9).

A pale-coloured but rich duck or goose stock can be made by boiling the bird (and boiled duck was a regular favourite in the eighteenth century) but a more deeply coloured and very good stock can be made from the giblets and carcass of a braised or roast duck. From the point of view of the soup, your duck should be rather under-roasted – cook it at 425°F (220°C, Gas 7) for 1 hour – so that the carcass does not dry up.

carcass and giblets from a
cooked duck, plus the scrapings from the roasting tin
4 pints (2.3 l) water
4 oz (110 g) trimmings from
carrots, onions and celery

2 bay leaves *or* 8 allspice berries
1 sprig thyme, marjoram or
oregano
2 parsley stalks
10 peppercorns

When you have enjoyed your roast duck, put a pint or so of water
into the roasting tin and boil it up on top of the stove, stirring and
scraping until all the delicious caramelized bits have dissolved into
the water. Put the carcass, chopped into several pieces, any skin, all
the giblets, the feet and the contents of the roasting tin into a large,
heavy pan. Add the rest of the cold water and bring to the boil. Turn
the heat down and skim off any scum that rises. Then add the
vegetable trimmings, bay leaves or allspice berries, herbs and
peppercorns. Simmer the stock for 2 to 3 hours, then strain and cool.
There will be quite a lot of fat, which is easily removed, when the
stock is cold, for storage in the fridge. If you are lucky enough to
have a lot of stock, it can be reduced to a glaze in the same way as
chicken stock (see p.118) for convenient long-term storage.

PURÉE OF DUCK AND CELERY

Duck stock is so richly flavoured in itself that soups can be made from
it using very simple ingredients, and extra flavourings and
enrichments become superfluous. If you have no duck meat left, use
another stick or two of celery, cut into fine dice and simmered with
the puréed soup for 5 to 10 minutes before serving. This soup keeps
and freezes well and is best made a day in advance.

1 small head celery – 8 oz (225 g)
after trimming
1 small onion
1¼ pints (750 ml) duck stock (see
above)
salt
a thin ½ inch (1 cm) square piece
of orange rind

1 dessertspoon potato or rice
flour (optional)
2 to 4 oz (60 to 110 g) cooked
duck meat
freshly milled pepper
2 slices wholemeal bread

Chop the celery and onion roughly and simmer them with the duck
stock, a little salt and the orange rind in a tightly-covered, heavy pan
for 30 minutes or until the celery is tender. Put the soup through the
medium plate of a food mill, or blend it and then sieve out the

stringy celery bits. If the soup has reduced too much during cooking
– you should have a little less than 1½ pints (900 ml) – add more water
or stock. At this point the soup can be stored overnight or longer in
the fridge. If you think it is too thin, mix the potato or rice flour with
a little cold water and whisk it into the soup.

Now reheat the soup. Remove all fat and skin from the cooked
duck meat and cut it into small, neat dice. Add to the soup when it is
hot, and taste. Add more salt, and some pepper if necessary. Leave
the soup just below simmering point while you dice the wholemeal
bread and fry the cubes in duck fat. Drain the croûtons on kitchen
paper. Serve the soup without reboiling, and hand the hot croûtons
separately.

Variations

1. This soup is also very good made with a rich chicken, turkey,
   goose, pheasant or partridge stock, but with game stock 1 to 2 oz
   (30 to 40 g) butter must be added at the beginning of cooking.
2. The croûtons can be omitted and the soup served plain or with a
   few tablespoons thick cream and some finely chopped celery
   leaves stirred in just before serving.

DUCK AND CUCUMBER SOUP

While the barnyard duck has been a favourite for centuries on the
tables of the landed gentry and *haute bourgeoisie* of Europe, it has
never quite made it as a ceremonial dish. Not so the Chinese duck
which, cooked in all kinds of lengthy and sophisticated ways, has
been the star attraction at feasts through many a dynasty and still
holds pride of place today. Soup is served by the Chinese at the end
of the meal and is therefore often of a light, refreshing nature. Given
some good duck stock, this can be made in a few minutes – most
dramatically at the table in one of those Chinese charcoal burners
with a moat for the soup. It should be eaten immediately, while the
vegetables are still crisp.

8 oz (225 g) hothouse cucumber,
    ber, unpeeled
1 bunch spring onions
½ inch (1 cm) piece of fresh
    ginger

1 pint (600 ml) well-flavoured
    duck stock, strained and with
    the fat skimmed off (see Duck
    Stock)
2 tablespoons dry sherry

150

| 2 tablespoons soy sauce | salt |
| 2 to 4 oz (60 to 110 g) cooked duck meat, preferably breast, cut into fine strips | freshly milled pepper |

Cut the cucumber into thin strips about 2 x $\frac{1}{2}$ x $\frac{1}{4}$ inch (5 x 1 x $\frac{1}{2}$ cm). Peel and trim the spring onions into $\frac{1}{2}$ inch (1 cm) lengths. Peel and grate the fresh ginger. Put the duck stock into a heavy pan or the moat of a charcoal burner, and add sherry and soy sauce. Bring to the boil. Add the cucumber and spring onion and simmer for 3 to 5 minutes, until the vegetables are bright green and slightly tender. Add the duck meat. Simmer for 1 minute. Taste, and add more salt, pepper and soy sauce if necessary. Serve at once.

Variations

1. This soup can also be made with goose, boiling hen or turkey.
2. If you like a slightly thicker soup, stir 1 dessertspoon arrowroot into 2 tablespoons cold water to make a smooth paste, and whisk into the soup before the meat is added. Arrowroot is not always easy to find, but gives a clear thickening, unlike cornflour, which makes the soup opaque and rather gluey.
3. Water chestnuts, bamboo shoots, bean sprouts or Chinese cabbage, or any combination of these, can be used instead of the cucumber.
4. If you cannot find fresh ginger, cook a little piece of dry root ginger with the soup and remove it before serving. Do not use powdered ginger, which will make the soup cloudy.

Duck Livers

See under:
Cream of Chicken Liver and Madeira, Variation 3

Eel

EEL SOUP

Eels may not look glamorous, squirming blackly in the fishmonger's bucket, but both their life cycle and their flavour belie their slightly repulsive appearance. Spawned in the Sargasso Sea off Bermuda, the tiny, transparent larvae drift back to European or North American rivers, taking up to three years on their journey. There they live for between five and twenty years before swimming the three thousand miles back to the West Indies, where they spawn and die. This romantic creature is best eaten when 1 to 2 ft long. Ask the fishmonger to kill it and skin it for you. If you prefer, ask him to cut it up too, since the nerves of eels go on twitching for some hours after death and cutting up a flapping, wriggling eel is disconcerting, be it ever so dead. Eels are very gelatinous and the soup will set naturally when cold.

an eel or eels weighing 12 oz
    (350 g) after skinning
1¼ pints (750 ml) fish stock (see
    p.157)
1 very small onion *or* 2 shallots
squeeze of lemon juice *or* 1
    tablespoon wine vinegar

salt
2 tablespoons finely chopped
    parsley
2 tablespoons finely chopped
    chives
freshly milled pepper

Cut the eel into $\frac{1}{2}$ inch (1 cm) pieces and put it in a stainless or enamelled pan with the fish stock. Chop or grate the onion or shallot and add, along with the lemon juice or wine vinegar and a little salt, and bring to the boil. Simmer very gently for 15 to 20 minutes until the eel is tender. Stir in the chopped herbs, taste, and add more lemon or vinegar, salt and pepper to taste. Serve at once, or leave to cool and jelly.

Variations

1. Water or water and wine – 1 pint (600 ml) water and a glass of white wine – with a $\frac{1}{2}$ bay leaf and a blade of mace can be used instead of fish stock; alternatively a vegetable stock for fish (see p.157) can be used.
2. A little finely chopped or minced celery, bulb fennel or leek can be used instead of or as well as the onion or shallot – say 1 to 2 oz (30 to 60 g).
3. To make a more substantial meal, plain croûtons can be served with the soup (see p.27). Make them very fresh and hot.

Smoked Eel

See under:
Smoked Mackerel Soup, Variation 3

Eggs

See under:
Chicken, Egg & Lemon Soup
French Onion Soup, Variation 1
Basic Processes: thickening soups, p.21
Garnishes and Accompaniments: egg garnishes, p.30

Bulb Fennel

See under:
Bass, Vermouth and Garlic Soup, Variation 4
Celery and Tarragon Mousseline Soup, Variation 1
Crab and Red Pepper Bisque, Variation 1
Purée of Cucumber and Fennel

Fish

CHOOSING AND USING

Fish that is not perfectly fresh can sometimes be disguised in a main dish by a blanket of rich, powerfully flavoured sauce. In a soup, however, the fish must be very fresh indeed or the slight stale flavour will communicate itself irredeemably to the liquid. Very fresh fish, apart from being bright-eyed and firm-finned, have almost no smell and are covered with a transparent slime. Frozen fish are fresh enough when originally frozen, but lose some of their texture during freezing and defrosting. They are best used in soups where the flavour of the basic liquid does not depend on the fish or fish bones, such as Smoked Haddock Chowder, in which milk and vegetables give flavour, or Cod and Prawn Velouté, in which the prawn shells and vegetables make a well-flavoured stock.

Types of Fish

For a special velouté, there is no doubt that one of the expensive, firm-fleshed, delicately flavoured white fish such as turbot, halibut, Dover sole, monkfish, sea bass, etc. will make a soup of real distinction. On the other hand dabs, whiting, coley, cod, haddock, plaice, lemon sole and so on will make a very good soup, and if your choice lies between very fresh dabs and a slightly stale turbot, pick the dabs or other cheap fish every time.

Oily fish such as mackerel, herring and conger eel are not so versatile. The oil in them rapidly gets rancid and produces a powerful and not very pleasant flavour. However, fresh fish of this kind can be used very successfully in a soup with a slightly acid flavour, such as Mackerel and Lemon Cream. They can also be combined with white fish in fish stews.

Gutting, Filleting and Skinning

Fishmongers still consider at least the first two of these processes to be part of the job. Ready-filleted white fish is good if you are in a hurry to get your shopping done, but fish deteriorates more quickly off the bone. In addition, all the white fish bones may have been thrown out some time before the prospective soup-maker gets to the fishmonger's. It is preferable to choose a whole fish, then ask for it to be gutted and filleted and the head and bones included in the parcel.

Gutting
Fish are gutted by slitting their bellies from anus to throat and scooping out the innards. They should then be rinsed under the cold tap.

Filleting
This operation is not difficult but does need a very sharp, flexible knife. Press the knife against the bone near the tail of the fish on one side. Grasp the tail firmly in your other hand and, holding the knife nearly horizontal against the bone, work it up to the head with a delicate sawing motion. Turn the fish over and repeat the process on the other side.

Skinning
Lay the fish fillet on a board, skin side down. Dip your fingers in salt to prevent them slipping on the fish. Using the same knife as for filleting, grip the thin end of the fillet. Now slide the knife blade carefully through the flesh, with the blade starting up against, but pointing away from, the fingers of your other hand. When the knife meets the skin, slide and wiggle it, with the blade more or less flat between the skin and the flesh, to the far end.

Fish which has been frozen will not skin in this way. The skin of white fish will lift off very easily after cooking, but mackerel and herring skin is somehow knitted into the flesh and must be scraped away with great care.

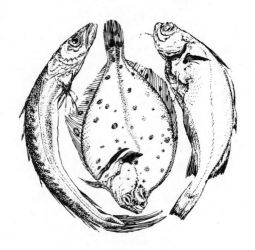

FISH STOCK

In *The Adventurous Fish Cook* George Lassalle sings the praises, for fish soup-making, of a steamer holding tiers of perforated metal baskets. Having acquired one of these relatively cheap marvels (see p.16) I soon realized that he was right. You can put fish bones and trimmings and flavouring ingredients in the bottom basket and then lower the next basket, containing the actual fish, to be poached or steamed for the appropriate time. You then simply lift out the upper basket and leave it to cool, instead of chasing elusive and fragmenting bits of fish around the pan with a fish slice.

With or without this piece of equipment, the actual making of a fish stock is extremely simple. The problem is finding a fishmonger who will supply the right fresh raw ingredients. These days people do not buy so many fillets of prime fish as they used to, and therefore the heads and bones are not readily available. Ideally, freshly filleted bones and heads of sole, plaice, whiting, haddock, halibut, turbot, bream etc. should be used. About 1 lb (450 g) bones will make 3 pints (1.75 l) stock. Stale, coarse or oily fish bones give a rank-tasting stock that will overpower other delicate flavours in a soup. If the right fish bits are not to be found, an aromatic stock of vegetables, wine and herbs makes a good substitute (see below).

Basic Fish Stock

1 lb (450 g) heads and bones
    from fresh raw white fish
4 pints (2.3 l) water
1 small peeled onion *or* 3 shallots
2 oz (60 g) celery or bulb fennel
    trimmings
1 bay leaf *or* 2 blades mace
2 parsley stalks
10 peppercorns

other herbs and garlic as appro-
    priate to the soup for which
    you will use the stock
2 to 4 tablespoons wine or cider
    vinegar
1 small glass dry white wine or
    dry vermouth or cider,
    according to the soup recipe
    you want to follow

Bring the fish trimmings and water to the boil in a stainless or enamelled pan and skim off any scum that rises. Add the other ingredients and simmer for 30 to 40 minutes. Strain and use or store. If the stock is kept boiling for any length of time, the bones will begin to dissolve and the stock will acquire a heavy, disagreeable flavour.

Vegetable Stock for Fish

Use the recipe above, omitting the fish bones etc. and with three times the quantities of onion and celery or fennel; simmer for 40 minutes.

ATLANTIC FISH STEW

With local differences in fish and seasonings, this stew or chowder is made in a great arc stretching from Newfoundland through Normandy to Norway. The British, who like all other food awash with either gravy or custard, like to have their fish in a solid, identifiable lump so that they can keep an eye on it, not floating fishily among lumps of vegetable. It is worth overcoming this prejudice, if you or your friends suffer from it, especially since the best and medium-grade white fish are now so expensive. This recipe uses cheaper fish and will feed 6 people on only 12 oz (350 g) fish. It makes a large quantity of soup, and half quantities can be made using only one or perhaps two kinds of fish.

For 3 pints (1.75 l)

2 oz (60 g) butter
1 medium leek
1 medium carrot
2 sticks celery *or* ¼ celeriac
1 clove garlic, peeled and
    crushed with a little salt
    (optional)
1 large potato
2 dessertspoons wine or cider
    vinegar

2½ pints (1.5 l) fish stock or
    vegetable stock for fish (see
    p.157) salt
freshly milled pepper
12 oz (350 g) fillets of very fresh
    fish such as coley, dabs,
    conger eel, whiting, mackerel,
    salmon trout, turbot, sole and
    skate
2 tablespoons chopped parsley

Melt the butter in a heavy stainless or enamelled pan. Cut the leeks in rings, wash them well, and add them with the carrot and celery, thinly sliced, and the optional garlic. Sweat together for 5 minutes. Cube the potato, add, and sweat for another minute. Pour in the vinegar and fish stock and bring to the boil. Add salt and pepper and simmer for about 7 minutes. Meanwhile skin the fish (see p.155) and cut it into chunks on the same scale as the vegetables and potatoes, but not less than ½ inch (1 cm). Add the fish, the thickest pieces first and the delicate, thin bits only a minute or two before serving: none of the fish will take more than 5 minutes to cook. Taste, and adjust seasoning. Stir in the parsley and serve.

Variations

1. If no fish bones are available or time is short, substitute water, a glass of white wine and some grated nutmeg for the stock.
2. Shellfish; mussels, prawns, clams, scallops and so on can be substituted for all or part of the fish.
3. A couple of rashers of smoked streaky bacon can be used instead of butter, or use cubes of salted belly of pork. In Newfoundland, little bits of crispy salt pork fat called scruncheons are used.
4. Instead of parsley, use any fresh green herb, such as chervil, chives, lemon balm, young marjoram etc., or watercress or sorrel.

FISH STEW WITH GARLIC, TOMATOES AND OLIVE OIL

To make a real Bouillabaisse it is necessary not only to have certain types of little fish from the Mediterranean, but to have both them and the shellfish in glorious abundance. That is why I have not included a classic recipe. This version uses a moderate quantity of northern fish, with Mediterranean vegetables and seasonings, and the result is delicious and glamorous. It is best eaten at once, but can be kept overnight and reheated with care. It is important that fish soups should be cooked for precisely the time stated and not left hanging around keeping hot, or worse, simmering. If you are preparing a fish soup in advance, cook the soup for the time stated and cool and refrigerate as rapidly as possible. This fish stew is a good soup for a party, since all the preparation can be done in advance. The more you make in one go, the more different kinds of fish fillets you can order from the fishmonger. For a larger quantity, shellfish can also be included (see Variation 3).

For 3 pints (1.75 l) soup:
2½ pints (1.5 l) white fish stock or
    vegetable stock (see
    pps.156-7) juice of ½ lemon *or*
    1 tablespoon wine vinegar
12 oz (350 g) ripe, red tomatoes
1 medium leek
1 small onion
4 tablespoons good fruity olive
    oil, extra virgin for preference
2 cloves garlic, peeled and
    crushed with a little salt

1 packet of saffron (optional)
1 bay leaf
a few fennel seeds
salt
slices of French bread, baked
    hard in the oven
12 oz (350 g) mixed fish fillets –
    some white, some oily fish,
    and all as fresh as possible:
    say cod, mackerel and
    monkfish
freshly milled pepper

Follow the instruction on p.157 for making either fish stock with heads and bones, or with vegetables only if fresh white fish trimmings are not available. Peel and core the tomatoes (see pps.247-8). Slice the leek and onion finely and chop the tomatoes. Sweat the leek and onion in the olive oil with the garlic for 5 minutes in a stainless or enamelled pan. Add the tomatoes and cook for another 5 minutes. Add the saffron, bay leaf, fennel seeds and a little salt. Stir in the fish stock and bring to the boil. Boil hard for 10 minutes, uncovered. The soup can be made in advance to this point.

Skin the fish fillets (see p.155) and cut into 1 inch (2.5 cm) squares. Put the hard baked slices of bread in the oven to heat up. Five minutes before serving the soup, bring it rapidly back to the boil and add the fish. Boil gently for 3 to 4 minutes until the fish pieces are just cooked. Taste and adjust seasoning, adding plenty of black pepper. Serve at once, ladled over the bread slices.

Variations

1. You may choose any sea fish and shellfish you like, being guided by what is freshest. It would be better to use only one-third oily fish, but if these are your freshest buy cut down the amount of olive oil and add a little more wine vinegar or lemon.
2. If you are using shellfish, remember that raw mussels, scallops and prawns take only a minute or two to cook and will lose their flavour and texture if overcooked.
3. Proportions of ingredients for a party soup for 20, allowing $\frac{1}{2}$ pint (300 ml) per person: about 7 pints (4 l) fish stock, $2\frac{1}{2}$ lb (1 kg) tomatoes, 1 very large onion, 4 leeks, $\frac{1}{3}$ pint (200 ml) olive oil, 6 oz (175 g) fillets of each of 3 kinds of white fish, 1 small bream or red mullet, 1 small mackerel *or* 2 squid, 30 mussels or prawns.
4. A small, bright red pepper can be substituted for the leek; and canned, peeled tomatoes can do duty for fresh ones, though it would be a pity not to use some fresh ones, say half and half.
5. Rouille or aioli (both garlic and olive oil sauces; see pps.44,39) are delicious stirred into the soup as it is served, in which case little or no garlic or oil should be used in making the soup.
6. This is an excellent soup for slimmers or those watching their animal fat intake. The amount of olive oil can be reduced if you like, but otherwise the soup needs no alteration. In fact a diet based on this soup, wholemeal bread and fruit or salad would be a very healthy way to slim and infinitely tastier than crispbread and cottage cheese.

FISH SLICE AND MUSHROOM SOUP

At the first dinner-party I went to after losing most of my sight we were served little white fish on the bone. It had not occurred to either my hostess or me that these would be hard for a blind person to manage, but I soon found this out and rapidly created a little panicky hell of fins, bones and skin for myself. A lot of normally sighted people have much the same feelings about the lurking, invisible contents of fish soups and so avoid them. This is a clear consommé-like soup of Chinese origin in which the little cubes of skinless boneless white fish along with dark brown mushrooms and bright green spring onions can be clearly seen and fearlessly enjoyed.

$\frac{1}{2}$lb (225 g) really good white fish
˙ – sea bass, monkfish, turbot
    or halibut
$\frac{1}{4}$lb (110 g) flat mushrooms
3 large spring onions with plenty
    of bright green stalk

1 tablespoon soy sauce
1 tablespoon arrowroot
3 tablespoons dry sherry
1 pint (600 ml) water
salt

Get the fishmonger to skin and bone your piece of fish, which should be 'lepping fresh'. Cut it into neat $\frac{1}{2}$ in (1 cm) cubes and put in a little bowl with the soy sauce, 1 tablespoon sherry and the arrowroot (You can use cornflour instead, but the arrowroot gives a lovely glistening clear finish.) Peel and trim the spring onions, leaving on most of the green and cut into slanting slices $\frac{1}{2}$ in (1 cm) long. Cut the mushrooms into neat $\frac{1}{2}$ in (1 cm) cubes too. Five minutes before you want to eat, put the water in a pan with the rest of the sherry and some salt. When it boils add the onions and mushrooms. After 30 seconds add the fish and its marinade, stirring until the soup comes back to the boil. Simmer for 2-3 minutes only. Adjust seasoning and serve at once.

Variations

1. You could replace the mushrooms with asparagus or bulb fennel, or even shreds of fresh spinach, but don't get carried away – the elegance of this soup lies in its simplicity.

SAFFRON FISH SOUP

You can still buy excellent quality fish for this soup for very little, provided you are lucky enough to use a fishmonger who also supplies hotels and restaurants. For he will be sending them evenly-sized, nicely-shaped cutlets and fillets of prime fish such as turbot, halibut and bass, and you, after suitable discussion of the weather and his grandchildren, will be able to buy the messy-looking but deliciously meaty heads and tails. You are then saved the bother of making a separate fish stock and this becomes a quick and easy soup.

1½-2 lb (675-900 g) meaty fish
heads and tails (see above)
1½ pints (900 ml) water
1 tablespoon wine vinegar or
lemon juice
a sprig of thyme or ½ teaspoon
dried thyme
1 packet saffron powder

½ brightly coloured sweet
pepper, preferably striped red
and green
4 tablespoons olive oil
1 clove of garlic
1 egg yolk
salt and pepper

Wash the fish heads and slice the pepper finely. Put 1 tablespoon of
olive oil in a stainless or enamelled pan over a gentle heat and cook
the sliced pepper in it for a couple of minutes. Add the water,
vinegar, thyme, a little salt and pepper and the fish heads. Bring to
the boil and simmer for 15 minutes. Lift out the fish and leave to
cool. You should now have just over a pint ((600 ml) of fish stock and
pepper mixture. Remove it from the heat temporarily. Crush the
garlic with a little salt, beat it with the egg yolk and then gradually
add the remaining olive oil to make a tiny garlic mayonnaise (see
p.39 for more details). Take the meat off the fish heads. Cut it into
fairly neat small pieces and add it to the stock. Add the saffron and
taste for seasoning. As well as salt and pepper, you may need a drop
more vinegar. Assemble your eaters, for this soup won't wait, then
stir a spoonful of the soup into the mayonnaise. Pour the mayonnaise
mixture back into the soup, stirring all the time and re-heat very
gently until hot but definitely not boiling. Serve with hot French
bread.

Variations

1. Failing the prime fish heads, you can, of course make this soup
   with 1 pint (600 ml) fish stock and ½ lb (225 g) white fish fillet (cod
   or haddock will do).
2. If the prospect of making a special mayonnaise daunts you, add
   the crushed garlic with the pepper right at the beginning, and stir
   in 2 tablespoons of commercial mayonnaise (first adding a little
   soup to the mayonnaise) just before serving.

FINNISH FISH SOUP

The time-consuming part of fish soup making is the fish stock. This
recipe which has been adapted from one in Alan Davidson's beautiful

book *North Atlantic Seafood*, uses only water and milk and is therefore not only quick, but has a clean, simple flavour which even non-fish-eaters might like. This recipe makes 3 pints (1.75 litres)

8-10 oz (225-280 g) firm white
    fish, skinned and filleted (cod,
    haddock, or monkfish)
a large onion about 5 oz (140 g)
½ lb (225 g) new potatoes
¾ pint (450 ml) water
1 pint (600 ml) milk mixed with

1 heaped tablespoon flour
2 oz (60 g) butter
salt, a few dill seeds, 6 allspice
    berries
2 tablespoons each chopped
    parsley and chives

Peel the onion and cut it into ½ in (1 cm) chunks. Put the chunks in a heavy pan with a little salt, the dill and allspice and the water. Bring to the boil and simmer for 10 minutes. Scrub the potatoes and cut in half. Add them to the onion and simmer another 10 minutes. Cut the fish into large chunks, the size depending on the size of your spoons and the occasion. Make sure the flour is thoroughly blended with the milk, then add both to the soup through a sieve, and stir continuously until the soup returns to simmering point. Add the fish and cook very gently for only 3-5 minutes until a chunk will just break when pressed. Add salt if necessary. Stir in the herbs and butter and serve.

Variations

1. You can vary the fresh herbs with marjoram or thyme, lemon balm, lovage, or even watercress or sorrel, but the milk, onion and potato are all necessary to the character of the soup.

SCHCHI (RUSSIAN FISH AND SPINACH SOUP)

In the original, this soup contains sorrel (see Variation 1) and even black treacle. It is essentially a purée of green leaves poured over little crispy bits of fried fish and garnished with spring onions and sour cream. It is absolutely delicious. The purée can be made a few hours in advance, but the fish should only be fried at the last moment. This recipe makes 3 pints (1.75 litres) but half quantities work perfectly well.

163

1 lb (450 g) fresh spinach
1 bunch watercress
1 medium onion
2 carrots
2 pints (1.2 litres) fish stock (see p.157)
2 tablespoons lemon juice
1 bay leaf
2 strips of lemon peel

2 oz (60 g) butter
1 tablespoon vegetable oil
2 tablespoons flour
$\frac{1}{2}$ lb (225 g) white fish fillets
salt and fresh pepper
Garnish
4 spring onions
2 hard-boiled eggs (optional)
$\frac{1}{4}$ pint (150 ml) sour cream

Strip away any tough stalks or yellow leaves from the spinach and watercress, and wash in two or three changes of water. Chop the peeled onion and carrots and fry gently in 1 oz (30 g) of the butter in a large, heavy stainless or enamelled pan (the type of pan is vital, or the soup will discolour horribly). Add the fish stock, bay leaf and lemon peel and bring to the boil. Simmer for 10 minutes. Add the spinach and watercress and cook for 3 minutes only. Put the soup through a food mill using the medium plate, or blend it and then sieve back into the rinsed-out pan. Season this purée with salt, pepper and lemon juice to make quite a sharp, peppery mixture. Meanwhile skin the white fish fillets and cut into cubes about $\frac{1}{2}$ inch (1 cm) depending whether you are aiming at an elegant first course or hearty main dish. Hard boil the eggs, peel and dice them into neat little pieces. Peel the spring onions and cut up. Mix the fish pieces with the flour, adding a little seasoning. When you are absolutely ready to eat, with the egg, spring onion and sour cream in bowls on the table, re-heat your spinach purée and fry the fish bits seaparately in the oil and remaining butter for about 3 minutes over quite high heat, until they are cooked and crispy.

Put some fish bits in each bowl, ladle over the spinach purée and allow people to try out different combinations of garnish.

Variations

1. Substitute about 2 oz (60 g) sorrel for the watercress and omit the lemon juice.
2. A simpler but still delicious soup can be made leaving out the spring onion and optional egg garnishes and even, perhaps, the sour cream. In this variation, the spinach and watercress is more carefully prepared, with all tough bits of stalk removed. The leaves and tender stems are then finely sliced (cutting across a few times as well, otherwise you get spinach-spaghetti drooping from the

spoon), and the onion and carrot chopped finely or grated. The method is the same as before but the soup is not puréed, but simply ladled over the fried fish.

3. A small fresh green chili, seeded and chopped, can be added with the carrot and onion.

VELOUTÉ OF WHITE FISH

My attempts at this soup have been many, and finally I realized that it was beautiful but temperamental. Neither the fish stock nor the soup can be left, like a good-natured meat stock, to simmer for 15 minutes extra while something else is being done. It must be made quickly and precisely to time. It can, however, be made a day in advance. While cooking the piece of fish, it is convenient to keep it separate from the bones and heads in the pan. This is easily done with the steamer/stockpot described on p.16, or by lowering the piece of fish into an ordinary pan in a chip basket or sieve.

For the soup base:
8 oz (225 g) white fish heads and bones (see p.156)
1½ pints (900 ml) water
juice of ½ lemon *or* 2 tablespoons wine vinegar
1 very small onion *or* 2 to 4 shallots
1 stick celery
1 blade of mace
½ bay leaf
8 peppercorns
2 parsley stalks
a 6 oz (175 g) fillet of good white fish such as sole, turbot,

halibut, monkfish, cod or haddock

To finish the soup:
6 tablespoons double cream
2 egg yolks
2 tablespoons fruity white wine or madeira
1½ oz (40 g) butter
2 rounded tablespoons white flour
salt
freshly milled pepper
lemon juice

Put the fresh, raw white fish heads and bones in a stainless or enamelled pan. Cover with the water, add the lemon or vinegar, and bring to the boil. Meanwhile peel the onion and roughly chop it and the celery. As soon as the fish stock begins to boil, turn the heat low and quickly skim off any scum. Add the vegetables and seasonings, and simmer for exactly 10 minutes. Add the piece of fish and simmer, with a bubble breaking the surface only every second or so, until the fish is just cooked – 6 to 10 minutes, depending on the thickness of the piece. Lift the fish out and leave to cool. Immediately strain the fish stock into a bowl and leave it to cool. Discard the heads and bones. Up to this point the soup can be made in advance.

The final stage of the recipe must be done quickly, so assemble everything before you begin. Measure 1 pint (600 ml) of the fish stock into a stainless or enamelled pan. Add the cream. Remove any skin and bone from the piece of fish and divide it into its natural flakes. Whisk the egg yolks with the white wine or madeira. Make a *beurre manié* (see p.22) by mixing the butter with the flour. Heat the soup, taste, and adjust the seasoning with salt, pepper and extra lemon juice if needed. Whisk in little lumps of the *beurre manié* until the soup is the consistency of thin cream. Whisk a ladleful of the soup into the egg mix, then whisk the egg mix into the soup. The soup should thicken very slightly. If not, go on heating and whisking with great care, since egg curdles and cooks at a relatively low temperature. When you are satisfied with the thickness of the soup, remove it from the heat, stir in the fish flakes and serve. The soup may be cooled and stored overnight before the egg yolks are added. If you are doing this the fish should not be flaked until shortly before it is needed.

Variations

1. If no suitable fish bones are available, make the vegetable stock on p.157. Alternatively, if small white fish such as dabs or whiting are cheap, cook them instead of heads and bones. Remove their heads and bones and put their flesh through a food mill with the stock to form a thin purée of fish. Then proceed with the main recipe.
2. To make a mushroom and fish velouté, halve the quantity of fish fillet, and cook 3 oz (90 g) sliced button mushrooms with 1 oz (30 g) shallot or onion in $\frac{1}{2}$ oz (15 g) butter, to be added when the soup is reheated.
3. A dessertspoon of paprika can be whisked into the fish stock to give a pretty colour and an interesting flavour. A very little grated orange or lemon rind may be added to the soup just before the final stages.
4. Although the egg yolks are a classic finishing touch in a velouté, they can be replaced by $\frac{1}{4}$ pint (150 ml) double cream.

See also:
Bass, Vermouth and Garlic Soup, Variation 1
Atlantic Fish Stew
Fish Stew with Garlic, Tomatoes and Olive Oil

VELOUTÉ OF COD AND PRAWNS

Here is a really showy soup that is not extravagant. It is absolutely delicious but a hard act to follow. You could either make it the central dish of the meal, or the overture to something plain and simple but excellent. It keeps well overnight in the fridge but would be spoilt by freezing. Since this really is a silk purse soup don't try to make it out of sow's-ear ingredients; make sure everything is very fresh.

For the Stock
shells from 3-4 oz (90-110 g)
    prawns (unshelled weight)
½ lb (225 g) white fish bones and
    heads
5 tablespoons fruity white wine
1 sprig parsley
a small strip of lemon rind pared
    thinly
½ bayleaf
6 peppercorns
½ pint (300 ml) water

For the Soup
3 very ripe tomatoes
6 oz (175 g) cod fillet
1½ oz (40 g) butter
1 rounded tablespoon flour
1 small leek peeled and trimmed
the shelled prawns
¼ pint (150 ml) single cream
salt
freshly milled pepper
a squeeze of lemon
2 egg yolks (optional)

The prawns may have gluey lumps of spawn between their feelers. If so remove them with the body shell, pull off the prawn heads and put all these bits in a large stainless or enamelled pan. Add the white fish bones if you have them. If the cod still has skin on, remove it with a sharp knife (see p.155) and add the skin to the stock pan along with the wine, parlsey, lemon rind, bayleaf, peppercorns and water. Bring slowly to simmering point and skim off any scum. Pop the tomatoes into the boiling stock for a minute, then lift them out and peel off their skins. Remove the cores and dice the flesh. After the stock has simmered for 15 minutes (don't overdo this) add the cod fillet in a sieve or basket for easy removal and poach for 6-8 minutes until it is creamy and just flakes under the finger. Lift it out and leave to cool. Meanwhile melt the butter in another stainless pan and add the flour. Cook this roux for a minute or two stirring lest it brown. Strain the fish stock and make it up to 1 pint (600 ml) if necessary with water. Add it little by little to the roux, stirring the sauce completely smooth between each addition. Bring this soup base to the boil and simmer for 10 minutes. Wash the leek, finely slice it, then add it to the soup

167

with the tomato dice. Separate the cod into big flakes, removing every lurking bone as you go. After the leek and tomato have simmered for a couple of minutes, add the flaked fish and prawns. Remove the pan from the heat. Add the cream, salt, pepper and lemon to your taste. At this point the soup can be cooled and stored in the fridge until the next day, or served as it is. However a classic velouté is traditionally enriched further with egg yolks. Beat the 2 yolks in a small bowl with a little more lemon juice, whisk in a ladleful of the hot soup, then transfer the whisk to the pan and whisk in the egg mixture. Serve without re-boiling.

Variations

1. Any fresh white fish can be used in this soup, but if only the delicate fragmenting type like dabs or plaice are available, use only 4 oz (110 g) of fish and extra prawns.
2. If good ripe tomatoes aren't available, substitute 2 oz (60 g) of cup or button mushrooms – sauté them finely sliced in a very little butter or oil before adding to the soup with the prawns.

Green Leaves

CHOOSING AND USING

Delicate green-leaved vegetables such as lettuce, spinach, beet leaves, watercress, young nettles – find them in May and early June – and wild sorrel can all be used to make delicious soups. If you have quite a lot of your chosen vegetable, say 1 lb (450 g) or more, use the recipe for Purée of Lettuce with Sour Cream. If you have only about 8 oz (225 g), try the velvety spinach soup called Crème Florentine. Smaller amounts can be used for Zuppa di Verdura, a lovely combination of green vegetables, olive oil, garlic and herbs, or for Spinach, Green Pea and Lettuce Purée. The last two soups mentioned follow here; all the other recipes will be found under their main ingredient. Other possibilities are Variation 3 of Potato and Parsley Soup, Cream of Watercress Soup.

Whatever your choice of recipe, use these delicate leaves as freshly picked or bought as possible, wash them thoroughly, especially spinach, which may need several changes of water before all the sand is out, and remove any fibrous ribs or stalks. To remove the central rib of a fresh spinach or beet leaf, hook your thumb and forefinger round the stalk from the back, just below the leaf, and pull the stalk sharply towards you with the other hand. The leaf will rip neatly away.

For information about the tougher green leaves of members of the cabbage family, see under Cabbage.

SPINACH, GREEN PEA AND LETTUCE PURÉE

This recipe and the Italian green vegetable soup that follows are nice examples of how different culinary traditions use the same ingredients to create different results. The Italians leave the green vegetables as pieces floating in a broth enriched and robustly flavoured with garlic, olive oil, Parmesan and basil, while their neighbours the French use fewer ingredients and blend them to a subtly textured purée enriched with butter and cream. This soup is adapted from Elizabeth David's beautiful Purée Léontine and is well worth the small trouble of preparing the fresh vegetables. It is best served at once, but will keep and freeze satisfactorily.

1 oz (30 g) butter
6 shallots *or* 1 small onion
1 lb (450 g) fresh green peas
1 pint (600 ml) boiling water
salt
½ small round lettuce

12 oz (350 g) fresh green spinach
¼ pint (150 ml) single cream
juice of 1 small lemon
freshly milled pepper
1 tablespoon chopped parsley
1 tablespoon chopped chives

Melt the butter in an enamelled or stainless pan. Chop the shallots or onion and sweat in the butter over a low heat for 5 minutes. Pod the peas and add them and the boiling water, plus a little salt. Simmer, covered, for 10 to 15 minutes, until the peas are nearly tender. Meanwhile wash the lettuce, and particularly the spinach, very thoroughly; remove the central rib of the spinach (see p.169). Discard any yellowed or sagging leaves. Add the spinach and lettuce and simmer for a further 5 minutes. Put the soup through the medium plate of a food mill, or blend it, in which case try to leave a little texture by blending in short bursts only. Add the cream and the lemon juice. At this point the soup can be stored overnight in a non-metal container, or frozen. Reheat uncovered in a clean stainless or enamelled pan and check the seasoning when hot. Serve without reboiling, sprinkled with the chopped herbs.

Variations

1. You can of course use frozen leaf spinach and peas. The spinach does very well but I do think frozen peas, though a great standby, would be a sad comedown for this distinguished soup.
2. For a low calorie, low animal fat soup reduce the amount of butter to 1 teaspoon or use just a little oil, or leave the fat out altogether. Omit the cream and the lemon and substitute 3 to 4 oz (90 to 110 g) cottage cheese, added to the soup in the blender.
3. If you are blending the soup, you may like to reserve 2 leaves each of the lettuce and spinach, roll them into a cigar shape and slice across very thinly into a chiffonade (see p.31). Add to the soup when you begin to reheat it, to give a more interesting texture.

ZUPPA DI VERDURA: ITALIAN GREEN VEGETABLE SOUP

In my limited experience of restaurants in Italy, this soup is far more likely to be on the menu than a Minestrone. The *verdura* in the *zuppa* can, if you are unlucky, be limited to a large and solitary spinach leaf highlighted by a single lump of carrot, but the soup should be a gorgeous mixture of vegetables, the green predominating, seasoned with garlic, olive oil and Parmesan. It needs no stock, takes perhaps 30 minutes to prepare and cook, and is very rich in vitamins C and A and in iron.

1 small potato, peeled or
    unpeeled as you prefer
1 small carrot, peeled or
    unpeeled
2 ripe tomatoes
1 large clove garlic, peeled and
    crushed with a little salt
4 tablespoons good olive oil
2 oz (60 g) fresh spinach, lettuce,
    beet or young green cabbage
    leaves

$\frac{1}{2}$ bunch watercress
2 sprigs parsley
6 to 8 basil leaves
1 courgette
2 oz (60 g) runner or French
    beans, topped and tailed
2 pints (1.2 l) water
salt
freshly milled pepper
2 tablespoons grated Parmesan,
    fresh if possible

Peel the potato and carrot, or just scrub them and cut into $\frac{1}{2}$ inch (1 cm) dice. Skin (see pps.247-8), core and roughly chop the tomatoes. Put these ingredients with the garlic in a heavy stainless or enamelled pan with the oil and sweat them over a low heat for 5 minutes, stirring ocasionally. Wash the green vegetables well, and chop them into $\frac{1}{2}$ inch (1 cm) square pieces, discarding any tough or yellow parts. Chop the parsley and basil leaves into rough shreds – this is a chunky soup – and slice the courgette and beans. Add the water to the oil and vegetable mixture, bring to the boil and simmer for 10 minutes. Add the green vegetables and simmer for 10 minutes longer. Taste, and add salt and pepper. Serve at once, with Parmesan sprinkled on top.

Variations

1. There is no need to use so many different ingredients unless you have them on hand, or are making the soup for a special occasion in large quantities. So long as the ingredients are all young and fresh, and the green leaves slightly predominate, you have endless scope for invention. Try broccoli or green peas instead of beans, mushrooms instead of tomatoes, and $1\frac{1}{2}$ oz (40 g) small pasta instead of the potato. Either the watercress or spinach can be omitted and more of the other ingredient used, or you can use more parsley.
2. An Italian acquaintance sent this spring herb variation. Translated, her letter read, 'In spring every little herb that lifts its head is good for soup. Use the gramophone needles (youngest shoots) only of mallow, nettles, parsley, daisy, violet, primrose and other little weeds. Wash them and add them to the soup a minute or two before serving.'

See also:
Beans: White Haricot Bean and Watercress Soup, Variation 2

Grouse

See under:
Pheasant and Quince Cream, Variation 1
Pheasant and Lentil Soup

Haddock

SMOKED HADDOCK CHOWDER

Chowder came to Britain from India, via the East India Company, but only became really popular after it reached America by way of the early settlers. Honest young America did her own cooking, with none of the sophisticated equipment and underpaid kitchen maids of decadent old Europe, so the great tradition began. Chowder is just the thing for holiday food, for it needs only a knife, a spoon, a pan and a source of heat. This chowder is very nearly a complete food, containing plenty of protein, calcium and other minerals, as well as vitamins A, B and D. Pale brown smoked haddock, if you can get it, is much more authentic than the golden variety.

8 oz (225 g) smoked haddock
1 pint (600 ml) creamy milk
1 bay leaf *or* 7 allspice berries *or* a
    small piece of nutmeg
freshly milled pepper
1 small carrot

1 small leek
1 oz (30 g) butter
1 matzo cracker *or* 2 unsweetened
    wholemeal biscuits, crumbled
1 tablespoon chopped parsley
salt

Cover the haddock with the milk in a heavy pan and add the bay leaf or other spice and some pepper. Bring to the boil and simmer until the fish is just beginning to flake – 7 to 10 minutes. Meanwhile cut the carrot and leek into small, even pieces. Wash the leek thoroughly in plenty of cold water (see p.183). Lift out the cooked haddock and leave to cool. Put the leek, carrot and butter in the milk and simmer for 20 minutes or until the vegetables are tender. Meanwhile flake the smoked haddock carefully, removing all the skin and bones but retaining the delicate, curving flakes of fish. The soup can be prepared in advance to this point.

Five minutes before serving, remove the bay leaf or other spice and add the crumbled biscuit, flaked fish and half the parsley. Bring to just below boiling point. Do not reboil or the luscious, smooth flakes of haddock will become dry fragments. Serve sprinkled with the remaining parsley.

Variations

1. Two rashers of bacon are a nice and typical addition. Cut the rashers into small squares and fry them in their own fat until they are crisp and brown, then add to the soup with the flaked fish. Omit the butter.
2. Ham or bacon stock can be used instead of $\frac{1}{2}$ pint (300 ml) of the milk, but make sure it is not too salty.
3. A small onion and 2 tablespoons canned sweetcorn can be used instead of the leek and carrot.
4. A medium potato or 2 heaped tablespoons fresh breadcrumbs can be added for extra bulk. Put the diced potato in with the other vegetables; add the crumbs with the biscuit.

SMOKED HADDOCK CREAM

My soup-tasting guests while I was preparing this book could be divided loosely into three categories: those who had spent the previous hour in the pub and whose comments were rather unreliable; those who arrived covertly or overtly appalled at the prospect of five strange soups in a row instead of a proper dinner; and those who had eaten nothing but water biscuits all day, determined to detect every nuance of texture, flavour and appearance, and made invidious comparisons with soups eaten in New York, in the Dordogne or at their Polish grandmother's. Here is a soup that has pleased all three types, being simple, hearty, familiar and yet sophisticated. The flavour is improved by a night in the fridge. Try and get pale brown haddock if you can.

$\frac{3}{4}$ pint (450 ml) milk
2 shallots *or* a $\frac{1}{2}$ oz
(15 g) piece of peeled onion
$\frac{1}{2}$ bay leaf *or* 1 clove
freshly milled pepper
6 oz (175 g) smoked haddock

1 small potato, peeled and grated
salt
8 tablespoons, $^1/_5$ pint
(125 ml), double cream
2 tablespoons finely chopped parsley

Put $\frac{1}{2}$ pint (1.75 l) of the milk in a heavy pan with a capacity of at least 3 pints (300 ml) to minimize the risk of boiling over. Add the peeled shallots or onion piece, the $\frac{1}{2}$ bay leaf or clove, some pepper and the piece of smoked haddock. Bring to the boil over a low heat and simmer very gently, with a bubble breaking the surface only every second or so, for 10 minutes or until the fish just flakes under the pressure of a finger. Lift out the fish. Add the grated potato and simmer for a further 10 minutes, stirring occasionally. When the haddock is cool enough to handle, discard the skin and bones and separate the fish into individual flakes. Keep 2 tablespoons of the best flakes aside and add the rest to the soup. As soon as the potato is cooked, blend the soup with the remaining $\frac{1}{4}$ pint (150 ml) of the milk. At this point the soup is best poured into a container or bowl, the reserved flakes of haddock added and the whole thing stored overnight in the fridge.

When you are ready to serve it, reheat the soup very gently in a clean pan, being careful not to let it boil or the delicious texture of the haddock flakes will be lost. Taste the soup when it is very hot and add more pepper and some salt if needed. Stir in the cream and serve with the finely chopped parsley.

Variations

1. Another smoked white fish such as smoked cod can be used instead of haddock.
2. Two heaped tablespoons mashed potato can be used instead of raw potato. It can be blended without further cooking.
3. A rounded tablespoon potato flour or instant mashed potato could be used instead of fresh potato.
4. The potato can be left out altogether and the milk in which the haddock was cooked made into a soup base. Make a roux of 1 oz (30 g) butter and 1 heaped tablespoon plain flour, stirred together over a low heat. Add the strained fish milk by degrees, stirring each addition to smoothness. Simmer this base very gently over a very low heat, or on a heat-absorbant mat, while the haddock is blended with the extra milk. Finish with haddock flakes and cream as before.

174

Ham

See under:
Bacon and Ham: Goulaschsuppe
Chinese Chicken Soup
Green Pea and Ham Soup
Tripe: Zuppa di Trippa alla Milanese, Variation 3

Hare

HARE SOUP WITH MADEIRA AND BREAD BALLS

Hare is by far the best value game around. You can get a good big meal for 4 from the saddle and back legs and still have the carcass and fore legs left for this robust soup. Buy your hare with the head on and the blood correctly caught inside its rib cage. If you do not need the blood for the main dish, it will be an excellent enrichment for the soup. This soup keeps well; minus the bread balls and the blood it also freezes well.

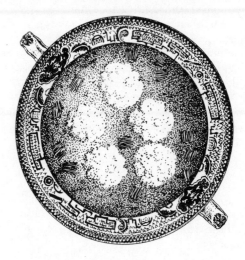

For the stock:

the front half of a hare, *or* the raw carcass and about 3 oz (90 g) cooked hare meat

3 pints (1.75 l) water

1 small onion, 1 small carrot and 1 stick celery, all peeled,*or* 4 oz (110 g) trimmings from these vegetables

2 parsley stalks

1 bay leaf

5 allspice berries

10 peppercorns

5 tablespoons wine or cider vinegar

To finish the soup:

1 oz (30 g) bacon

1 oz (30 g) onion

2 slices bread, soaked in water or stock

1 dessertspoon chopped fresh thyme or marjoram (optional)

1 egg yolk

salt

freshly milled pepper

5 tablespoons Madeira

1 heaped teaspoon sharp fruit jelly – redurrant, quince, rowan or crab apple

Put all the ingredients for the hare stock, excluding any cooked hare meat, in a covered ovenproof dish and leave in a slow oven (300°F, 150°C, Gas 2) for at least 4 hours. The stock can also be made in the ordinary way on top of the stove, but the oven method produces a stock of particularly fine flavour. Strain the stock and reduce it by fast boiling to just over 1 pint (600 ml).

Remove the hare meat from the bones. If you are using meat from the saddle, it has a tough second skin which must be removed. Cut the meat into small, neat slices or dice it. Now for the bread balls. Squeeze out the soaked bread. Chop or mince the bacon and onion finely and fry them together for 2 to 3 minutes. Remove from the heat and stir in the bread mush, the herbs, the egg yolk and salt and pepper. Form this mixture into about 12 tiny balls.

Add the Madeira and jelly to the hare stock. Taste it and adjust the seasoning. If you have hare blood, whisk a ladleful of the hare stock into the blood, and reserve. Put the hare meat and bread dumplings into the soup and simmer for 1 to 2 minutes, taking care that the soup does not boil or the hare meat will deteriorate. Whisk the blood mixture into the soup and serve immediately, without reboiling. If boiled, blood curdles in the same way as eggs.

Variations

1. If the hare is not at all high, you may like to leave out both the vinegar and the fruit jelly; if it is very high the quantities of both may be increased.

2. The spices in the stock can be varied with cloves, cinnamon, mace or nutmeg, ginger, juniper and strips of orange or lemon rind. However, the final reduced broth should be only faintly spicy, so don't get carried away.
3. If the hare blood is not available, an enrichment of 4 to 6 tablespoons thick cream can be added with the hare meat and bread balls.
4. The hare broth and meat are nutritious and low calorie, so for a slimmer's soup simply leave out the dumplings. If the vinegar is left out of the stock, a ladleful of broth can be mixed with 4 to 5 tablespoons yogurt and then whisked back into the soup as a finishing touch.

See also:
Rich Venison Soup with Port, Variation 1

Herbs

Most of the recipes in this book contain fresh herbs; only those which are particularly significant are mentioned here.

See under:
Green Leaves: Spinach, Green Pea and Lettuce Purée
Green Leaves: Zuppa di Verdura
Leek and Potato Soup, Variation 4
Pork Gravy Soup with Madeira, Variation 2
Cream of Tomato Soup
Tomatoes: Gazpacho
Tomato and Red Pepper Soup
Vegetables: Minestrone
Vegetables: Pistou
Enrichments: bacon, parsley and onion, especially Variation 3, p.41; pesto, p.43

Herrings

See under:
Mackerel and Lemon Cream Soup, Variation 1
Smoked Mackerel Soup, Variation 3

Lamb and Mutton

CHOOSING AND USING LAMB AND MUTTON

How much easier life would be if the food that was good for you was also the most delicious, morally upright and agriculturally prudent, but alas in this world of woe one can only make a reasonable compromise. Sheep meat, for instance, is ecologically good because sheep feed on high pasture or rocky soils that would not support a crop. It is also morally okay, that is if you are going to eat meat at all, because although the sheep or lamb's life is cut short, it is led in reasonably natural circumstances, not crowded into cages or pens. Because a sheep is not so valuable as a beef steer nor so accessible as a battery chicken, it is less prone to injections of hormones antibiotics and other uglies. But lamb and mutton are bad for the health if you belong to the low animal fat brigade. They are also considerably less versatile in cooking than less morally sound beef, chicken and pork, because they have a dominant flavour which easily swamps other ingredients.

Having decided to buy lamb or mutton for soup, you must then choose between mutton, sold almost exclusively in Afro-Muslim butchers, and British or New Zealand lamb. Mutton is sheep meat over 18 months old and has a good but powerful flavour best used with other strong flavours. Besides the recipes which specifically call for mutton, it could be used in game soup recipes such as those for hare or venison. The cheap cuts recommended for lamb can be used but will take longer to cook. Alternatively you can use the better cuts from the leg or loin.

Lamb signifies an animal between 4 and 12 months old. British lamb is available from March, but is cheapest in the autumn. Lamb from down under is available during winter and spring. British lamb should have bright, dark red flesh and creamy fat. Australian and New Zealand lamb has all been frozen and both meat and fat are paler. On the whole the brighter the colour the less time in the deep freeze.

Scrag end and middle end of neck are the best cuts for soup. They are cheap and have enough meat for a soup and plenty of flavour in the bones. Shank end of leg is good too but works out more expensively. It takes a while to strip the cooked meat off the bones in these cheap cuts, so a more expensive piece of lamb from leg or loin plus some raw bones may suit you better.

LAMB AND GREEN PEA SOUP

With fresh peas, English lamb and an egg and cream enrichment (see Variation 1), this soup would make a lovely summer lunch dish, but even with frozen peas and New Zealand lamb it is still a very pleasant, filling main course soup. It works well in large quantities and can be frozen, though if you are using frozen peas much of their texture will be lost in refreezing.

a shank end of leg of lamb *or* 8 oz (225 g) neck of lamb (see p.178)
2 pints (1.2 l) water
vegetable trimmings as available, for stock
1 bay leaf
1 sprig thyme or marjoram
2 parsley stalks
6 to 8 peppercorns
1 small potato
salt
freshly milled pepper
a generous 8 oz (225 g) peas in the pod – 3 to 4 oz (90 to 110 g) after podding
4 lettuce leaves
1 tablespoon chopped parsley, mint or chervil

Put the lamb in a stainless or enamelled pan with the water and bring to the boil. Lower the heat and skim off any greyish scum that rises. When only white foam is left, add a few celery, carrot and onion or leek trimmings if you have them, the bay leaf, thyme, parsley stalks and peppercorns. Lower the heat until a bubble breaks the surface only every second or so, and simmer for 1 hour or until the lamb is tender. A slow cooker or pressure cooker could also be used for this part of the recipe.

When the lamb is cooked, lift it out and leave to cool. Strain the stock into a measuring jug and remove the fat. You should have 1 pint (600 ml); if you have much less, make it up with water, and if much more, reduce it by fast boiling before adding the potato. Return the stock to the rinsed-out pan and add the potato, cut into ½ inch (1 cm) square dice. Bring the soup back to the boil and add salt and pepper. Add the peas and simmer for 10 minutes, or longer if the peas are old. Remove the bones, gristle and fat from the meat and cut it into large dice the same size as the potatoes. Roll the washed lettuce leaves into a cigar shape and slice across into fine strips. Add them to the soup with the chopped herbs. Taste, and adjust the seasoning. Add the meat and simmer for a minute more. Serve, or cool and store. If you intend to freeze the soup, it is better to add the potato, already cooked, when the soup is defrosted.

179

Variations

1. Reduce the stock to rather less than 1 pint (600 ml) before adding the vegetables. Beat 5 tablespoons double cream with 2 egg yolks and 1 dessertspoon lemon juice. When the soup is ready to serve, beat a ladleful of the soup broth into the cream mixture, then remove the soup from the heat and stir in the cream mixture very quickly and thoroughly. The soup should thicken a little. If not, return it to the heat for a minute until it does, stirring all the time.
2. An equal quantity of mushrooms, leeks, onions or carrots can be used instead of potato.
3. If you are in a hurry, the vegetable trimmings can be left out and the bay leaf, thyme and parsley stalks tied together for easy removal. The lamb should be cooked for 40 minutes or so, then the potato added and so on. The lamb can either be boned as you eat, or removed and boned just before serving.

MUTTON, RICE AND APRICOT SOUP

Rice and dried apricots are as everyday in Iran as potatoes and carrots are in Scotland, and this main course soup is really a kind of Persian Scotch Broth. It is pretty, very filling and highly nutritious, since, provided you use brown rice – which the Iranians don't, but should – the soup has good quantities of protein and vitamins A, B and C. It is best served at once.

1 lb (450 g) middle or scrag end of neck of mutton or lamb – 3 to 4 oz (90 to 110 g) meat	crushed with a little salt salt
2 pints (1.2 l) water	$\frac{1}{2}$ oz (15 g) dried apricots
1 teaspoon coriander	1 oz (30 g) brown rice
$\frac{1}{2}$ teaspoon cumin	1 medium pepper, red for preference
1 clove garlic, peeled and	freshly milled pepper

Cover the mutton with the water in a heavy pan and bring to the boil. Reduce the heat and skim off the greyish scum as it rises. When only white foam is rising, add the spices, crushed garlic and a little salt. Simmer for about 1 hour, until the meat is well cooked, then lift it out and leave to cool. Check that you still have 1$\frac{1}{2}$ pints (900 ml) liquid and top up with water if necessary. Cut the apricots in small pieces. Add the rice and apricots, cover the pan tightly and simmer

180

until the rice is nearly tender. Meanwhile dice or slice the pepper, and cut the meat away from the fat and bone and dice it. Add the pieces of pepper to the soup and simmer for 10 minutes. Check the seasoning and add more water if the soup has reduced too much. Add the meat, taste again, but do not reboil the soup or the meat will go stringy. Serve at once.

Variations

1. Shin of lamb can be used for this soup, but it works out rather more expensive. Breast of lamb is also good, or the remains of a joint cooked for a previous meal, but if no stock or scrapings from the roasting tin are available the soup will not have the same depth of flavour.
2. Dried prunes would make a good substitute for the apricots – use 1 oz (30 g) because of the stones. You could also use fresh apricots, plums, or a small amount of quince, a common fruit in Iran.
3. For a special occasion, use the cooked lamb and rice to make the meat balls on p.34. Poach them in the soup for 5 minutes.

SCOTCH BROTH

Neck of lamb or mutton is still an economical cut, even allowing for the fact that two-thirds of the weight is bone. If you make a stew from middle or scrag end of neck and vegetables, and include 1 lb (450 g) extra neck plus an extra pint or two of liquid, with very little effort you can use it the following day to make a Scotch Broth. If you want to make it from scratch, and it certainly is worth making in large quantities, turn to Variation 1. Scotch Broth freezes well.

2 pints (1.2 l) lamb stock, mutton stock, or stock and water	1 largish onion
	1 medium carrot
	1 small parsnip
1 oz (30 g) pearl barley	2 oz (60 g) cooked lamb or mutton lean scraps
salt	
freshly milled pepper	2 tablespoons chopped parsley

Remove most or all of the fat from the stock. This is very easy if the stock has been in the fridge overnight, since the fat will have formed a solid, white lid. Put the stock in a heavy pan and add the barley and some salt and pepper. Bring to the boil and simmer, half-covered.

Peel the onion and dice it large for a main course or small for a starter. The carrot and parsnip may be peeled for appearance or left unpeeled for vitamins. Dice them the same size, removing the core of the parsnip if it is hard and fibrous. After the barley has been cooking for $\frac{1}{2}$ hour, add the vegetables to the broth and continue simmering. Remove all the fat and gristle from the lamb or mutton scraps and cut into dice. When the barley is cooked, after 1 to $1\frac{1}{2}$ hours, taste the soup and correct the seasoning. Add the meat and chopped parsley and serve, or cool and store in the fridge, where it will keep for several days, or freeze.

Variations

1. Put 8 oz (225 g) neck of lamb or mutton, plus 1 lb (450 g) or so extra raw bones if the butcher has them, in a large pan and cover with 3 pints (1.75 l) cold water. Bring to the boil and turn down to simmer. Remove the greyish scum as it rises. When only white foam remains, add 1 bay leaf, 1 sprig or $\frac{1}{2}$ teaspoon thyme, rosemary or marjoram, 8 or so peppercorns, 3 or 4 parsley stalks, and the peelings and ends from the onion, carrot and parsnip. Simmer for $1\frac{1}{2}$ hours, or until the meat is tender. Lift out the meaty bits and leave to cool. Strain off 2 pints (1.2 l) stock. Remove most of the fat with a large metal spoon. Now proceed with the main recipe.
2. Turnip can be used instead of parsnip, and potatoes – 2 to 4 oz (60 to 110 g) – instead of barley.
3. For a low calorie soup, be absolutely scrupulous about removing all the fat. You may also like to omit the barley or the meat.
4. For a main course soup, the quantity of meat may be increased to 3 to 4 oz (90 to 110 g), the barley to $1\frac{1}{2}$ oz (40 g), and the pieces of meat and vegetable cut in $\frac{1}{2}$ inch (1 cm) cubes or larger.

See also:
Dried Mixed Beans: Harira, Variation 2

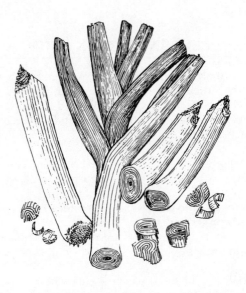

Leeks

CHOOSING AND USING

Leeks are in season all through the autumn and winter, but are only rarely available in summer. Choose medium-sized ones, 1 inch (2.5 cm) or so thick, and with about 6 to 8 inches (15 to 20 cm) of white stem. The white part should not be dirty, lumpy or broken. By the time you have skinned and trimmed a leek it will have lost nearly half its original weight, so they are twice the price they appear to be. To clean, cut off the root and remove one skin. Trim off all the dark green leaves with slanting cuts away from the root, tapering the end to a point. You will be left with a fat, green and white pencil. Cut the pencil in 2 or 4 vertically, and then cut it across into thin slices. Leave these slices to soak in cold water for 15 to 30 minutes before using them, since grains of sand and soil get trapped between the skins of the leek. When you have soaked the leek slices, scoop them off the surface of the water, leaving the grit at the bottom.

LEEK AND LEMON SOUP

The pungent combination of garlic, lemon and spice which is so common in the Eastern Mediterranean make this soup memorable. It is suitable for a really hot day, when the acid lemon tang will seem very attractive. It can be served hot or iced and will keep a day or so, but isn't worth freezing.

about $1\frac{1}{4}$ lb (560 g) leeks
1 large lemon
2 tablespoons oil
1 clove garlic or more to taste, peeled and crushed with a little salt
$\frac{3}{4}$ flat teaspoon turmeric

$\frac{3}{4}$ flat teaspoon cumin
$\frac{1}{4}$ teaspoon chili, cayenne or tabasco
just under 1 pint (600 ml) water
salt
$\frac{1}{4}$ pint (150 ml) plain yogurt
freshly milled pepper

Cut the leeks into thin slices $\frac{1}{4}$ inch ($\frac{1}{2}$ cm) wide and clean them as described on p.183. Grate the lemon rind and extract the juice. Put the oil in a stainless or enamelled pan, add the garlic and spices and stir over a low heat for a minute. Add the leeks and sweat gently for 5 minutes. Pour in the water and bring to the boil. Add the lemon juice, rind and a little salt and simmer for 15 minutes. Blend or put through the medium plate of the food mill. If you are blending and prefer a soup with texture, leave a ladleful unblended. Return to the rinsed-out pan and reheat. When the soup is very hot, put the yogurt in a bowl and very thoroughly stir in a ladleful of soup, then beat the yogurt mixture into the soup. Taste, and add salt and pepper and more spice as you think fit. Serve at once, since it is risky to allow yogurt to boil, for it may curdle. The soup is also good served ice. Chill it thoroughly and check the seasoning again when very cold. You may want to thin it with a little water or yogurt when serving iced.

Variations

1. A really good chicken stock would lift this soup from very pleasant to first class.
2. For a slightly different flavour, use $\frac{1}{2}$ lemon rind and $\frac{1}{2}$ orange rind. Use only lemon juice, though, because orange would be too sweet. The rind and juice of 2 or 3 limes should work well, too.
3. The leek slices could be left intact and the yogurt served in a

dollop on each bowlful.
4. For a more varied texture 8 oz (225 g) trimmed leeks can be used, and 2 to 3 tablespoons cooked rice added a couple of minutes before serving.

LEEK AND POTATO SOUP: POTAGE PARMENTIER

When you are feeling old and disappointed, when days are dark and summer is far away, or when human beings are behaving even more inhumanly than usual, a bowl of Leek and Potato Soup will put you at peace with the world. It is quick and cheap, keeps well, though not in the freezer, and the ingredients are available everywhere; yet if carefully made it is as subtle, comforting and delicious as any of its grand cousins. If you have to blend this soup, it will have the texture of glue for several hours afterwards, so prepare it well in advance. The soup is an excellent base for other flavours, and the variations given are only a small selection which any imaginative cook can easily augment.

2 medium leeks
1 small onion
1 large potato – a floury white one is best – 7 oz (200 g) after peeling
1 oz (30 g) butter

1 pint (600 ml) chicken stock or water
salt
freshly milled pepper
nutmeg
¼ pint (150 ml) single cream
1 dessertspoon chopped parsley

Wash the leeks as described on p.183. Thinly slice them with the onion and potato, and sweat for 10 minutes in the butter in a heavy-bottomed stainless or enamelled pan, stirring occasionally. Do not let them stick or brown, and keep the lid on between stirs. Add the stock or water, salt, pepper and a little grated nutmeg, and simmer the soup, half-covered, for about 15 minutes or until the potatoes and leeks are soft. You may like the lumpy texture of the soup without sieving, or you can put it through the medium or coarse plate of the food mill. Return to a clean stainless or enamelled pan for serving, and reheat with the cream and the parsley. Add a little milk if you like a thinner soup. Taste when the soup is hot, and adjust the seasoning. Serve sprinkled with the chopped chives. The soup improves if it is kept in the fridge overnight.

Variations

1. Use 4 oz (110 g) potato, and double cream instead of single. Blend and sieve to a velvet texture. Chill thoroughly, then adjust the seasoning. This is real Crème Vichyssoise.
2. Use milk, low fat milk powder and water, or light ham stock for the liquid.
3. Use only 5 oz (140 g) potato, and add 4 oz (110 g) wiped, quartered button mushrooms to the butter, leek and potato mixture at the beginning.
4. Use 6 oz (175 g) potato and add 4 oz (110 g) finely sliced sorrel or spinach or 3 heaped tablespoons chopped, minced fresh herbs such as watercress, parsley, chervil, chives, basil, marjoram or tarragon. Do not use dried, strongly flavoured or bushy herbs. Stir any of these alternatives into the soup with the cream, and simmer for 2 minutes before serving.
5. Without using any butter, make a simple soup base of the leek, onion, potato and stock or water. Boil it until cooked, then sieve or mill it. Dilute the base with more stock, water or milk and season it sparingly. Now enrich it with pesto (p.43), fricassée (p.41), a mixture of onion, garlic and parsley, or peperonata (p.43).

See also:
Chicken: Cock-a-Leekie
Cream of Mushroom Soup, Variation 2
Oatmeal and Vegetable Soup, Variation 3
Cream of Onion Soup, Variation 2
Potatoes: Potage Bonne Femme
Tripe: Zuppa di Trippa alla Milanese

Lemon

Lentils

LENTIL AND SAUSAGE SOUP

A slow cooker has the curious but useful property of softening the toughest meat or pulse, while leaving vegetables still almost chewy after 8 hours' cooking. Except for red kidney beans, most of the bean and pea soups in this book can be slow-cooked very successfully. This one takes only 5 to 10 minutes to prepare in the morning and will present you with a simple but hearty main course soup on your weary evening return. It can also be cooked in the ordinary way, of course. It keeps and freezes well. Continental pork sausage with garlic makes the most interesting soup, but ordinary pork sausage can be used (see Variation 1).

1 small onion
3 to 4 oz (90 to 110 g) sausage
1 dessertspoon oil
2 oz (60 g) green or brown lentils
2 to 2½ pints (1.2 to 1.5 l) water
   – just over 1 pint (600 ml) for
   a slow cooker
½ bay leaf
½ teaspoon oregano or
   marjoram
salt
freshly milled pepper
1 medium potato, peeled or
   unpeeled
chopped parsley or croûtons (for
   garnish)

Chop the onion and sausage into large or small pieces according to your preference. Put them in a heavy pan or frying pan and fry them together in the oil for 5 minutes. Add the washed lentils, water and seasonings. If you are using a slow cooker, cube the potato, add it now with the sausage, onion, lentils and smaller amount of liquid, and switch on. Otherwise simmer the soup for 45 to 60 minutes, until the lentils are nearly tender, then add the potato cut into cubes. Simmer for another 15 minutes, until the potato is cooked. Taste, and adjust seasoning. Serve with parsley or croûtons on top.

Variations

1. Ordinary British bangers may be used instead of fresh continental sausage. They can be chopped in pieces, or the skins twisted at 1 inch (2.5 cm) intervals to form lots of tiny sausages. Cut the twisted bits with scissors. Good-quality salami can also be used: 2 oz (60 g) will be plenty, and 1 oz (30 g) extra lentils should be used.
2. If you do not like potatoes and lentils in combination, use an equal weight of carrots, celery, parsnip or turnip.
3. Instead of water use pork bacon, vegetable or beef stock, or $1\frac{1}{2}$ pints (900 ml) water and a 14 oz (400 g) can of peeled tomatoes, roughly chopped.

SPICY LENTIL AND VEGETABLE SOUP

While the previous recipe, for Lentil and Sausage Soup, contains manufactured pork products, which some people think not only dangerous but immoral to eat, this soup has no animal products at all. Eaten with wholemeal bread it provides good levels of protein, iron and vitamins A, B and some C. It is very simple to make and keeps and freezes well. Flat brown lentils taste much better than the prettier pinky-orange ones.

1 small onion	water
1 small carrot	salt
1 small turnip or $\frac{1}{2}$ celeriac	freshly milled pepper
2 tablespoons oil	grated rind of $\frac{1}{2}$ a small lemon
1 flat teaspoon coriander	juice of $\frac{1}{2}$ to 1 lemon
1 clove garlic, peeled and crushed with a little salt	pinch of cayenne *or* dash of tabasco
3 to 4 oz (90 to 110 g) flat brown lentils	1 small onion (for garnish) parsley or mint (for garnish)
$1\frac{1}{2}$ to 2 pints (900 ml to 1.2 l)	

Chop the onion, carrot and turnip or celeriac and put them in a heavy pan with the oil, coriander and garlic, if you only like a mild flavour of garlic. (If you like the garlic more predominant, add it with the lemon at the end.) Sweat the vegetables over a low heat for about 15 minutes, stirring occasionally and keeping the pan covered in between stirs. Then add the washed lentils and the water, bring to the boil, add a little salt and pepper and simmer, uncovered, for 45 to 60 minutes, or until the lentils are a mush. Add the lemon rind and juice, and cayenne or tabasco. Taste the soup and adjust the seasoning. At this point it can be cooled and stored overnight or frozen. To serve, slice $\frac{1}{2}$ a small onion paper-thin and separate the rings. Coarsely chop the parsley or mint and float the onion rings and herbs on the reheated soup before you serve it.

Variations

1. Vegetable broth (see pps.263-4), vegetable extracts or a stock cube can be used instead of or with the water, but commercial products tend to be higher in salt than in real flavour. Alternatively $\frac{1}{2}$ pint (300 ml) or so of tomato juice or vegetable juice can replace part of the water. Add it when the lentils are cooked.
2. Other root vegetables such as Jerusalem artichokes and potatoes can be substituted for the vegetables given.
3. To make a more substantial meal, put a boiled potato or 1 heaped tablespoon cooked rice in the centre of each bowlful of soup, or serve with plain or herb croûtons (see pps.27-8).
4. A heaped teaspoon of curry powder or paste, or your own home-made combination of coriander, cumin, turmeric, cayenne, cardamom, garam masala etc. can be used instead of coriander. This could be a real blast as a curried soup, which would be good served with yogurt.

See also:
Dried Mixed Beans: Harira
Mung Bean and Black Olive Soup, Variation 1
Pheasant and Lentil Soup

Lettuce

PURÉE OF LETTUCE WITH SOUR CREAM: POTAGE
DU PÈRE TRANQUIL

This is a most delicately flavoured soup which would be wasted on palates dulled by too much alcohol or nicotine. It is lovely on a hot day; Variation 1 has only 50 calories per 8 fl oz (250 ml) portion.

2 large round or Cos lettuces
3 shallots *or* 6 large spring
   onions
1 oz (30 g) butter
1½ pints (900 ml) chicken stock
   or half milk half stock

salt
freshly milled pepper
1 teaspoon sugar
2 teaspoons lemon juice
¼ pint (150 ml) *crème fraîche* (see
   p.142) or sour cream

Discard any wilted or grubby lettuce leaves and pull the lettuces to pieces. Wash all the leaves, then roll a few at a time into cigar shapes and cut across into ½ inch (1 cm) slices with a stainless steel knife. Keep a handful of inner leaves aside. Roll these up, slice very finely – ¼ inch (½ cm) or less – and reserve as a chiffonade. Peel and chop the shallots or spring onions into small pieces, and sweat them for 5 minutes in the butter in a heavy stainless or enamelled pan over a low heat. Add the lettuce, except the reserved leaves, and stir over the heat until it wilts and begins to shrink. Add the chicken stock or stock and milk and the seasoning, bring to the boil and simmer for 15 minutes. Put the soup through the fine plate of the food mill, or blend and then sieve it. Return to a clean stainless or enamelled pan. Taste, and add more salt, sugar, pepper or lemon juice as necessary. Add the reserved lettuce chiffonade and reheat the soup. Simmer for 3 minutes, taste again, and serve with a swirl of *crème fraîche* or sour cream stirred into each bowlful.

Variations

1. Sweat the onion in 1 teaspoon butter or good olive oil. Add chicken stock, or half chicken stock half milk made with ¾ oz (25 g) skim milk powder, and serve with plain yogurt instead of cream. You may like to omit the lemon juice since the yogurt is

190

itself sharp.

2. You can use spinach, sorrel, young nettle tops, beet leaves or watercress in this recipe. If you are using sorrel or watercress, halve the quantity, and cut up a large potato into small pieces and add it to the butter, onion and green leaves mixture.

3. If you like a slightly thickened soup, add 1 dessertspoon plain flour to the butter and onion mixture and stir for a minute before adding the lettuce or other green leaves. For a more delicate way of thickening the soup, add 1 to 1½ oz (30 to 40 g) ground almonds with the lettuce and garnish with toasted almonds.

See also:
Green Leaves: Spinach, Green Pea and Lettuce Purée
Green Pea and Ham Soup
Purée of Green Peas with their Pods
Cream of Watercress, Variation 4

Lime

See under:
Tomato and Orange Soup, Variation 3

Lobster

CHOOSING AND USING

Lobsters are in season from April to November and these days fetch such ludicrously high prices that it is perhaps only worth making a real Lobster Bisque if you are personally acquainted with your fishmonger, or even better with a fisherman. The price is no guarantee of high quality – rather the reverse in fact – and it is frustrating to lavish money and care on an old or out-of-condition creature which inevitably tastes muddy and dull.

To make the perfect Lobster Bisque one must be not only extravagant but murderous. Because of the speed at which their delicate flesh putrefies, lobsters are generally bought alive, when they are navy blue, and killed either by boiling or, more humanely, by driving a large knife right through the spinal cord. If you can't face doing this, the fishmonger can kill it while you wait, provided you intend to use it at once. Only buy a cooked lobster from a very reputable shop that cooks them daily. For cooked or canned lobster use the Shellfish Cream recipe. If you are discouraged by the money and mayhem involved in a Lobster Bisque turn to Crab Bisque. Crabs are a quarter of the price of lobsters, and the bisque equally delicious. Those still determined to pursue the perfect coral and rose pink Bisque d'Homard, with its rich, sweet shellfish flavour, cut by the merest whisper of brandy, read on.

A lobster is in its prime for eating when it weighs about $1\frac{1}{2}$ lb (675 g). Chefs often choose hen lobsters for their vivid coral roe, but a cock lobster costs the same and may have slightly more meat on it. (Why crustaceans are sexed in the poultry yard is a mystery.) Lobsters which are much larger or much smaller that this ideal weight should be avoided, especially large hen lobsters which are generally full of roe and have little body meat. Ask your fishmonger to pick out a lively lobster that is heavy for its size, and postpone your dinner party if he says that none of them is just the right weight.

You may buy a live lobster the day before you cook it and make the soup the day before you eat it, for the bisque will improve with 24 hours in the fridge. If you buy the lobster the day before, keep it overnight in the bottom of the fridge in a large plastic or heavy paper bag with air holes. Do not attempt, as I once did, to give it a comfortable last night in the condemned cell by mixing a salt solution in the washing bowl. The next morning the lobster was dead and the water tinged with pink – I had killed it by osmosis, for the heavy salt solution had sucked the poor thing's vital juices. The degree of saltiness, I discovered later, is very critical, and fresh water will suffocate it.

Killing a Lobster

When the hour of execution has arrived, wash the lobster under cold running water, and lay it on its back on a chopping board standing, if possible, on a deep-rimmed tray to catch any juices. Hold it firmly down with a cloth if you like (its claws will be pegged or fastened with elastic bands). Plunge a heavy knife straight between the row of feelers just below the head. At this point the lobster is technically dead, though it will flap around a bit while you cut down to the tail, right through all the flesh to the back shell. When you reach the tail, which is marked in blue and yellow as delicately as a butterfly's wing, use a pair of heavy scissors to cut up the middle of the back shell to the top of its head. The lobster is now cut in half lengthways except for its head. Grasp the lobster by its claws and pull it apart. In the head you will find a stomach sac with an intestinal tube running from it towards the tail; remove and discard both of these. If you have cut the sac in two, just throw away both bits. The sac is quite large and pale, with gristly bits at one end. Scoop out any black, shiny roe and greenish 'cream' and keep them in the fridge. Pull away and discard the triangular, fibrous gills which lie under the body shell, and twist off the claws, dividing them into their separate joints and cracking each joint slightly with a heavy knife. You are now ready to make your Bisque.

BISQUE D'HOMARD

This is the ultimate soup, beloved of French restaurants with long menus and brigades of harrassed little commis chefs ready to pound the lobster shells to powdery fineness. To make the soup at home you need either a pestle and mortar and a lot of spare time, a stout-hearted blender, or an electric food processor. Before you embark on this epic soup, please read the information on buying and preparing the lobster. This recipe makes 3 pints. (see above)

4 oz (110 g) butter – unsalted is better
2 tablespoons olive oil
1 fresh raw lobster weighing 1½ lb (675 g), prepared as above
1 small onion *or* 8 to 10 shallots
3 sticks celery
2 cloves garlic, peeled and crushed with a little salt
6 tablespoons reasonable-quality brandy
2½ pints (1.5 l) white fish stock (see p.157) or water

salt
freshly milled pepper
3 thin strips lemon rind
1 oz (30 g) uncooked white rice
cayenne or tabasco
squeeze of lemon juice

If you have a hen lobster and want to make a coral butter garnish:
2 oz (60 g) unsalted butter
lemon juice
salt
freshly milled pepper
cayenne

Melt 1 oz (30 g) of the butter with the olive oil in a heavy frying pan over a medium heat, and fry the lobster pieces in the shell a few at a time, turning them until every side has changed from blue-black to brilliant orange-red. Lift out the pieces as they are done, and finally fry the lobster cream for a moment or two. If you want to make coral butter, do not wash up the pan.

Meanwhile melt 2 oz (60 g) butter over a low heat in a heavy stainless or enamelled pan of 7 pints' (4 l) capacity. Slice the onion and celery finely, and sweat them in the pan with the garlic. When the vegetables are slightly soft, put the lobster pieces on top and scrape in all the juice from the pan and any that has collected on the preparation tray and board. Also add the fried lobster cream.

Cover the pan and heat the lobster and vegetables through for a minute, then pour over 4 tablespoons of the brandy. When you have removed the brandy bottle, light a match and touch it to the pan; shake it and stir the contents so that everything comes into contact with the burning alcohol. When the flames have died, pour in 1 pint (600 ml) of the fish stock or water. Add a little salt, pepper and the lemon rind, cover, and simmer on a very low heat for 15 minutes. Lift out the lobster pieces and leave them to cool. Meanwhile boil the rice with salt and pepper in another $\frac{1}{2}$ pint (300 ml) of the fish stock or water for 12 minutes or until tender.

When the lobster is cool enough to handle, lift out the tail meat with your fingers if possible, keeping it intact. Break or chop the body shell and feelers into $\frac{1}{2}$ inch (1 cm) pieces and set aside. Crack the claw shells open with a heavy knife but a light hand, so that little bits of shell are not pressed into the lobster flesh. Ease out the lobster meat as delicately as possible, keeping it in large pieces and removing the piece of cartilage from the centre of the claw meat. You may find a skewer useful for pushing out the last fragments from the tough central joint. Cut the better half of the lobster flesh into slices for a garnish. Cover all the meat and put it in the fridge.

Unless you have an unusually powerful and well-made blender or processor, discard the claw shells since they are much tougher than the body shell. Grind the body shell and feelers in the processor, or purée them in the blender with some of the remaining fish stock. You can, of course, pound them by hand in the time-honoured way, or put them twice through the fine plate of an electric mincer. Add the shell purée to the vegetables in the pot, with some of the remaining stock if you ground the shell dry, and simmer the mixture for another 10 minutes, stirring occasionally. Blend the mixture thoroughly and put it through a fine sieve, or through the fine plate of a food mill. Do not use a wide-meshed sieve, or unpleasant little chunks of shell may be left in the soup. If you have a hen lobster, and are not serving a separate coral butter, fry the roe in the remaining butter and flame it with the rest of the brandy for a minute. Scrape everything into the blender, blend it with the rice mixture, then sieve or mill it into the shell and vegetable mixture. Swill out the frying pan, blender and sieve with the last of the fish stock, and scrape any bits from the bottom of the sieve into the soup.

Now at last you can admire your Bisque. Taste it and add salt, pepper, cayenne and lemon juice, and enjoy its brilliant, shifting shades of flame pink and orange. Add the reserved slices of lobster meat to the soup and store it, well covered, for several hours in the fridge, and preferably overnight to allow the flavours to mature. Reheat very gently without boiling, or the lobster slices will become stringy. Serve accompanied only by thin slices of home-made bread.

Coral Butter

Melt half the butter in a small frying pan. Add the shiny black raw roe and sauté gently for a minute or so until it has turned a brilliant coral colour. Add a squeeze of lemon, salt, pepper and a pinch of cayenne. Scrape into a small bowl and mash thoroughly with the rest of the butter. Taste – it should be sharply flavoured. Put it into a butter paper or small piece of greaseproof paper, roll into a small log, and put in the fridge. When you serve the Bisque, float a slice of the coral butter on top of each bowl. If you are using cooked lobster roe, proceed in exactly the same way, but warm the roe through in the melted butter rather than actually cooking it any more.

Variations

1. If you are using a lobster that has been cooked by the fishmonger, read the instructions on pps.191-2. Cut the lobster in half and discard the stomach etc., then remove the lobster meat from the shell. Cover the meat and coral and put it in the fridge. Sweat the vegetables as in the main recipe, then add the body shell and feelers, broken into very small pieces. Flame and simmer as in the main recipe. After 30 minutes blend the shell, vegetables and stock very thoroughly and push through a fine-meshed sieve. If you are not making separate coral butter turn the lobster meat and roe in butter over a very low heat, and then flame them with the rest of the brandy – you are not cooking the meat, merely impregnating it with the brandy and butter. Slice the best pieces (about half) of the lobster neatly for garnish, and blend the rest with the roe and rice. Finish the soup as in the main recipe.

2. You can of course add all kinds of other wines and flavourings and enrichments to a Lobster Bisque, but I consider that the time and money would be better spent getting the very best lobster. No art can disguise an out-of-condition or stale lobster, while tampering further with a prime, fresh specimen would be a coarse gilding of the lily.
3. If you want to be frugal, use some of the lobster tail meat for another dish.

See also:
Shellfish Cream

Mackerel

MACKEREL AND LEMON CREAM SOUP

Oily but delicately flavoured fish such as mackerel, and the poor over-fished herring which is now so expensive, do make good soups. It is very important to get fresh fish with no rank oiliness about them, or the flavour will be spoilt. This soup is very simple; getting the skin off the cooked mackerel is the only fiddly bit. It is best eaten at once, but can be prepared in advance and the egg yolks added on reheating.

1 small mackerel – 6 oz (175 g) after filleting – with its head and bones
8 oz (225 g) white fish heads and bones (optional)
1½ pints (900 ml) water
juice of ½ to 1 small lemon
2 strips lemon rind
pinch of fennel seeds *or* ½ a fennel bulb

10 peppercorns

To finish the soup:
5 tablespoons *crème fraîche* (see p.142) or sour cream
salt
freshly milled pepper
2 egg yolks
lemon juice

If the fishmonger has filleted the mackerel, well and good; if not, turn to p.155. Put the head and bones, plus other bones if you have them, in a non-aluminium pan with the water and lemon juice. Bring to the boil and quickly skim off any scum that forms. Add the 4 strips of lemon rind, fennel seed or fennel bulb cut in small pieces, and the peppercorns, and simmer for 15 minutes. Add the mackerel fillets, preferably in a perforated tray or sieve so that they can be removed easily, and simmer very gently for a further 6 to 8 minutes, until the mackerel gives under the pressure of a finger. Leave the mackerel to cool, strain the stock at once, and discard the head and bones.

Measure the stock into a clean pan: you should have 1 pint (600 ml). If you have too much, bring it to the boil and reduce by hard boiling, but do not leave it on the heat longer than necessary or the flavour of the stock will deteriorate. If you have too little, make it up with water. Meanwhile peel the skin off the mackerel; this is a bore, but most of the skin can be removed without breaking up the fillets, though it takes patience. Flake the fish. Add the cream to the stock, taste it, and add salt, pepper and lemon as needed. Whisk the egg yolks with a squeeze of lemon juice. Take the soup off the heat if it is still on, beat a ladleful of the soup into the egg and lemon mixture, then beat that mixture into the soup. It should thicken just a little. If not, return the pan to a very low heat and stir continuously until the soup thickens slightly. (Eggs scramble well below boiling point, so watch it like a hawk.) Stir in the flaked mackerel, and serve.

Variations

1. A medium, very fresh herring can be used instead of mackerel. Since it is difficult to fillet herrings thoroughly, it might be better to bone it after cooking, when the bones will just lift out.
2. If you like a light, lemony, slightly acid flavour with fish, there is no reason why you should not use this recipe with any fish; salmon and salmon trout would be particularly suitable.
3. Dill seeds or weed can be used instead of fennel. Watercress, or fresh green herbs such as parsley, chervil or chives, can be used to flavour the soup. Chop them and stir them in with the flaked fish.
4. For a low calorie soup, use yogurt instead of cream and/or egg yolks. You may want to reduce the lemon juice, since the yogurt is itself acid. Add the yogurt in the same way as the eggs in the main recipe.

SMOKED MACKEREL SOUP

Fish can be cold-smoked, like haddock, cod and kippers, which need further cooking, or hot-smoked, like mackerel, buckling, and smoked trout and eel, which are ready to serve. These hot-smoked fish have become very popular hors d'oeuvres in recent years and are available in most good supermarkets. Any of them can quickly be converted to a tasty soup, the only problem being the careful removal of all bones, since cooked fish is difficult to sieve or mill. It is important to use freshly smoked fish, since aging smoked fish acquires a rank flavour which is particularly noticeable in a soup. The soup is not really worth freezing and will only keep a day in the fridge.

1 small smoked mackerel – 8 oz (225 g) after skinning and boning
¾ pint (450 ml) milk
1 tablespoon paprika
sprinkle of cayenne
1 tablespoon rice flour or potato
flour or cornflour
¼ pint (150 ml) single cream
1 tablespoon wine vinegar
salt
1 tablespoon finely chopped chives or parsley

Skin the mackerel, lift out and discard the backbone, and flake the fish very carefully in order to extract every single bone. Reserve about a quarter of the flesh, including the best pieces. Put the rest of the fish with the milk, paprika, cayenne and rice, potato flour or cornflour in the blender and liquidize thoroughly. A few minutes before serving, pour the mixture into a stainless or enamelled pan; watch the last little bit carefully for bones. Put in the cream and the reserved mackerel pieces, and heat to just below boiling point, stirring as you heat. Add wine vinegar and salt to taste, and serve sprinkled with the chopped herbs.

Variations

1. Fish stock, or vegetable stock for fish (see p.157), can be used instead of milk.
2. A sherry glass of fruity white wine can be added instead of an equal amount of milk or stock.
3. Any of the hot-smoked fish mentioned in the introduction to the recipe can be used instead of mackerel.
4. The paprika gives a pretty colour and pleasant flavour, but is not essential. It can be omitted, in which case the soup will taste of just smoked mackerel and cream. A few fennel or dill seeds or a few leaves of dill or tarragon can be substituted for the paprika.

Melon

ICED MELON AND FRESH GINGER SOUP

This is very nearly an instant soup if you have a blender. Considering how luxurious it tastes, it is surprisingly low in calories and is altogether a useful beginning to a summer dinner. Test melons for ripeness by pressing the non-stem end, which should give a little. Chicken glaze gives the soup a much richer flavour than that achieved with a stock cube.

1 piece of green ginger about
  ½ inch (1 cm) square
1 ripe melon weighing 1½ to 2 lb
  (675 g to 1 kg) when whole –
  14 oz (400 g) pulp
2 cubes chicken glaze (see p.118)

or 1½ chicken stock cubes
8 tablespoons boiling water to
  dissolve glaze or stock cubes
¼ teaspoon salt if you use glaze
pinch of cayenne
½ pint (300 ml) plain yogurt

Peel the ginger with a potato peeler and chop to peppercorn size. Cut the melon in half. Discard the seeds and scoop all the soft, ripe flesh into the blender jar, reserving 2 large scoops for the garnish; if you have a ball cutter cut out 12 or so melon balls for garnish before you start scooping. Add all the other ingredients, including the defrosted cubes of glaze diluted with cold water, or the stock cubes dissolved in the boiling water, plus salt if you are using glaze. Blend thoroughly, making sure that the glaze has dissolved. Taste and add more grated ginger, salt and cayenne as you like. Bear in mind that iced food needs more seasoning than hot food. Put the soup to chill in the freezer for 30 minutes before moving it to the fridge. Stir in the finely diced melon or the little melon balls.

Variation

A vegetarian stock cube works very well, as does a not too salty ham glaze or a ham stock cube. For a richer soup all or part of the yogurt can be replaced by sour cream or *crème fraîche* (see p.142).

Minestrone

See under:
Vegetables

Mint

See under:
Iced Cucumber and Yogurt Soup, Variation 1

Red Mullet

See under:
Sea Bass, Vermouth and Garlic Soup, Variation 1

Mulligatawny

See under:
Chicken

Mushroom

BLACK MUSHROOM SOUP

I adapted this soup years ago from the Veronese Mushroom Sauce in Elizabeth David's *Italian Food*. Since then I have tried it out with several different stocks and seasonings. Given fresh, flat mushrooms, it has a delicately sensuous fragrance and texture, which even the best creamy mushroom soup lacks. It is at its best immmediately it is made. If you are in the country and can really use 'morning-gathered, dew-fresh' field mushrooms, your soup will have a flavour that would make a truffle jealous. Most people, though, are not in this lucky position, and will have to content themselves with flat mushrooms (not cups, and still less buttons) that are as fresh as possible, with damp, velvety, dark undersides.

12 oz (350 g) mushrooms, preferably flat	1 pint (600 ml) delicate beef or vegetable stock
1 small onion	salt
2 tablespoons fruity olive oil *or* 1 oz (30 g) butter	freshly milled pepper scrape of nutmeg
1 large clove garlic, peeled and crushed finely with a little salt	2 tablespoons finely chopped parsley or fresh marjoram

Chop the mushroom stalks and slice the caps finely; keep the two separate. Slice the onion finely and put it with the oil or butter and garlic in a heavy pan; add the chopped mushroom stalks. Sweat gently, half-covered, over a low heat for 10 minutes, stirring occasionally. Add the stock and seasoning and bring to the boil. Simmer, partly covered, for 15 minutes, then add the mushroom caps and simmer for a further 5 minutes. Adjust the seasoning, stir in the chopped herbs, and serve.

Variations

1. Duck or a lightly flavoured game stock are the very best for this soup, but chicken stock will do, or even water. Don't on any account sully its glorious mushroominess with a bought stock cube. If you are using water, 5 tablespoons good white wine or the juice of $\frac{1}{2}$ a small lemon could be added.
2. Although this soup should be kept simple, it could be served with tiny plain croûtons fried in olive oil (see p.27), or fresh Parmesan, bought in a lump and grated at home.
3. For a low calorie soup, use 1 teaspoon only of a very fruity, first-pressing olive oil.

CREAM OF MUSHROOM SOUP

The canned version of this soup is a perennial bestseller, in spite of the fact that much of the fragrance and texture of the mushrooms are lost during canning. A beautifully made, fresh mushroom soup will make any guest feel relaxed and comfortable. If you consider this quantity of mushrooms an extravagance for a single soup, make a plain vegetable purée, such as broad bean, white bean, or potato; add a mushroom and onion enrichment at the end (see red pepper and onion, Variation 4, p.43). Field mushrooms have the best flavour but will turn the soup rather dark brown.

12 oz (350 g) cup or button
   mushrooms, as fresh as
   possible
1 medium onion
1 oz (30 g) butter
1 rounded tablespoon plain or
   rice flour
1½ pints (900 ml) milk, or milk
   and water mixed

a little grated nutmeg
salt
freshly milled pepper
1 sprig of fresh marjoram *or* ½
   teaspoon dried marjoram or
   basil
squeeze of lemon juice (optional)
¼ pint (150 ml) single or double
   cream

Wipe any compost off the mushrooms. Pull off their stalks and dice them with the onion. Sweat them for 6 to 7 minutes in half the butter in a heavy pan over a very low heat, stirring occasionally. Keep the pan covered. Cut the mushroom caps into ¼ inch (½ cm) slices or quarters, depending on whether you are aiming at elegance or heartiness. Put the remaining butter in a small pan with a lid. Add the mushroom caps and sweat them very gently for a few minutes until they are just soft, then set aside.

Stir the plain flour, if you are using it, into the butter, onion and mushroom stalk mixture. Stir it in thoroughly and cook over a low heat for a minute or two. Now add the milk a little at a time, stirring it in thoroughly after each addition, until you have a thin, beige sauce. If you have rice flour, dissolve it in a little of the cold milk. Add the rest of the milk to the butter, onion and mushroom stalks, and, when it is barely boiling, whisk a little of it into the rice flour mixture. Transfer the whisk to the pan and pour the rice flour mixture into the pan, whisking as you do so.

Add a little grated nutmeg, a little salt, some pepper and marjoram and simmer the soup, partly covered, for 15 minutes. Put the soup through the fine plate of the food mill, or allow it to cool a little and then blend and sieve it. (You can, of course, leave the soup chunky.) Add the mushroom caps and their butter. At this point the soup can be stored in the fridge or frozen, but it is best served immediately. Taste when very hot and add more seasoning and a little lemon if you like. Stir in the cream, heat for another moment and serve.

Variations

1. Any fresh-flavoured, light stock, ham, beef, chicken, duck or vegetable, can be used instead of part or all of the milk.
2. The white part of 2 small leeks can be used instead of onion. If you like a thick soup, use 1 oz (30 g) butter to fry the onion and mushroom stalks and add 1 heaped tablespoon flour.
3. For an exhibitionist soup, use just under 1¾ pints (1 l) good light stock and 5 tablespoons fruity white wine, and softly whip about 8 tablespoons double cream. With a sharp knife scallop the edges of 12 little mushroom caps, and sweat them in an extra ½ oz (15 g) butter very gently, so that they do not shrink, for 3 to 4 minutes. Serve each bowlful of soup garnished with a swirl of whipped cream and 3 to 4 of the little mushroom caps.

See also:
Broad Bean and Mushroom Soup
Beetroot: Borscht with Mushrooms and Sour Cream
Crab and Mushroom Chowder
Leek and Potato Soup, Variation 3
Potato, Mushroom and Sour Cream Soup
Pork Gravy Soup with Madeira, Variation 3
Shellfish Cream, Variation 3
Devilled Turkey Soup
Rich Venison Soup with Port, Variation 2
Enrichments: red pepper and onion, Variation 4, p.42
Garnishes and Accompaniments: mushrooms, p.32.

Mussels

CHOOSING AND USING

Mussels are the last of the great shellfish and crustacean delicacies to be found cheaply and easily in fishmongers, and although their preparation and cleaning is lengthy and rather tedious, they are worth buying regularly during their winter season. By the time our grandchildren are grown up mussels will no doubt be an extravagant luxury like oysters or lobsters. However, quite a lot of prejudice exists against mussels and many people either are, or think they are, allergic to them, so check with your prospective guests before buying. Mussels should be eaten as soon as possible after purchase. Many fishmongers go to market on Tuesdays and Fridays, so these may be good days for mussel buying. They should be eaten at once, but leftover cooked mussels can be kept overnight in the fridge and eaten cold with vinaigrette or as part of a rice salad.

Cleaning

If you think the mussels may be gritty or you have gathered them yourself, put them into a washing-up bowl full of cold lightly-salted water, along with a few tablespoons flour or oatmeal and leave them overnight. Mussels bought from a reputable fishmonger should not require this treatment. To clean them, take a short, stout vegetable knife and scrape off any barnacles as well as removing as much as possible of the beard, which is the little fibrous string dangling from the hinge of the mussel. As you clean them, keep a sharp eye out for any that are cracked or not tightly shut – discard them at once, including any that seem even a little less than tightly shut. Mussels occasionally open in the water, but if in good condition will snap shut when picked up. Give the cleaned mussels a gentle rinse in fresh water and leave in a cool place. They can be safely left for an hour or two, but if you have to keep them overnight they are best left uncleaned, wrapped in wet newspaper in the fridge.

MOULES MARINIÈRE

It is difficult to estimate quantities of mussels for other people, since those who like them usually love them, besides which there are always 10 to 20 per cent broken or dead mussels in any purchase. The position is further complicated by the extent to which mussels vary in size, and by the fact that many fishmongers now sell them by the pound, while the old-fashioned ones still sell by the pint or quart. The quantities given here are intended to provide a hearty starter-cum-main course, more mussel than soup, for 4, while the following recipe gives quantities for a more delicate soup-with-mussels-in version. In both recipes real mussel aficionados will want to increase the quantities.

For the main course for 4:
1 small leek
1 bunch of very fresh parsley
4 shallots *or* 1 small onion
½ pint (300 ml) dry white wine of respectable quality
½ pint (300 ml) fish stock or water

5 to 6 fennel seeds *or* 2 sprigs of dried fennel
2 to 2½ lb (about 1 kg) live mussels in the shell – 3 to 4 quarts
salt
freshly milled pepper

Very finely chop or mince the leek, parsley stalks and shallot or onion. Put them in the bottom of a pan holding 1 gallon (5 l) or more. Add the wine and water or stock, the fennel and the mussels, prepared as described above. Put a lid on the pan, heat it gently, and simmer for 2 minutes only. Remove from the heat and leave with the lid on for a further minute. Lift the lid and make sure that all the mussels have opened. If not, return the pan to the heat for another minute. If one or two are still reluctant to open, discard them. Put the mussels into warmed soup bowls or a tureen. Place the liquor back on the heat. Taste, season with salt and pepper and stir in the chopped parsley. Pour over the mussels and serve.

Variations

1. If you have good fish stock, nearly a pint (600 ml) can be used plus the juice of a large lemon or 2-3 tablespoons wine vinegar.
2. A little crushed garlic can be used – ½ clove is enough, and the parsley varied with watercress, chervil, marjoram or other fairly delicate green herb.

CREAM OF MUSSEL SOUP

This is the delicate dinner-party version of the previous soup, though, of course, it is far, far higher in calories. If the occasion is not appropriate for slurping, you can remove the mussels from their shells altogether, or you can leave them in the half-shell.

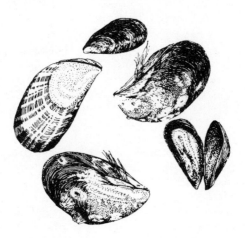

20-24 good-sized mussels	$1\frac{1}{2}$ oz (40 g) butter
3 shallots or $\frac{1}{2}$ a bunch of spring onions	2 oz (60 g) cup or button mushrooms
a small handful of fresh parsley	4-6 tablespoons of thick cream
$\frac{1}{2}$ pint (300 ml) dry white wine	salt and fresh pepper
$\frac{1}{2}$ pint (300 ml) fish stock or water	a blade of mace or $\frac{1}{2}$ a bay leaf
1 oz (30 g) plain flour	

Clean and prepare the mussels as described on p.204, discarding ruthlessly any which are cracked or not quite shut. Knead the butter and flour together to form *beurre manié* (p.22). Peel and chop the shallots and parsley stalks and put them with the wine and fish stock, fresh pepper and mace into a large stainless or enamelled pan with a good lid. Bring to the boil and simmer for 10 minutes. Add the mussels. Cover the pan tightly and cook for 3-4 minutes shaking the pan occasionally until all the mussels are open. Remove from the heat. Chop the parsley finely and chop or slice the mushrooms. You can prepare the soup to this point an hour or so ahead, but not much more or the mussels will get that dull bistro flavour.

Five minutes before serving, strain the liquor into a clean stainless pan. You should have a little over $\frac{3}{4}$ pint (450 ml). Remove half or all of each mussel shell. Bring the soup base to the boil and add the mushrooms and parsley. Whisk in little pieces of the beurre manié quickly but thoroughly. Add the cream at once. Taste and adjust seasoning with salt, pepper and more wine. Add the mussels and serve immediately.

Variations

1. For even more luxury, beat 2 egg yolks with a little lemon juice and whisk a ladleful of the finished soup into it, then whisk the egg mixture back into the soup and serve at once. This is a velouté of mussels.
2. Mussels can be varied with oysters, clams and fresh scallops.
3. 2 very ripe tomatoes, peeled, cored, seeded and diced (see pps.247-8) can be used instead of the mushrooms.

Nettle Tops

See under:
Green Leaves: Zuppa di Verdura. Variation 2
Purée of Lettuce with Sour Cream, Variation 2
Spinach: Crème Florentine, Variation 3
Cream of Watercress, Variation 4

Noodles

See under:
Chicken Noodle Soup
Garnishes and Accompaniments: noodles, p.37

Oatmeal

OATMEAL AND VEGETABLE SOUP

Soup recipes which use oats as a thickening agent generally begin by frying the oats in butter, which provides a pleasant toasted 'flapjack' flavour but also a porridge-like consistency. This recipe is merely one example of the many possibilities. For those who enjoy oatiness, any of the recipes for lentils or split peas can be used, substituting the same quantity of oats. Oatmeal soups taste better the day after they are made.

selection of winter vegetables weighing 8 oz (225 g) after peeling, e.g. 1 small leek, 1 medium carrot, 1 stick celery, 1 small potato
$1\frac{1}{2}$ oz (40 g) butter
1 oz (30 g) oatmeal–quick cooking for speed, pinhead for texture and flavour
$1\frac{1}{2}$ pints (900 ml) water or stock
salt
freshly milled pepper
2 tablespoons parsley

Cut the leek into 4 lengthways and then in $\frac{1}{2}$ inch (1 cm) slices. Put the slices in a bowl of cold water (see p.183). Roughly dice the other vegetables. Melt the butter in a heavy-bottomed pan, add the oats and fry them, stirring regularly for 5 to 10 minutes until they are brown. Put in the leek, carrot and celery and fry for a further 5 minutes. Then add the potato and the stock and bring the soup to the boil. Add salt and pepper. Now simmer the soup for 15 minutes to 1 hour, depending on the type of oats and your schedule. The glueyness of oats makes them tend to stick and burn, so turn the heat as low as possible and/or put a mat between the stove and the pan bottom. Cover the pan while it simmers, but remember to stir it occasionally to make quite sure that the soup is not sticking. When the oats are well cooked, either cool the soup and store overnight, or taste and add more liquid and seasoning as required. Stir in the parsley and serve.

Variations

1. Robin Howe, in her useful book called simply *Soups*, suggests that a game stock is the best for oatmeal soups. I have not tried it, but have certainly found that more strongly flavoured stocks such as bacon, ham or beef improve these soups.
2. A highly seasoned vegetable stock, or 1 pint (600 ml) water plus $\frac{1}{2}$ pint (300 ml) tomato juice, or $1\frac{1}{4}$ pints (750 ml) water plus a 7 oz (200 g) can peeled tomatoes, can also be used.
3. Omit the other vegetables and use just 12 oz (350 g) leeks, plus oatmeal, salt, pepper, parsley and a little mace or nutmeg. If you like to keep some texture in leeks, add them only about 10 minutes before the end of the cooking time.

See also:
Rich Venison and Port Soup, Variation 3

Black Olives

See under:
Mung Bean and Black Olive Soup
Tomatoes: Gazpacho

Onions

CREAM OF ONION SOUP

This recipe is adapted from Julia Child and colleagues' tremendous work, *Mastering the Art of French Cooking*. One friend of mine, who ate his way through 30 or more trial soups while I was testing the recipes in this book, remembers 'that creamy onion soup' as the pinnacle of his gastronomic experiences.

4 medium onions
1 oz (30 g) butter
1 dessertspoon plain flour
1 pint (600 ml) milk
1½ oz (40 g) white rice
salt

freshly milled pepper
½ bay leaf
5 tablespoons dry white wine or
　　dry white vermouth
¼ pint (150 ml) double cream

Slice the onions as finely as you can and put them with the butter in a heavy pan over a very low heat. Sweat them gently for 10 minutes, stirring occasionally, by which time they should be very pale gold. Now stir in the flour and allow this roux mixture to cook gently for a minute. Pour in the milk a little at a time, stirring each addition smooth before making the next. When all the milk is in, stir in the rice, salt, pepper and bay leaf. Watch it while you bring it to the boil (it will boil over as you turn your back) and simmer, partly covered, for 20 minutes. Put the soup through the fine plate of the food mill, or allow it to cool a little and then blend. Pour in the white wine or vermouth. At this point the soup can be cooled and stored in the fridge overnight, but it is just as good served at once. Return to a clean pan, reheat gently, and taste when very hot. Add more seasoning if necessary. Stir in the cream just before serving, or whip it to a soft peak and put a dollop on each bowlful of soup.

Variations

1. Chicken, mild ham or vegetable stock, if light in colour, can be used instead of milk.
2. An equal weight of trimmed leeks can be substituted for all or part of the onion.
3. For a richer soup with a fine texture, leave out the rice and beat 3 egg yolks with the wine or vermouth. Make the soup as in the main recipe. Reheat the thin purée and, when it is very hot but not boiling, and the seasoning is to your taste, whisk a ladleful of the soup into the egg and wine mixture. Take the soup from the heat, transfer the whisk to the soup pan, and whisk in the egg mixture. The soup will thicken slightly. Serve with or without the cream.
4. The best 'garnish' for this soup is a rich-coloured bowl or tureen to set off its delicate paleness. If you have only white china, sprinkle a few chopped chives or watercress leaves on the soup.

FRENCH ONION SOUP

It is a common misapprehension that restaurants choose menus to suit their customers; they do no such thing. Dishes are actually chosen because they are convenient or economical to prepare. As long as they can then be made to sound glamorous they can be sold to a diffident clientele. French Onion Soup cooks better in large quantities and keeps well, and the commis chef can gussie it up with a toasted cheese garnish just before serving. The soup is therefore a favourite with chefs, and has become so with customers through habit. That is how fashion so often comes about – not chosen by the consumer but dictated by the supplier. Fortunately, a well-made version of this soup also tastes good.

The initial reduction of the raw onion to a mahogany-coloured semi-melted state takes at least 45 minutes. If you hurry or use a thin pan, the soup will have black flecks and a bitter taste. If you are short of time make Variation 1. Try and use fresh Parmesan if possible, because it has so much more flavour than the ready-grated kind.

4 large onions, 1½ lb (675 g) after peeling
1 oz (30 g) butter
2 tablespoons oil, olive for preference
1½ pints (900 ml) good beef stock
salt
freshly milled pepper
1 oz (30 g) grated Gruyère and ½ oz (15 g) grated Parmesan *or* 1½oz (40 g) grated good, sharp Cheddar
4 slices French bread (optional)

Choose a heavy pan, preferably with a small base so that the onions will form a really thick layer after slicing. The thicker the onion layer, the better they brown and reduce, which is why the soup works well in bulk. Quarter the onions and slice or chop them about ¼ inch (½ cm) thick. You may leave the onion in whole or half rings if you wish, but they tend to slide off the spoon and are irritating when you eat the soup. Put the butter and oil in the pan over a very low heat. Add the onions and stir them a little. At first you need only stir occasionally, but as the onions lose their water and begin to colour you will have to stir frequently, or they will stick and burn. Do not cover the pan at all during this stage. After 45 minutes or so, when the onions are really deep mahogany brown but in no way burnt, add the beef stock and a little salt and pepper. If you get impatient and add the liquid when the onions are golden, the final soup will be insipid and yellowish instead of a deep, rich brown. Simmer the soup, partly covered, for 30 minutes. Check the seasoning. At this point the soup can be chilled and put in the fridge overnight. It will keep longer than this in cool weather, but onion sours easily in hot or muggy weather.

Serve accompanied by a little bowl of grated mixed cheese – Gruyère and Parmesan are ideal, but a good Cheddar will do; alternatively toast the slices of French bread, pile the grated cheese on to them, and grill until golden. Float a toasted cheese slice in each bowlful of soup. If your soup bowls are ovenproof, the slices of cheese-covered toast can be floated in the soup first and then browned under the grill. For a party, make the soup in a larger quantity in a cast-iron casserole and cover the surface of the cold soup with pieces of cheese-sprinkled toast. Then put the whole casserole, uncovered, in an oven preheated to 350°F, 180°C, Gas 4 to heat through and brown on top for 45 minutes or so.

Variations

1. If you are short of time, sweat the sliced or chopped onion in the

butter and olive oil in a covered pan for 15 minutes, until soft but not brown. Add the stock and seasoning and simmer for another 10 minutes. Serve with lots of chopped parsley and, for a main course meal, slip a poached egg into each portion as you serve it.

2. The soup can be made with mild ham or bacon stock, or vegetable stock or water. You can try a little beef extract or a stock cube in an emergency, but the soup will taste more of the cube than of the onions.

3. If you are using water or rather insipid stock, add a bay leaf, a sprig of thyme or marjoram and a couple of parsley sprigs, tied up with string attached to the pan-handle for easy removal. Some people like to include a tablespoon of cider or wine vinegar, or a small glass of rich red wine or port.

4. The cheese can be left out and the soup served with chopped parsley and plain or herb croûtons (see pps.27,28) or 3 or 4 rashers streaky bacon, fried very crisp and crumbled into the soup.

See also:
Tomato, Onion and Potato Soup
Enrichment: red pepper and onion, Variation 3, p.42
There is some form of onion in nearly all the soups in this book, but the proportions are mostly small. The ones above contain a larger quantity.

Orange

See under:
Carrot and Coriander Soup, Variation 5
Carrot and Lemon Soup, Variation 2
Leek and Lemon Soup, Variation 2
Tomato and Orange Soup

Oxtail

See under:
Beef: Oxtail, Bacon and Vegetable Soup
Beef: Pepperpot Soup, Variation 4

Oysters

OYSTER CREAM

Charles Dickens characterized the mean streets of nineteenth-century London as being the ones with oyster shells on the ground. Even when James Beard, the fine American cookery writer, was a boy in Portland, Oregon, he collected oysters on the beach. Now one only collects oysters from the smartest fishmongers in exchange for large sums of money. Still, they are worth it for a really posh dinner. This recipe, adapted from James Beard's mother's oyster stew, is one of the simplest and most delicious in this book.

12 large or 18 small oysters in their shells	a little lemon juice
½ pint (300 ml) milk	salt
½ pint (300 ml) double cream	freshly milled pepper

Opening oysters is not an easy job without an oyster knife. On the other hand oysters opened by the fishmonger will deteriorate very quickly and lose most of their delicious juices on the way home. If you are a novice at oyster opening, wear a thick glove on your left hand; insert an oyster knife or stout, short but sharp vegetable knife at the hinge of the shell, and twist the blade to force the oyster open.

Put the oysters and all their juice into a bowl. Pour the milk and cream into a heavy stainless or enamelled pan on the top of a double boiler, and add lemon juice and salt. Cut the oysters in half and add them and their juice to the cream mixture. Heat very, very slowly to near simmering. Cook at this temperature for 2 to 4 minutes until the oysters are just firm but tender. Taste and add more salt and lemon juice and some pepper. Serve and eat at once.

Variations

1. Any extra ingredients in this stunning soup really detract from its glory, but no more than 1 oz (30 g) diced, smoked bacon can be dry-fried in the pan for a moment before the cream and milk are added. However even this slight addition takes away from the flavour of fresh oysters and is only recommended if canned oysters are being used. American whole or minced canned oysters have quite a good flavour – use 7 to 10 oz (200 to 280 g).
2. If you long for a garnish to the soup, use finely snipped chives, not parsley, but it is better to leave it out and use deeply coloured soup bowls to set off the paleness.
3. Four large raw scallops, cut in pieces, can be used instead of oysters.

See also:
Mussels: Moules Marinière
Shellfish Cream

Parsley

See under:
Potato and Parsley Soup with Cream
Many of the recipes in this book contain parsley, but in too small quantities to mention individually.

Parsnips

SPICED PARSNIP PURÉE

This soup is a blast of parsnip – sweet, spicy and totally comforting. If you are still recovering from school parsnips, begin with Variation 3.

1 small onion
1 small clove garlic, peeled and
  crushed with a little salt
1 flat teaspoon curry powder
2 tablespoons mild-flavoured oil
  or 1 oz (30 g) butter

3 to 4 parsnips, 11 oz (310 g)
  after peeling and topping
3 2-inch (5 cm) strips of lemon
  rind removed with a peeler
1 pint (600 ml) milk

Slice the onion and sweat it for 5 minutes with the garlic and the curry powder in the butter or oil in a heavy-bottomed, lidded saucepan. Slice the parsnips and add them to the pan with the lemon rind. Sweat the mixture for another 10 minutes, shaking the pan occasionally. Add the milk, salt and pepper. Simmer for 20 minutes; watch it for the first few minutes as it will long to boil over. The best texture is achieved by putting the soup through the fine plate of the food mill, but if you decide to blend, sieve it afterwards to remove any stringy bits. The flavour matures if it is made a day in advance. Reheat gently, without boiling, in a clean pan. Add extra salt and a little grated lemon rind if you like.

Variations

1. The very best liquid for this soup is a spicy, but not too salty, ham or salt beef stock. If you think the soup too rich with all milk try half milk half water, or just stock. Buttermilk gives the soup a pleasant tang. If you would like to use plain yogurt, cook the soup in ¾ pint (450 ml) milk or water and turn to p.21 for instructions on adding ¼ pint (150 ml) plain yogurt.
2. Substitute ½ teaspoon each of cumin and coriander, or 1 teaspoon garam masala, for the curry powder. Orange rind can be used instead of lemon rind, especially if you have ham stock in the soup.
3. Use 2 parsnips, 1 very small onion, 1 small carrot, and 1 small

potato, and follow the main recipe.
4. A slimmer's soup can be made by sweating the vegetables either
   dry or with 1 teaspoon butter or oil, and using as the liquid ham
   stock, buttermilk, or yogurt and water.

Partridge

See under:
Purée of Duck and Celery, Variation 1
Pheasant and Quince Cream, Variation 1
Pheasant and Lentil Soup

Pasta

See under:
Chicken Noodle Soup
Tripe: Zuppa di Trippa alla Milanese, Variation 5
Vegetables: Minestrone, Variation 3
Vegetables: Pistou
Garnishes and Accompaniments: ravioli, p.36; noodles, p.37

Dried Green or Yellow Split Peas

QUICK SPLIT PEA SOUP

A split pea soup generally takes 1 hour or more to cook, or a little
less if the peas have been soaked in advance. In this recipe the peas
are ground to a powder, so the whole of the preparation and cooking
take not more than 30 minutes. Alternatively, it may be convenient to
cook it very slowly. Most bean and dried pea soups, including this
one, are very successful in slow cookers. If you are using one, the peas
need not be ground up or soaked, but simply slow-cooked for 5 to 8
hours (see Variation 1).

2 oz (60 g) green or yellow split peas	tablespoons oil
1½ pints (900 ml) water or bacon stock	2 raw pork sausages
	½ teaspoon garam masala or curry powder
freshly milled pepper	½ teaspoon coriander
1 large onion	salt
1 oz (30 g) lard or butter *or* 2	

Reduce the dry split peas to a coarse powder in a coffee grinder or food processor. Put the powdered peas and stock or water in a large pan (it tends to boil over easily), add pepper and stir well. Bring the pan to the boil and let it simmer for 15 minutes. Meanwhile, slice the onion and fry it in the fat or oil for 5 minutes. Cut the sausages into ½ inch (1 cm) pieces, add them with the spices, and fry for another 10 minutes. Put the sausage mixture into the soup and simmer for 5 minutes. Taste, and add salt if needed. The soup can be served at once, or cooked and stored overnight in the fridge, or frozen.

Variations

1. Put the split peas straight into a slow cooker and add 1 pint (600 ml) only of water or bacon stock. Fry the onion, sausage and spices as in the main recipe, but for only 5 minutes with the heat fairly high so that the sausages are browned. Then scrape the sausage mixture into the slow cooker, stir, and cook for at least 5 hours. The soup will not spoil if it is left cooking for a further 3 to 4 hours.
2. The raw British sausages can be replaced with 4 oz (110 g) salt or fresh belly of pork, weighed after skinning and boning. Cut the pork into small pieces and use in the same way as the sausages. Cooked sausages such as frankfurters, knackwurst etc. can be used instead of raw ones, in which case they should either be sliced and added to the onion for just a minute or two, or left whole and added when the onion and split pea mixture are put together.

SPLIT PEA AND BACON SOUP

A robust and warming winter cousin of the graceful Green Pea and Ham Soup, this recipe can be made either with the remnants of a bacon joint and its stock (see pps.55-6) or with sliced streaky bacon as in Variation 1. It is a very easy-going soup and can be kept hot for hours without damaging its flavour. A good choice for a winter picnic or bulk catering, it also keeps and freezes well.

3 oz (90 g) dried split green or
yellow peas, or 2 oz (60 g) for
a thin purée
1 pint (600 ml) bacon stock or
water
½ bay leaf threaded on a clove
freshly milled pepper

1 small onion
1 small carrot
2 small sticks celery *or* 1 small
parsnip
2 oz (60 g) piece of white cabbage
2 oz (60 g) cooked gammon or
bacon scraps

If you soak the peas overnight they will cook more quickly, but it is not essential. Put the peas in a pan with the stock or water, the clove and bay leaf, and grind in some pepper. Bring to the boil and simmer, covered, for 45 to 60 minutes, until the peas are mushy. Take out the bay leaf and clove and add the onion, carrot and celery or parsnip, all peeled and cut into ½ inch (1 cm) cubes. Simmer for 15 minutes and add the cabbage, cut in squares. Dice the bacon or gammon scraps, removing all skin, fat and gristle. After 5 minutes, when the cabbage is nearly tender, add the bacon. Taste the soup and add salt if necessary and some pepper. The soup can be served immediately, but its flavour will mature if it is cooled and kept overnight in the fridge. If you want to keep the soup hot for some time add more liquid, say ¼ pint (150 ml), and put a stove mat between the pan and the heat.

Variations

1. Cook the peas in 2 pints (1.2 l) water, with a ham stock cube if you like. Bone and rind 4 oz (110 g) streaky sliced bacon and cut it across into ½ inch (1 cm) pieces. While the peas are cooking, fry the bacon for 10 minutes in its own fat in a heavy pan, stirring occasionally, until it is slightly crisp and brown. Add all the other vegetables except the cabbage and fry them together for another 10 minutes over a low heat. When the peas are cooked, add the vegetables and bacon with its fat and proceed with the main recipe.
2. If you are using water, or ham stock from a bought cube, you may like to add 1 teaspoon garam masala, or ½ teaspoon mixed spice and ½ teaspoon coriander, or ½ teaspoon ginger plus some grated nutmeg.
3. Three ripe tomatoes, peeled and cored (see p.247), can be added

instead of cabbage; alternatively use a 7 oz (200 g) can of peeled tomatoes and leave out $\frac{1}{2}$ pint (300 ml) stock or water. Put in the roughly chopped tomatoes with the root vegetables.

Green Peas

CHOOSING AND USING

Frozen peas are consistent and convenient and useful when fresh peas are not in season, but they have neither the delicacy of flavour nor the granular texture of fresh ones. Peas in their pods are available in most greengrocers between the end of June and September, and it would be a pity to ignore them, especially since podding them is such a pleasant job. Choose pods that are nicely full, but not yellowish or showing the shape of individual peas through their sides. To pod peas, sit in the sun and hold the pod in your left hand with the cut stem in the heel of your palm and pointing outwards. At the front end of the pod a curved corner will be pointing upwards. Press down with your right thumb on this corner, and the pod will pop satisfyingly and split. Slide your thumb backwards to open up the pod and forwards again, scooping the peas into the pan. If your peas are small and the pods tender, make the Purée of Green Peas with their Pods. If the pods are faded and elderly, discard them and try Green Pea and Ham Soup. A pound of peas in the pod will yield approximately 6 oz (175 g) peas.

GREEN PEA AND HAM SOUP

Peas and ham are one of the great culinary combinations and this soup appears wherever peas are grown and pigs are raised. In Holland it is almost a national dish. The soup is nutritious and sustaining, with a rich flavour and satisfying texture, besides keeping and freezing very well and looking very beautiful. Several good canned pea soups are available, but before you reach for one of these or a packet of frozen peas do try making it from scratch – it is quite a revelation. If the stock is not salty, reverse the quantities of stock and milk.

1 small onion
¼ of a lettuce
2 oz (60 g) cooked lean ham or
gammon
1 oz (30 g) butter
1 to 1½ lb (450 to 675 g) peas in
the pod – the larger amount if
the pods are flattish
½ pint (300 ml) ham or gammon
stock
1 pint (600 ml) milk
freshly milled pepper

Chop the onion roughly. Roll the washed lettuce leaves into a cigar shape and slice thinly with a stainless knife. Dice the ham or gammon. Melt the butter in a heavy stainless or enamelled pan. Add the onion and lettuce and sweat gently for 6 to 7 minutes, stirring occasionally. Put in the peas and stir them round in the butter and onion mixture for a minute or two. Pour in the ham stock and ¼ pint (150 ml) milk and cook, half-covered, for 20 to 40 minutes, depending on the hardness of your peas. When they are soft, blend or mill the soup. If you want a main course soup, use the coarse plate of the food mill, or blend half the soup and leave the rest. Use the remaining milk to rinse the last bit out of the blender jar or food mill. Add the diced ham or gammon. At this point you can store or freeze the soup. Reheat in a clean stainless or enamelled pan, taste, and add pepper; it is unlikely that you will need salt.

Variations

1. For what one friend called a 'fairy soup', leave out the ham stock and make the soup with all milk or half milk half water. Add fine slivers good cooked ham just before serving.
2. Use chicken stock, and chicken meat instead of ham. You will need to add some salt for this variation.
3. For a thick, filling soup, use a ½ lettuce and add a small potato, diced, with the peas, or leave out the lettuce and add the potato with 1 small carrot and 1 stick celery.
4. For a slimmer's soup use all stock, or stock and water; use only 1 teaspoon butter, or sweat the vegetables without fat.

PURÉE OF GREEN PEAS WITH THEIR PODS

While green pea soup made with frozen or tinned peas is pleasant enough, a purée of fresh young peas with the extra flavour and texture from their sieved pods is a great delicacy. It is altogether superior, besides being a most alluring colour. The pods must be young and squeaky fresh.

1½ lb (675 g) peas in the pod	½ a small lettuce
1½ pints (900 ml) boiling water	5 spring onions *or* 2 shallots,
salt	peeled and trimmed
1 teaspoon sugar	¼ pint (150 ml) *crème fraîche*
2 oz (60 g) or more butter	(optional; see p.142)

Pod the peas and, using a sharp knife, cut the pods into ½ inch (1 cm) slices. Mind your fingers, since the pods are tough and will slip. Discard any bits of stem as you go along. Put the pods in a stainless or enamelled pan and pour the boiling water over them. Add ¼ teaspoon salt and the sugar, and simmer, partly covered, for 30 minutes. Meanwhile melt the butter in another heavy stainless or enamelled pan. Slice the lettuce and spring onions or shallots finely with a stainless knife and add to the butter with the peas. Turn the heat very low, or put the pan on a stove mat. Cover, and leave to simmer for 10 to 15 minutes. Stir regularly, because if the mixture sticks or browns at all the colour will be spoilt. When the pods are tender, blend and then sieve them, or put them with their water through the medium plate of a food mill. Scrape the last bits from the bottom of the sieve or mill and return the purée to a clean pan. Blend or mill the pea and lettuce mixture, keeping a spoonful of peas whole if you like, and add this purée to the pod mixture. At this point the purée can be refrigerated overnight; it will taste even better the next day. Reheat, adjust the seasoning when hot, and serve with or without *crème fraîche*.

Variation

Make a simple purée using just the pods from 2 to $2\frac{1}{2}$ lb (1 kg) peas, about 2 pints (1.2 l) water, and a little salt. Use this purée in the ways described for the purée of broad beans in Broad Bean and Mushroom Soup.

See also:
Green Leaves: Spinach, Green Pea and Lettuce Purée
Lamb and Green Pea Soup

Peanut Butter

See under:
Chicken, Pumpkin and Peanut Butter Soup

Red and Green Peppers

See under:
Almond Cream Soup, Variation 3
Aubergine, Red Pepper and Coconut Soup
Sea Bass, Vermouth and Garlic Soup
Majorcan Cabbage Soup
Sweet Corn Chowder
Crab and Red Pepper Bisque
Fish Stew with Garlic, Tomatoes and Olive Oil, Variation 4
Mutton, Rice and Apricot Soup
Tomato and Red Pepper Soup
Enrichments: red pepper and onion, p.42; peperonata, p.43

Peach

PEACH AND BLACKBERRY SOUP

My husband, who has become an extremely discerning, not to say hypercritical soup eater in the last two years, slurped this down at high speed, saying very nice through the peach slices. Later he remarked that the British would never eat a hot fruit soup! This soup is perfectly pleasant when chilled, but hot it has real oomph.

3 large ripe peaches ($\frac{3}{4}$ lb 350 g before peeling)
4 oz (110 g) blackberries
1 flat tablespoon arrowroot (cornflour will do, but gives an opaque finish to the soup)

$\frac{1}{2}$ oz (15 g) sugar
2 good pinches salt
juice of 1 large lemon and 1 orange
$\frac{3}{4}$ pint (450 ml) water
$\frac{1}{2}$ capful of good brandy

Pour boiling water over the peaches. Leave them for a minute, then drain off the water and peel the peaches under the cold tap with a little knife. Slice them very thinly. Put all the other ingredients in the blender (except the brandy) and blend to a smooth cream. If your guests have false teeth (or you do) it may be kind to sieve the mixture at this point. Pour it into an enamelled or stainless pan and bring to the boil stirring all the time. As soon as it boils and thickens, taste and adjust the seasoning. Stir in the peach slices and the brandy and serve.

Variations

1. Red currants, black currants, damsons, blueberries or any other well-flavoured dark red fruit could be used instead of the blackberries.
2. A fruit eau de vie, such as framboise or kirsch could be used instead of brandy, or a glass of fruity white wine be substituted for the brandy and $\frac{1}{4}$ pint (150 ml) of the water.

Pheasant

PHEASANT AND LENTIL SOUP

I have chosen pheasant for this game soup recipe and the following
one because, if you have to buy it at the butcher's, pheasant is much
better value than grouse or partridge. However Elizabeth David's
recipe, from which this is adapted, uses patridge, and any well-hung
game bird will do. Don't be tempted to use the pinky-orange lentils
which don't taste of anything. The soup freezes well, though it is at its
best the day after making. Although it is a rather dull mushroom
colour, both flavour and texture are exquisite, so don't waste this
marvel on undiscriminating eaters.

$\frac{1}{2}$ a pheasant, or the legs and
    back – about 12 oz (350 g)
    meat and bones
2 oz (60 g) butter, duck fat, goose
    fat or strained pork fat
onion peelings
celery trimmings
2 parsley stalks
8 peppercorns

1 bay leaf
1 sprig of thyme
2 cloves *or* 6 allspice berries
about $3\frac{1}{2}$ pints (2 l) water
1 medium leek
2 oz (60 g) green or brown lentils
salt
$\frac{1}{4}$ pint (150 ml) double cream
freshly milled pepper

Smear the pheasant with butter or other fat and roast it at 450°F
(230°C, Gas 8) for 25 minutes. Pre-roasted pheasant can be used, but
some of the depth of flavour will be lost if the scrapings from the
roasting dish have already been used for another dish. Serve half the
meat, or reserve it for another meal. To make the stock, put the
carcass, together with any other poultry or game bones that you
happen to have on hand, in a large pan with the vegetable trimmings,
parsley, spices, herbs and water. Bring to the boil and simmer,
uncovered, for 2 hours. Add more water if necessary. Cut the leek in
thin rings and wash in plenty of cold water. Neatly dice the best bits
of pheasant meat.

    When the stock is ready measure out $1\frac{1}{2}$ pints (900 ml) of it – if you
have too little, add water; if too much, reduce by boiling. Add some
of the stock to the scrapings in the roasting tin and heat the tin on top
of the stove; stir and scrape all the bits off the bottom. Strain with the
rest of the stock into a stainless or enamelled pan and add the lentils

and leek rings. Cover tightly, bring to the boil, and simmer for 45 minutes or until the lentils are cooked. Add salt to taste and the scrappy bits of pheasant. Blend or put through the medium or coarse plate of the food mill. At this point the good pieces of pheasant meat can be added and the soup stored overnight in the fridge. Reheat in a clean pan with the cream. Taste when hot and add pepper and more salt if needed.

Variations

1. This is a very rich soup, and the amount of cream can be reduced according to your taste, but remember that game birds have no opportunity to get fatty and need plenty of lubrication while roasting.
2. I wouldn't sully the flavour even with parsley, but if you feel a garnish is called for you could use chives, or very thin rings of leek boiled for 3 minutes in a little water, drained, and put in cold water.

PHEASANT AND QUINCE CREAM

Quince earns its place in the title of this soup not through the quantity needed but through its assertive flavour. A small quince of no more than 2 inch (5 cm) diameter, as grown on any suburban japonica, packs sufficient punch to compete with six times its weight of well-hung pheasant. Unless you have a gun or the right friends the pheasant will not be so cheaply obtained, but the legs of an elderly

225

specimen may be a bigger asset to the tureen than to the roasting dish. The pheasant meat should be gamey but not green, and the soup is best made a day in advance.

½ a pheasant or its legs and back
2½ oz (75 g) butter plus a little extra for frying the croûtons
1 bay leaf
1 sprig of thyme
onion peelings
celery trimmings
8 peppercorns
3 pints (1.75 l) water

1 small quince
1 small onion
2 sticks celery
salt
freshly milled pepper
¼ pint (150 ml) cream
4 tablespoons sherry or madeira
2 slices wholmeal bread

As in the previous recipe, preheat the oven to 450°F (230°C, Gas 8). Put the pheasant in a small roasting tin, smear it with 2 oz of the butter and roast for 25 minutes. Serve half the meat, or reserve it for another meal. You should have about 6 oz (175 g) left for soup.

Cut the best-looking pieces of flesh into neat dice and separate them and the scrappy bits. Meanwhile put the carcass, herbs, vegetable trimmings and peppercorns with the water in a pan and bring to the boil. Simmer the stock for 2 hours, adding more water if necessary – you want to end up with 1¼ pints (750 ml) stock. Strain some of the stock into the roasting tin and put the tin over a low heat to melt and amalgamate all the caramelized juices.

Melt ½ oz (15 g) butter in a heavy pan, add the sliced quince, onion and celery and cook gently for 10 minutes, stirring occasionally. Now strain in the stock from the roasting tin plus enough from the stock pan to make 1¼ pints (750 ml). Add also the scrappy bits of pheasant, salt and pepper. Bring to the boil and simmer for 20 minutes, then blend the mixture thoroughly or put it through the medium plate of the food mill. At this point the soup should be stored overnight. Reheat with the cream and sherry and taste when hot. The rich, gamey flavour should be balanced by, but not overpowered by, the exotic, acid quince. Dice the bread, fry very quickly in a little hot butter, and put to drain. Stir the pheasant meat dice into the soup and serve, handing the croûtons in a separate bowl.

Variations
1. Any well-hung game bird can be used. You need about 12 oz (350 g) raw, plucked partridge, grouse, pigeon, woodcock or whatever comes your way.

2. Crab apples would be a good substitute for the quince; otherwise part of a cooking apple with some lemon juice could be used – it will give a pleasant result though without the panache of quince.

See also:
Purée of Duck and Celery, Variation 1

Pigeon

See under:
Pheasant and Lentil Soup
Pheasant and Quince Cream, Variation 1

Pistou

See under:
Vegetables

Plum

ICED PLUM SOUP WITH SOUR CREAM

The main recipe is for a quick blender soup which improves if made the day before. Variations 1 and 3 are much more extravagant. All are best served thoroughly chilled and almost icy. Use plums which are ripe but not over-sweet or mushy.

1 pint (600 ml) water *or* ¾ pint (450 ml) water and ¼ pint (150 ml) riesling or other fruity white wine
1 oz (30 g) sugar – less if the plums are sweet
salt
1 2-inch (5 cm) strip each of

orange and lemon rind, thinly peeled
1¼ inch (3 cm) piece of cinnamon stick
1 clove
1 lb (450 g) dark red plums
¼ pint (150 ml) *crème fraîche* (see p.142) or sour cream

Put the water and/or wine, sugar, a little salt, citrus rind and spices into a heavy saucepan. Bring to the boil and simmer gently for 10 minutes. Lift out the spices and discard. Meanwhile cut the plums in half from top to bottom and prise out the stone with the point of a knife. Add the plum halves to the fruit 'stock' and simmer, covered, for 8 to 10 minutes until the plums are just soft. Blend to absolute smoothness, making sure that all the citrus rind has been thoroughly integrated. Leave the soup to cool a little. Set the fridge at its coldest, then put the cooled soup either in the freezing compartment for 1 hour, or just below it for at least 4 hours. Taste, and adjust the sugar, salt and spice. If you need more spice, try a pinch of mixed spice or nutmeg, but be sparing with the cinnamon because it is easy to overdo it. Serve with a dollop of *crème fraîche* or sour cream on top of each bowlful.

Variations

1. Instead of the water, use a half bottle of riesling or other fruity white wine, plus 4 tablespoons kümmel or brandy and ½ pint (300 ml) sour cream or *crème fraîche*. Add the spirit, as you blend, with ¼ pint (150 ml) of the sour cream. Refrigerate overnight to let the flavours blend and mature, and serve with the rest of the cream on top.
2. Substitute for the clove and cinnamon ½ teaspoon or more ground ginger, or, better, a ½ inch (1 cm) square of fresh ginger, peeled and grated.
3. Use 2 lb (1 kg) morello (sour) cherries, which are in season at the beginning of August. You will need this apparently large quantity because the stones comprise nearly half the fruit. Proceed as in Variation 1. Using ordinary cherries is a waste, and the result not nearly as good as the plum version.
4. Raspberries, redcurrants, blackcurrants, blackberries or bilberries can be substituted for the plums. In case some of your guests wear dentures it is kind to put the soup through a fine sieve before chilling it. See Iced Raspberry Yogurt Soup for another way of using berry fruit.

Pork

PORK GRAVY SOUP WITH MADEIRA

Up to the First World War just about anyone who could afford a servant would have more than one kind of meat and fowl on the table at dinner. As a result there were piles of bones, stock and scrappy meat to be used up, and gravy soups were a common way of doing this. Nowadays if you were invited to a dinner party which included a joint of beef, a ham, a chicken and a partridge or two, as well as fish, you would think that your host had either come into a large fortune or lost his marbles. Most of us, however, can still afford a hand or leg of pork. If the butcher bones and rolls the joint and puts the bones and trotter in the parcel, you will be equipped to produce at least one good roast and this delicious soup for the next day.

1 small onion	to 8 allspice berries
1 carrot	about 10 black peppercorns
2 small sticks celery	the scrapings from the roasting
the trotter and bones from a	tin
hand or leg of pork	salt
3 pints (1.75 l) cold water	freshly milled pepper
a little piece each of cinnamon	1 oz (30 g) cooked pork scraps
and nutmeg and 1 clove *or* 1	(optional)
flat teaspoon mixed spice *or* 6	3 to 4 tablespoons madeira

Peel the onion and carrot and trim the celery. Put the bones and trotter in a heavy pan with the water and bring to the boil. Skim off any grey scum that rises to the surface. When only white foam is left, add the spices and peelings and trimmings from the vegetables. Leave to simmer for 3 to 4 hours. Strain and leave to cool. If it is left overnight the fat will form a thick white crust of lard which can easily be removed. When the joint has roasted, pour off nearly all the fat from the roasting tin and add a few tablespoons of the stock. Put the tin over a low heat, and as the stock comes to the boil stir and scrape to dissolve into it all the caramelized meat juice. When you are satisfied that you have got most of the flavour off the bottom of the tin, strain this juice into the stock. Put the stock into another heavy pan – you should have 1½ pints (900 ml); if less add water, if more reduce by boiling – and add salt and pepper to taste. Cut the onion,

229

carrot and celery into matchsticks or dice. When the stock is boiling, add the vegetables and simmer for about 8 minutes or until they are crisp but cooked. Add the pork scraps and madeira, taste the soup and adjust the seasoning. Serve at once or cool and keep overnight in the fridge.

Variations

1. If you have no roasting juices to give the stock colour and body, a similar effect can be achieved, though to a lesser extent, by browning the trotter and bone in a very hot oven. Brown on one side for 20 minutes, then turn and brown for 10 minutes on the other side. Proceed with the stock as in the main recipe.,
2. Add 2 tablespoons chopped parsley, chives, fresh marjoram or rather less sage, since this last is an easy herb to overdo.
3. Two ounces (60 g) mushrooms, sliced or diced, are a pleasant substitute for the carrot, and parsnip or turnip for the celery.
4. For a one-pot meal, add 6 to 8 oz (175 to 225 g) diced pork scraps, with all fat and gristle removed, just before serving; 1 to 2 oz (30 to 60 g) pearl barley or 1 medium potato can also be included for an extra-filling soup. The barley takes 45 to 60 minutes to cook; dice the potato and add it with the other vegetables.

See also:
Vegetables: Garbure
Cabbage Soup with a Meat Crust, Variation 2
Chinese Chicken Soup

Potatoes

POTAGE BONNE FEMME

Thanks to Elizabeth David and many other good writers, the standard of cooking in British homes has improved immensely in the last twenty years. However we still do not rely enough on our own taste buds to tell us what is good, turning instead – particularly when entertaining – to recipes with many expensive ingredients. With the addition of a few other fresh, cheap foods, potato-based soups can become truly sophisticated dinner party fare. This soup should be made a day in advance to let the flavour mature, and can be left chunky for a main course soup or served with an elegant garnish (see Variation 3).

1 medium leek	salt
1 large, floury white potato	about 4 tablespoons thick cream
2 medium carrots	2 tablespoons roughly chopped
2 oz (60 g) butter	parsley
1¼ pints (750 ml) water	

Cut the leek into rings after trimming and put them to soak in plenty of cold water for 15 minutes or so. Cut the potato and carrots into ½ inch (1 cm) cubes. Put all the vegetables and the butter into a heavy stainless or enamelled pan over a low heat, cover, and sweat gently for 30 minutes, stirring occasionally. A stove mat between pan and heat is useful, since the vegetables ought not to stick or brown at all. Now add the water and a fair amount of salt, because the potatoes tend to absorb it. Bring to the boil and simmer for another 10 minutes. Put the soup through the medium or coarse plate of a food mill, or blend it, reserving a ladleful unblended to give texture. Cool and refrigerate overnight. Reheat over a low heat, stirring occasionally, and taste when hot. Stir in the cream and the parsley, bring the soup to just below boiling and serve.

Variations

1. The soup can be made with milk or with chicken or vegetable stock instead of water.
2. For a main course soup do not blend or mill the soup, but serve as it is; 2 to 3 tablespoons diced cooked bacon, ham or chicken can be stirred in, or the same quantity of grated cheese sprinkled on top, but I would prefer to serve this famous soup in its delicious simplicity and save the cheese for afterwards.
3. For a special occasion, reserve ½ a carrot and ¼ of the leek before cutting them up. Cut the reserved carrot in thin, delicate julienne strips (see p.31), and the reserved leek into the thinnest possible rings. Chop the parsley finely. Drop the carrot and leek garnish into ½ pint (300 ml) boiling salted water and boil for 3 minutes only. Drain, and cover with cold water. Make the soup as in the main recipe, adding up to another 4 tablespoons extra cream. When the soup is reheated and ready to serve, stir in the garnish and the parsley, leaving a little to sprinkle on the surface of the tureen or bowls.

POTATO, MUSHROOM AND SOUR CREAM SOUP

Here is another lovely potato soup, using slightly more exotic ingredients but still as easy as pie. Button mushrooms have less flavour and are more expensive, but flat or field mushrooms make the soup an unattractive grey. Variation 1 comes from South Africa and uses rice and spinach instead of potatoes and parsley.

2 medium floury white
   potatoes
½ pint (300 ml) water
½ pint (300 ml) milk
1 small leek
3 oz (90 g) button mushrooms

¼ pint (150 ml) sour cream or
   crème fraîche (see p. 142)
salt
freshly milled pepper
1 tablespoon chopped parsley

Cut the potato in small cubes and boil it, uncovered, in the salted water for 10 minutes or so until cooked. Put the potato mixture and the milk through the medium plate of a food mill. Return to a clean pan. Meanwhile, cut the leek into fine rings and soak in plenty of cold water. Slice the mushrooms. Put the leek, mushrooms and sour cream into the rinsed-out pan, bring to simmering point and cook very gently, using a stove mat if possible, for 10 minutes. Add the potato mixture. Bring back to just below boiling, taste, season, stir in the parsley and serve.

Variations

1. Cook 2 oz (60 g) rice in the water instead of the potatoes. If you are using brown rice, use 1 pint (600 ml). Make the recipe as above, but instead of parsley shred 4 or 5 fresh spinach leaves, or a small handful of sorrel leaves, and add them 2 to 3 minutes before serving.
2. Yogurt can be used instead of sour cream and low fat dried milk instead of fresh, in which case this soup will be very low in calories and animal fat. It is curious how the poor potato gets blamed for being fattening, while the real culprits are, of course, fat and sugar.
3. Finely chopped onion or spring onion can be used instead of leek. Lettuce, watercress or any fresh green herb can substitute for parsley.

POTATO AND PARSLEY SOUP WITH CREAM

If I were to be shipwrecked on a desert island with only eight of the soups in this book, this would be one of them. It has every virtue, being cheap, quick, easy and beautiful, though like all potato dishes it freezes rather badly (not a problem on most desert islands). The bacon or ham stock suggested in the main recipe gives extra body to the soup, but milk and water as in Variation 1 will do very well. Avoid using a blender if possible, because it makes the soup gluey for a time.

1 lb (450 g) floury White potatoes
1 pint (600 ml) not too salty
   bacon or ham stock
1 small clove garlic, peeled and
   crushed with a little salt
1 tablespoon chopped celery
   trimmings *or* ½ teaspoon

celery seed
4 shallots *or* 1 very small onion
freshly milled pepper
¼ pint (150 ml) single or double
   cream
2 tablespoons chopped parsley

Peel the potatoes, cut into 1 inch (2.5 cm) cubes, and put them in a heavy pan with the bacon stock, garlic, celery, roughly chopped shallots or onion, and some pepper. Cover the pan and bring to the boil. Simmer for 12 to 15 minutes, until the potatoes are just cooked. Put the soup through the medium or coarse plate of a food mill, or mash the potatoes with a potato masher, or, if you must use the blender, use it in short burst of a second or so in order to leave some texture in the soup. At this point the soup can be cooled and kept in a non-metal container overnight in the fridge. If you have used waxy potatoes and the consistency has become gluey through blending, a few hours in the fridge will put matters right. Reheat the soup in a clean pan with the cream and chopped parsley. Taste when hot and adjust seasoning. If the soup is too thick, add a little water, stock, milk or cream. Serve immediately – if you leave it simmering after it is cooked, it will acquire that horrid canteen potato flavour.

Variations

1. The potatoes and other vegetables can be cooked in ½ pint (300 ml) water and then milled or blended with ½ pint (300 ml) milk. Alternatively 1 pint (600 ml) milk can be used, in which case

watch that it doesn't boil over during cooking. Beef, chicken or vegetable stock can be used instead of bacon.
2. A $\frac{1}{2}$ bay leaf or a little grated nutmeg may be added, especially if you are using milk or milk and water for the liquid.
3. A $\frac{1}{2}$ bunch of watercress can be used instead of parsley. Add the chopped stalks with the potatoes, onion etc., and the chopped leaves just before serving. The celery can be omitted if watercress is used.
4. Potatoes have an undeservedly bad reputation among slimmers, for they contain less than 30 calories per ounce when boiled. If the soup is made with an extra $\frac{1}{4}$ pint (150 ml) stock instead of cream, and a little nut of butter is stirred in at the end of cooking, a medium-sized bowlful will only contain 130 calories.

See also:
Leek and Potato Soup
Green Pea and Ham Soup, Variation 3
Tomato, Onion and Potato Soup
Turkey Chowder
Cream of Turnip Soup
Garnishes and Accompaniments: potato dumplings, p.33

Prawns

See under:
Chinese Chicken Soup, Variation 1
Cream of Chicken Soup, Variations 1 and 2
Velouté of Cod and Prawns
Shellfish Cream
Shrimp and Salmon Cream

Prunes

See under:
Chicken: Cock-a-Leekie
Mutton, Rice and Apricot Soup, Variation 2

234

Pumpkin

See under:
Chicken, Pumpkin and Peanut Butter Soup

Quinces

See under:
Pheasant and Quince Cream

Rabbit

RABBIT AND CIDER CREAM SOUP

Wild rabbit is a bit more expensive than chicken but considerably more interesting to eat. Tame, or farmed rabbits are very dull. If you oven casserole a good-sized wild rabbit with the best bits (thighs and saddle sections) on top and the fore-legs and ribs, head and offal at the bottom and do it slowly with plenty of root vegetables, herbs and water, you will have a big casserole for 4 and the lowly bits of rabbit and extra stock will provide the base for this ace soup.

1½ pints (900 ml) rabbit stock
1 bay leaf with 2 cloves threaded into it
1 sprig of thyme or ½ teaspoon dry thyme
2 strips of thinly-pared orange peel
1 medium onion
3 sticks non-stringy celery

½ pint (300 ml) dry cider (preferably the real undyed kind)
¼ pint (150 ml) single cream
2 teaspoons cornflour or potato flour
3-4 oz (90-110 g) cooked rabbit
salt and fresh pepper

Bring the rabbit stock to the boil with the herbs, cloves and orange peel, plus the peelings and trimmings from onion and celery. Let it boil briskly and reduce to 1 pint (600 ml). Meanwhile dice the onion and celery and put them in another pan with the cider. Let them also come to the boil and reduce till the cider is only a tablespoon or two. Strain the stock on to this mixture and add a little salt and pepper. Mix the cornflour with the cream to a smooth paste and add this through a sieve, stirring as you do so. The soup is best made the day before to this point, for the flavours blend and mature overnight. Just before re-heating, slice the cooked rabbit into neat little pieces, add to the soup but don't let it boil, or they'll get tough. Taste and serve.

Variations

1. For a main course soup, double the quantity of cooked rabbit meat and vegetables. If you have no more cooked rabbit, make the bread and bacon balls described in Hare Soup with Madeira (pps.175-6).
2. Bacon and rabbit go well together so you could use bacon or ham stock instead of rabbit and/or fry 2 rashers streaky smoked bacon (rinded and diced) with the onion and celery before adding the cider. In this case the soup will be rich enough without the cream.

Raspberries

ICED RASPBERRY YOGURT SOUP

This recipe works equally well with strawberries and blackberries, but the raspberries give a particularly intense colour and flavour. You can also use sugarless frozen raspberries, in which case follow Variation 1.

2 tablespoons orange juice
2 teaspoons sugar *or* 1 tablespoon honey
salt

12 oz (350 g) raspberries
¾ pint (450 ml) plain yogurt
mint leaves (garnish)

Put the orange juice, sugar or honey and a pinch of salt in a heavy pan over a very low heat until the sugar has dissolved. Add the raspberries, cover and cook, shaking the pan, for 3 to 4 minutes until the raspberries are just soft. Purée the raspberry mixture with the yogurt in the blender, or put through the food mill. (If you have elderly guests it would be kind to strain out the seeds.) Put in the freezing compartment of the fridge for 1 hour or just below it for 3 to 4 hours. When very cold, taste and add more orange, sugar or salt. Serve decorated with whole or chopped mint leaves.

Variations
1. Purée the fruit raw with the yogurt and seasonings. Chill, taste, and serve. This method also works with redcurrants, blackcurrants and bilberries.
2. Use buttermilk, sour cream or *crème fraîche* (see p.142) instead of yogurt.
3. The fruit can be chopped instead of being puréed, or some berries left whole.

See also:
Iced Plum Soup with Sour Cream, Variation 4

Rice

See under:
Mutton, Rice and Apricot Soup
Cream of Onion Soup
Potato, Mushroom and Sour Cream Soup, Variation 1
Spinach: Crème Florentine
Tomato and Red Pepper Soup
Vegetables: Minestrone, Variation 3

Salami

See under:
Vegetables: Minestrone, Variation 2
Vegetables: Pistou, Variation 1
Enrichments: bacon, parsley and onion, Variation 2, p.41; red pepper and onion, Variation 1, p.42

Salmon and Salmon Trout

GREEN SALMON SOUP

It isn't the salmon that is green, you may be relieved to hear, but its vegetable companions in this pretty pastel pink and green soup. As salmon gets more and more extravagantly priced, rather than leave it out of your life altogether, buy a salmon head, cut generously to include a few ounces of the flesh and enjoy the lovely texture and flavour in a soup.

a salmon head with an extra $\frac{1}{2}$
    inch (1 cm) of salmon flesh *or*
    a 3-6 oz (90-175 g) salmon
    steak plus 1 lb (450 g) white
    fish heads and bones
2 oz (60 g) spring onions with
    plenty of bright green stalk
a tablespoon of chopped parsley

$\frac{1}{2}$ bunch watercress
4 oz (110 g) courgettes
2 small glasses fruity white wine

To finish the soup
2-3 egg yolks
the juice of a small lemon
salt and fresh pepper

Put the salmon head or fish bones in a non-aluminium pan with the bay leaf, 1 glass wine and cold water to cover. Bring to the boil, skim off any scum that rises and simmer very gently for 20 minutes. Lift out the salmon head and leave to cool. Strain the stock and reduce to $1\frac{1}{2}$ pints (900 ml) by fast boiling. Meanwhile peel and trim the spring onions and chop them into $\frac{1}{4}$ inch ($\frac{1}{2}$ cm) pieces. Discard any yellowing watercress leaves and hairy ends of stalks and chop into $\frac{1}{2}$ inch (1 cm) pieces. Cut the courgettes in four lengthwise and then into $\frac{1}{4}$ inch ($\frac{1}{2}$ cm) slices. Have the strained reduced stock ready boiling in a stainless or enamelled pan. Add the second glass of wine, the courgettes, watercress and parsley. Boil for 3-5 minutes until the courgettes are soft but not falling to bits. Skin and bone the cooked salmon easing all the little flakes of meat out from the cheeks and jaw of the salmon head. Remove the soup from the heat, taste and add salt and freshly milled pepper. Put 2 large or 3 medium egg yolks in a small bowl and stir in the strained lemon juice. Add a ladleful of the soup mixture to the eggs, then strain the eggs into the soup, whisking all the time. Add the salmon pieces and return to a low heat for half a minute stirring continuously. Serve at once.

Variations

1. The herbs could be varied with sorrel (in which case leave out the lemon juice), chives, chervil, lemon balm or fennel, and the courgettes varied with cucumber (which should be cooked on its own in the stock for 10 minutes before the herbs are added).
2. Salmon trout (sea trout) would be just as good as salmon and any prime white fish such as turbot, halibut or monkfish would make a good, though less pretty, soup.
3. 4 tablespoons of thick or sour cream or *crème fraîche* can be used instead of the yolks.

See also:
Mackerel and Lemon Cream Soup, Variation 2
Shrimp and Salmon Cream

Sausages

See under:
Bacon and Ham: Goulaschsuppe
Hungarian Cabbage Soup, Variation 1
Lentil and Sausage Soup, main recipe and Variation 1
Vegetables: Minestrone, Variation 2
Vegetables: Pistou, Variation 1

Scallops

See under:
Mussels: Cream of Mussel Soup, Variation 2
Oyster Cream, Variation 3
Shellfish Cream

Scotch Broth

See under:
Lamb and Mutton

Shellfish

SHELLFISH CREAM

When only canned or frozen shellfish is available it is better not to attempt a bisque, which needs the crushed shells to give the splendid flavour that makes the effort worthwhile. Instead make this extremely simple cream soup, which effectively disguises the supermarket origin of the ingredients. Canned American minced clams and oysters are packed in well-flavoured juice and should form half the quantity of shellfish used or more; otherwise use prawns, shrimps, crab meat, scallops, lobster etc. Avoid shellfish in vinegar. Serve the soup plain with crisp, hot bread or toast.

8 to 10 shallots *or* 1 bunch spring onions
2 small sticks celery
2 oz (60 g) butter
10 to 12 oz (280 to 350 g) canned or frozen shellfish
5 tablespoons sherry or madeira
$\frac{1}{2}$ to $\frac{3}{4}$ pint (300 to 450 ml) single cream
salt
freshly milled pepper

Mince the shallots or onion and celery, or chop them to a near slush. Sweat them in the butter in a heavy enamelled or stainless pan for 10 minutes. Keep a lid on the pan, since the vegetables should neither stick nor brown. Cut any large shellfish, such as scallops, into $\frac{1}{2}$ inch (1 cm) pieces. Add to the pan the sherry or madeira and the shellfish and its juice, and simmer for a minute or two. Pour in the cream and add a little seasoning; freshly milled white pepper rather than black prevents little dark specks appearing in this pale-coloured soup, but specks are better than the stale flavour of packaged ground white pepper. Bring the soup very, very slowly to simmering point. In his lovely book *Delights and Prejudices* James Beard, the American gourmet, says that a shellfish cream should be heated in a double boiler to give it gentle all-round heat. If you have a stainless or enamelled double boiler this is a good idea, otherwise a heavy-bottomed pan and a stove mat will do. Taste the soup when it is hot, and adjust the seasoning. Serve at once, or cool and refrigerate as soon as possible and reheat equally gently a few hours later.

Variations

1. A pinch of cayenne or dash of tabasco and/or 1 dessertspoon paprika can be added to the vegetables as they sweat.
2. A capful of good brandy or whisky and a little lemon juice can be used instead of sherry.
3. Use 2 oz (60 g) button mushrooms instead of celery. Cup or flat mushrooms will give a better flavour but may discolour the soup.

See also:
Atlantic Fish Stew, Variation 2
Fish Stew with Garlic, Tomatoes and Olive Oil, Variation 2

Shrimps

SHRIMP AND GREEN PEA PURÉE

This soup started off as a mere variation of Green Pea and Ham Soup, and if you use frozen peas and peeled shrimps or prawns, that is all it deserves to be. If, however, you are prepared to spend a little time easing fresh peas and shrimps out of their overcoats and making a stock out of both pods and shells, you will create a soup of delicacy and distinction.

1½ lb (675 g) fresh peas in the pod (about 9 oz (250 g) after podding)
½ lb (225 g) shrimps or prawns in the shell
1 small onion
1 medium-sized carrot
½ small glass of fruity white wine
5 tablespoons thick cream
a piece of mace or nutmeg
salt and freshly milled pepper
2 pints (1.2 l) water

Pod the peas and shell the shrimps, putting all the peelings into a saucepan as you go. Add the onion and carrot peel, the mace or nutmeg and the water and bring to the boil. Simmer for 25 minutes, skimming off any greyish scum that may rise after the first minute. Strain the stock about 1 pint (600 ml) into a clean stainless or enamelled pan and add the peas, the chopped carrot and onion and a little salt. Simmer until the peas are just cooked. Reserve 2 tablespoons of cooked peas and put the rest with the stock through the medium plate of a food mnill, or blend in short bursts so as to leave some texture. Return the soup to the rinsed out pan and add the wine, whole peas and shrimps. Re-heat and adjust the seasoning when hot. Stir in the cream and serve just before the soup boils.

Variation

For an exhibitionist soup, use another couple of tablespoons of thick cream and whip all the cream to a soft peak. Reserve 4 perfect shrimps in their shells and serve the soup with a big dollop of whipped cream in each bowl, supporting a reclining shrimp.

SHRIMP AND SALMON CREAM

The place to make this exquisite soup is Parkgate, beside the Dee estuary in Cheshire. All along the promenade, which now fronts not the sea, but a mile of marsh, are little fishmongers' shops. Throughout the summer they sell Dee salmon and piles of shrimps, caught by night in the estuary. Failing Parkgate, ask a good fishmonger for a salmon head with a bit of meat on it, and shrimps or prawns frozen in the shell.

1 lb (450 g) shrimps in the shell *or*
    6 oz (175 g) shelled shrimps
1 salmon head
3 pints (1.75 l) water
1 medium onion
2 sticks celery
1 thinly pared strip of lemon
    rind
2 sprigs of fennel *or* 5 fennel
    seeds
6 peppercorns
2 ripe tomatoes, 5 oz (140 g) after
    peeling and coring
up to 2 oz (60 g) unsalted butter
1 teaspoon plain flour
2 tablespoons brandy or whisky
¼ pint (150 ml) single cream
salt
freshly milled pepper

Peel the shrimps, eating not more than half a dozen, and put the heads and shells into a heavy, largish saucepan. Add the salmon head and cover with the cold water. Bring slowly to the boil and remove the scum which will form for the first 5 minutes or so. Lower the heat until a bubble breaks the surface only about every second, and then add 1 onion and 1 stick celery, both roughly chopped, the lemon rind, fennel sprigs or seeds, and the peppercorns. Simmer for 30 minutes, then lift out the salmon head and put it aside to cool.

Raise the heat under the fish stock, reduce it to about 1 pint (600 ml) and strain. Meanwhile chop the remaining onion and stick of celery into fine slices, and peel (see pps.247-8), core and slice the tomatoes. Sweat them all in the butter in a heavy stainless or enamel pan. After 6 to 7 minutes put in the flour, brandy and strained fish stock, stirring in the first ladleful very thoroughly before adding the rest. Let this soup base simmer for 10 minutes while you separate the flesh on the salmon head from the skin and bones; keep it in large flakes if you can. Reserve the best flakes and half the shrimps, and blend the scruffy salmon bits and the other half of the shrimps with the soup to a smooth, creamy consistency. Put it in a clean pan with the single cream and the reserved salmon and shrimps and heat gently. Taste, and add salt, pepper or lemon. Do not allow it to boil or the pieces of fish will be stringy.

Variations

1. A little mace or nutmeg and perhaps a pinch of cayenne can replace the fennel.
2. Provided that you have shrimp or prawn shells to flavour the stock, a delicious soup can be made without the salmon, using 8 oz (225 g) white fish heads and bones. Alternatively, if you have a good salmon head, a very good soup can be made from peeled

shrimps or prawns.

3. With good fish, a delicious low fat, low calorie soup can be made with only 1 teaspoon butter or oil and plain yogurt, or 2 tablespoons low fat milk powder mixed with $\frac{1}{4}$ pint (150 ml) water instead of the cream.

4. *Crème fraîche* (see p.142) makes a subtle change from single cream. A luxurious alternative is shrimp butter, made by blending 2 oz (60 g) shrimps, preferably in their shells, to a smooth paste with 2 oz (60 g) unsalted butter, a squeeze of lemon and a pinch of cayenne. Scrape this butter carefully out of the blender jar and add 1 tablespoon chopped chives or 1 teaspoon chopped fennel. Drop walnut-sized lumps of the shrimp butter into each bowl of soup as it is served, or spread it on thin slices of wholemeal bread to accompany the soup.

See also:
Chinese Chicken Soup, Variation 1
Cream of Chicken Soup, Variations 1and 2
Shellfish Cream

Sorrel

See under:
Chicken, Egg and Lemon Soup, Variation 3
Leek and Potato Soup, Variation 4
Purée of Lettuce with Sour Cream, Variation 2
Spinach: Crème Florentine, Variation 3
Cream of Watercress Soup, Variation 4

Spinach

CRÈME FLORENTINE

This is a luxurious and beautiful dinner party soup. It is very rich, and if the thought of accomplishing the egg yolk and lemon enrichment while simultaneously coping with guests daunts you, leave it out – you will still have a wonderful soup.

1 small onion *or* 3 shallots *or* 6
    spring onions
1½ oz (40 g) butter
1 lb (450 g) fresh, bright green
    spinach *or* 8 oz (225 g) frozen
    leaf spinach
1 pint (600 ml) good home-made
    chicken stock
1 heaped tablespoon rice flour

or potato flour *or* 1 oz (30 g)
    raw white rice
salt
freshly milled pepper
scrape of nutmeg
½ pint (300 ml) single cream
2 egg yolks
1 dessertspoon lemon juice

Chop the onion and sweat it in the butter in a heavy stainless or enamelled pan for 5 minutes or so. Add the well-washed fresh spinach (see pps.168-9 for preparation of spinach) or the defrosted frozen spinach, and stir for a couple of minutes. Add the chicken stock with the rice, or add the rice flour or potato flour whisked in the cold liquid. Season and bring to the boil. Simmer gently, half-covered, for 12 to 15 minutes, then blend the soup or put it through the medium plate of the food mill, which gives a more interesting texture. Pour the soup into a clean stainless or enamelled pan and add the cream. At this point the soup can be cooled and stored overnight in the fridge. Taste and adjust the seasoning, bearing in mind that you will add a little lemon at the last minute.

A few minutes before serving, put the soup to reheat over a low flame and whisk the egg yolks with the lemon juice for 2 minutes.

This beating makes the eggs less likely to curdle in the soup; you can also insure against curdling by adding 1 teaspoon plain flour to the yolks while beating, but this is cheating. When the soup is steaming but not yet boiling, pour a ladleful on to the yolk mixture, beating as you do so. Then add another ladleful. Remove the soup from the heat and, transferring the activities of the whisk to the soup pan, pour the egg yolk and soup mixture into the pan while whisking non-stop. The soup should thicken very slightly and acquire a velvety gloss. Taste the soup once more and serve immediately.

Variations

1. A very light ham or vegetable stock can be used instead of chicken.
2. Two tablespoons dry white wine can be used instead of lemon juice, but it is really gilding the lily.
3. Two bunches of watercress, or 8 oz (225 g) nettle tops or wild sorrel, or 1 lb (450 g) beet leaves can be used instead of spinach.

See also:
Beef: Pepperpot Soup
Chicken, Egg and Lemon Soup
Green Leaves: Spinach, Green Pea and Lettuce Purée
Green Leaves: Zuppa di Verdura
Leek and Potato Soup, Variation 4
Purée of Lettuce with Sour Cream, Variation 2
Cream of Watercress Soup, Variation 4

Strawberries

See under:
Iced Raspberry Yogurt Soup

Sweetcorn

See under:
Corn on the Cob

Tarragon

See under:
Beef: Consommé, Variation 3
Celery and Tarragon Moussseline Soup

Tomatoes

CHOOSING AND USING

Tomatoes are available in Britain all year round. In winter they are imported from the Mediterranean and especially the Canary Islands; Canary tomatoes, though they do not have a stunning flavour, set a consistent standard of sweet, sound fruit. In late spring tomatoes arrive from the Channel Islands; in my experience they are not as good as those from the Canaries, since they are woolly in texture and have no flavour to speak of. Then come the British hothouse tomatoes. The tiny cherry and plum tomatoes are often wonderfully sweet and fresh-flavoured and cheaper than the standard salad size; they are excellent for soup, as are the slightly soft, bright red tomatoes which the conscientious greengrocer often picks out of the box of salad tomatoes and is glad to sell you cheaply. Do not, however, buy tomatoes with yellow or brown marks on the skin, which often indicate something bad inside. The main crop of cloche and outdoor tomatoes come into the shops in September and October, which is the time to freeze or bottle, purée or chop tomatoes for soup bases. Big Mediterranean tomatoes like bright red and yellow peppers are sometimes available during the autumn and winter, but they don't seem to retain the wonderful flavour of Provence after their journey north.

Peeling and Coring

Ripe tomatoes are very easy to peel but ones with green or yellow sections may be more resistant. In either case drop the tomatoes into boiling water for $\frac{1}{2}$ to 1 minute. I generally wash them and then immerse them in the soup as it cooks. When you see the skins begin to split and wrinkle, lift out the tomatoes on a draining spoon and put them in a small basin of cold water until they are cool enough to handle. Pull off the skin with your fingers – the unripe tomatoes may need a little assistance from a vegetable knife – and cut out the core, which is the little piece of hard flesh just under the stalk. To do this, dig a sharp-pointed little knife into the tomato beside the stalk until it is one-third of the way into the fruit and cut out a conical section just below the stalk. For a special occasion you may like to remove the pips. Cut the tomatoes in quarters and scoop out the seeds with a teaspoon or your finger, then dice the flesh. This is called a *concasse* and was much called for in restaurants in the days when every chef had a couple of apprentices at his beck and call. These days we tend to make a virtue of necessity and consider throwing away the seeds very wasteful.

CREAM OF TOMATO SOUP

This soup is the national favourite, and though of course canned and dried tomato soups don't really taste of tomato but of a combination of sugar, salt and spices, over the years people have come to accept this flavour as Cream of Tomato. The real thing, made with ripe, tasty tomatoes, is quite different in colour – more of a deep peachy-orange – and has a sharp, tangy flavour the day it is made, maturing to a subtle sweetness after 24 hours. If you can't get rice flour (or potato flour) in your local delicatessen or specialist grocer, use corn flour; if only ordinary plain flour is available, turn to Variation 3. A thicker soup with more ingredients can be made from the recipes for Tomato, Onion and Potato Soup or Tomato and Pepper Soup.

1 lb (450 g) ripe tomatoes
1½ oz (40 g) butter
1 small clove garlic, peeled and crushed with a little salt
1 small strip of orange or lemon rind
½ pint (300 ml) milk and ½ pint

(300 ml) chicken stock *or* 1 pint (600 ml) milk
1 tablespoon rice flour
salt
freshly milled pepper
8 fresh basil leaves *or* ½ teaspoon dried basil

Peel the tomatoes as described on pps.247-8 and discard the cores. Roughly chop all but 3 of the tomatoes, and put the chopped ones in a heavy stainless or enamelled pan with the butter, garlic and citrus rind. Cut the reserved tomatoes in half and squeeze and scoop the seeds into the pan with the rest. Then neatly slice or dice these tomato halves for garnish, cover and put in the fridge. Cook the rest of the tomatoes over a low heat for 8 minutes, keeping them covered and shaking the pan occasionally. Meanwhile put the stock, milk and rice flour in the blender, if you are using one, or mix them thoroughly in a bowl. Add the tomato mixture to the liquid in the blender with some salt, pepper and a little of the fresh basil or all the dried. Blend thoroughly, or put through the fine plate of the food mill and mix with the liquid. Add the tomato garnish. At this point you can store the soup in the fridge until the following day.

Reheat in a clean pan. The soup will thicken slightly as it reaches simmering point. Simmer for 3 minutes, taste, and adjust the seasoning. Chop the rest of the fresh basil leaves and sprinkle on top of the soup.

Variations

1. A lightly flavoured beef, ham or vegetable stock is just as satisfactory as chicken.
2. Basil is tomato's best enhancer, but you can use $\frac{1}{4}$ teaspoon dried marjoram or oregano in the soup and serve it with chopped parsley, or use all fresh marjoram.
3. Rice flour gives this soup an instant delicate thickening without glueyness. Plain flour can, however, be used in the following way. Sweat the tomatoes in only $\frac{3}{4}$ oz (20 g) butter. Knead a rounded tablespoon flour into another 1 oz (30 g) butter to make a *beurre manié* (see p. 22). Purée the soup and begin to reheat it, but without the tomato garnish. When it approaches boiling point whisk in the *beurre manié* a little at a time, but working quickly. Add the tomato garnish as soon as the soup has thickened smoothly, and serve at once before the fresh flavour is lost.
4. Serve with *crème fraîche* (see p.142), sour cream or whipped fresh cream as a garnish.

GAZPACHO

This is the classic Spanish iced soup. It can be piquant and varied in flavour or very dull – if your tomatoes taste dull to start with, they will be even duller iced, so it would be better to make a hot Tomato and Orange Soup. Before starting, therefore, please read the general remarks on choosing and using tomatoes. Gazpacho should be made at least 2 hours before serving, but not more than 12 hours or the textures will deteriorate.

1¼ lb (560 g) good, ripe tomatoes
1 to 3 cloves garlic, peeled and finely crushed with salt
2 spring onions
1 2-inch (5 cm) chunk of cucumber *or* ½ a small fennel bulb
½ a small green pepper
2 heaped tablespoons chopped fresh herbs, e.g. parsley, chives, marjoram, basil or oregano

3 to 4 tablespoons really thick, fruity olive oil
3 to 4 tablespoons wine or sherry vinegar
salt
freshly milled pepper
cayenne or tabasco
¼ to ½ pint (150 to 300 ml) tomato juice
3 slices wholemeal bread
2 tablespoons oil
8 black olives, stoned

Begin making this soup several hours before you intend serving it, since the flavours need time to blend and the soup must be really icy cold. Peel the tomatoes as described on pps.247-8. Cut them up, discarding the hard core around the stalk; you may also discard the seed if you like (pps.247-8), but I like them in the soup. Put the tomatoes on a large board and chop them almost to a slush with a large knife. Scoop all the pulp into a non-metal container which will fit in the freezing compartment of your fridge or just beneath it. Add the garlic with the trimmed spring onions, chopped small. Seed the green pepper. Dice the cucumber or fennel and pepper into ¼ inch (½ cm) cubes, or cut them into julienne strips (see p.31) and add them too. Put in the chopped herbs, most of the oil and vinegar, and a little salt, pepper and cayenne or tabasco. Mix it all thoroughly and taste. Add more oil, vinegar and seasoning until you have a highly spiced mixture. If it is more porridge than soup dilute with tomato juice. Now chill thoroughly, which may take only 30 minutes in a really efficient freezer, but 3 hours or more in a fridge. Taste the soup again when chilled. It should be icy cold, though not frozen. Just before serving, cut the bread into small cubes and fry, preferably in olive oil. Drain the croûtons on kitchen paper when they are brown and crisp, and serve hot. Garnish with olives.

Variations

1. If you are in a great hurry, blend the roughly chopped tomatoes and other ingredients in a few short bursts of a second or so each. The different textures of the vegetables will be retained to a certain extent by this method if you blend only to large crumb size, but this more or less instantly prepared soup will not have the contrasting textures and general elegance of the hand-made variety.
2. For a slimmer's soup, reduce the quantity of olive oil (the fruitier the oil the less you will need) and either leave out the bread altogether, or add it to the soup in the form of crumbs before chilling.

TOMATO, ONION AND POTATO SOUP

Like Leek and Potato Soup and Purée of Broad Beans, this is both a dish in itself and a very useful base on which to build other soups. If you have a food mill it takes about 10 minutes to prepare, and in any case it takes less than 30 minutes to cook. The ingredients are quite ordinary, but if well made the soup has that refined simplicity which the British are often too lacking in confidence to attempt. Some people add sugar to tomato soups. I think this is a great pity since it tends to increase our already deplorable national sugar consumption.

$1\frac{1}{2}$ oz (40 g) butter
1 small onion
3 medium tomatoes
2 medium potatoes – white
  rather than reds
$\frac{1}{2}$ bay leaf
2 sprigs of fresh marjoram *or* $\frac{1}{4}$
  teaspoon dried marjoram and

1 tablespoon chopped chives,
  chervil or parsley
1 pint (600 ml) water
salt
freshly milled pepper
a few tablespoons top of the milk
  or single cream

Melt the butter in a heavy pan over a low heat. Finely slice the onion and add. Put a lid on the pan and sweat for 5 minutes, shaking the pan occasionally. Wash and chop but do not peel the tomatoes; add them and sweat for another 5 minutes, shaking the pan as before. Peel the potatoes and chop them roughly; add them with the bay leaf

251

and dried marjoram or 1 sprig of the fresh marjoram. Stir well and sweat for another minute. Add the water and a little salt and pepper, and put the lid on. Bring the soup to the boil and simmer for 15 minutes or until the potatoes are soft. Put the soup through the medium plate of the food mill, or allow to cool a little and then blend and sieve. Remember that the texture of potato soups is often gluey for several hours after blending. At this point the soup may be stored in the fridge until the following day. You can try freezing, but some texture and flavour are lost. When you want to serve it, return the soup to a clean pan with the cream and heat gently. Chop the other sprig of marjoram, if you have the fresh herb, for garnish. Taste the soup when hot and add more seasoning if necessary. Serve sprinkled with the marjoram, chives or parsley.

Variations

1. The soup can be made with part or all milk, in which case watch that it doesn't boil over, or part light stock – vegetable, chicken, beef, ham or duck – but be careful not to overpower the tomato flavour.
2. For a very quick soup, use half a 7 oz (200 g) tin of peeled tomatoes instead of fresh ones.
3. The soup can become a main course with the inclusion of other diced vegetables after sieving. The soup is then simmered for a further 10 to 15 minutes. More potato, celery, green pepper, carrot etc. would all be suitable, or 1 oz (30 g) long grain rice or small pasta can be cooked separately and added shortly before serving. Parmesan or other cheese can be sprinkled on top. The soup can also be served with cheese croûtons (see p.28), or a slice of toast with cheese on top can be floated in each bowl and grilled before serving.
4. Any of the concoctions of oil or butter and flavourings such as peperonata (p.43), pesto (p.43), aillade (p.40), mushrooms (p.32) etc. could be added for a more glamorous flavour, in which case you may wish to leave out the cream.

TOMATO AND ORANGE SOUP

This is a light, fresh summer soup, low in calories and high in vitamin C. It is immediately attractive even to the most conservative eaters and can be varied endlessly; it converts very well to a savoury water ice (Variation 3).

1 small onion *or* 4 shallots
1 clove garlic, peeled and
   crushed with a little salt
1½ oz (40 g) butter *or* 3 tablespoons oil
1½ lb (675 g) very ripe tomatoes

1 small orange
½ pint (300 ml) water
freshly milled pepper
salt
6 fresh basil leaves *or* ½ teaspoon
   dried basil

Peel and roughly chop the onion, and sweat with the garlic in the butter or oil in a heavy pan over a low heat for 15 minutes, stirring occasionally. Cut the tomatoes into quarters. Remove one-third of the orange rind very thinly with a potato peeler, leaving all the white pith on the orange. Put in the tomatoes, orange rind, strained juice and basil. Cook gently with the lid on for 5 minutes. Add the water, bring to the boil, and simmer for 6 more minutes. Put the soup through the fine plate of the food mill, or blend and then sieve it. The soup can be prepared in advance to this point. Reheat and adjust seasoning, adding mostly pepper and a little salt if you must.

Variations

1. The soup is delicious iced. Make it with oil instead of butter, and chill in the freezing compartment of the fridge or in the freezer until very cold indeed. Then taste and add more seasoning, including lemon juice if needed. Serve in pretty glasses, plain or with a dessertspoon of plain yogurt or *crème fraîche* (see p.142).
2. Ham, chicken, vegetable or shellfish stock may be used instead of water. For the shellfish stock see Shrimp and Salmon Cream. If you want to make the soup with milk, add 1 dessertspoon flour to the butter and onion mixture and stir it in well to prevent the milk curdling with the orange. The soup will be thicker than in the main recipe.
3. For a savoury summer water ice, make the soup without water and freeze it to a slush. Taste and add more seasoning, including cayenne or tabasco if necessary and lemon, lime or orange juice. Blend to smoothness and refreeze. Serve piled up in pretty glasses and garnished with orange dice and mint leaves.

TOMATO AND RED PEPPER SOUP

This is a pretty summer soup which almost everyone likes instantly. It is rich and filling and makes a good preface to a salad-based main course. It keeps well in the fridge for a day or two, and although some texture is lost during freezing it is still excellent after defrosting.

1¼ lb (560 g) ripe tomatoes
1 large or 2 small, brilliant red peppers
1 medium onion
1 to 2 cloves garlic, peeled and crushed with salt
1 oz (30 g) butter or 2 table-spoons olive oil
salt
freshly milled pepper
pinch of cayenne or dash of

tabasco
8 fresh basil leaves or ½ teaspoon dried basil
1 clove
scrape of nutmeg
1 oz (30 g) long grain white rice
½ pint (300 ml) water or a little more
¼ pint (150 ml) crème fraîche (see p. 142) or sour cream

Peel and core the tomatoes (see pps. 247-8). Seed the red pepper and trim away the white pithy bits. Cut both pepper and onion in quarters and slice them thinly. Using a heavy pan on a very low heat, sweat the pepper, onion and garlic in the butter or oil. Do not let the vegetables stick or colour. After 10 minutes add the roughly chopped tomatoes, a little salt, pepper, cayenne or tabasco, the dried or chopped fresh basil, the clove and nutmeg. Cover the pan and simmer for 15 minutes. Discard the clove, add the rice and the water, and simmer for a further 12 minutes or until the rice is just tender. At this point the soup can be stored in the fridge until the following day, or even the day after that in cold weather; the flavour will mature and improve. Reheat in a clean pan, diluted with a little more water if you like. When it is hot, taste and add more seasoning if necessary – the soup should be richly spicy. Serve with a dollop of crème fraîche or sour cream in each bowl.

Variations

1. If you have a food mill you can use a quicker though less elegant method. Roughly chop the onion, pepper and unpeeled tomatoes. Follow the recipe until you have sweated the onion and pepper and then the tomatoes. Put this mixture through the coarse plate of the food mill – most of the tomato skins will be caught in the plate. Then proceed with the main recipe.
2. Brown rice is more nutritious than white, but takes much longer to cook. If you want to use it, it is better cooked separately.
3. For a soup low in animal fat, use olive oil; leave out the garlic and

basil in the main recipe, and serve the soup with a pesto (p.43) or aillade (p.40) instead of the sour cream.
4. For a slimmer's soup, cut down the oil or butter at the beginning and leave out the cream. Keep the rice, though, and make the soup a sustaining low calorie main course.

See also:
Aubergine, Red Pepper and Coconut Soup, Variation 2
Sea Bass, Vermouth and Garlic Soup
Beef: Meat Ball and Tomato Soup
Beef: Wedding Soup
Cabbage: Majorcan Soup
Fish Stew with Garlic, Tomatoes and Olive Oil
Mussels: Cream of Mussel Soup, Variation 3
Split Pea and Bacon Soup, Variation 3
Shrimp and Salmon Cream
Tripe: Zuppa di Trippa alla Milanese, main recipe and Variation 4
Vegetables: Pistou, main recipe and Variation 2
Enrichments: aubergine and tomato, p.40; red pepper and onion, p.42; peperonata, p.43
Garnishes and Accompaniments: tomatoes, p.32

Smoked Trout

See under:
Smoked Mackerel Soup, Variation 3

Tripe

CHOOSING AND USING

White tripe is the second stomach of the ox or cow; black tripe, the first stomach, is much coarser and sold only in parts of Lancashire. The white variety is always sold scraped, bleached and cooked; when raw, tripe is covered with black or green furry matter and is attached to a tough, hide-like membrane. The whole white tripe weighs about 15 lb (7 kg) after cooking and dressing, and is then divided into three

parts: the thick seam, the honeycomb, and the 'face piece' or 'flat tripe'. The thick seam is the thickest and meatiest part of the tripe, and, according to Mr Harry Schiach, President of the National Association of Tripe Dressers, the very best part of the tripe to use for soup; the finest part of the thick seam is the knuckle, where 4 seams join. This part of the tripe, Mr Schiach says, will keep its texture best after further cooking at home. Honeycomb tripe, the second choice, comes from the bottom of the stomach, where the acid forms which breaks down the grass and other foodstuffs. The 'face piece' or 'flat tripe' is the thinnest, and most likely to dissolve into a jelly if cooked for a long time at home.

How much you cook the tripe yourself therefore depends on the type you have bought, but also on whether the tripe has been thoroughly cooked by the dresser and whether it comes from an old or a young animal. If the tripe is easily pierced by your thumbnail and feels soft throughout, 30 minutes' more cooking will do, but if your thumbnail bounces back at you, allow $1\frac{1}{2}$ hours or even more.

TRIPE CHOWDER

No tripe soup recipe is very quickly made because of the need to cook, or at least finish cooking, the tripe (see above). However, if you are making another tripe dish, cook 4 oz (110 g) extra and this rich, well-flavoured soup will take only 25 minutes. If you are starting from scratch, make two or three times the recipe and freeze the rest but without the potato, which should be added only when reheating. Simmer for 10 to 15 minutes before serving.

4 oz (110 g) tripe
2 tablespoons vinegar or lemon juice and water to soak the tripe
2 pint (1.2 l) water to cook the tripe
6 allspice berries *or* 2 cloves
freshly milled black pepper *or* 8 to 10 peppercorns
parsley stalks

celery trimmings (optional)
1 small onion plus a little extra for the stock
2 rashers unsmoked back bacon, 2 oz (60 g)
1 small potato
1 dessertspoon flour
$\frac{3}{4}$ to 1 pint (450 to 600 ml) milk
salt
2 tablespoons chopped parsley

If you are starting with tripe straight from the butcher, i.e. only partly cooked, leave it to soak in water with lemon or vinegar for 15 minutes, then rinse it. Put it in a heavy pan with the cooking water, bring to the boil and skim thoroughly as the grey scum rises. After 10 minutes or so, when only white foam is coming to the surface, add the cloves or allspice, peppercorns or a few grinds of pepper, and parsley stalks, celery trimmings and a little onion if you have them. Cover the pan and simmer for between 30 minutes and $1\frac{1}{2}$ hours (see p.256), until tender.

Meanwhile remove any bones and rind from the bacon and cut into $\frac{1}{2}$ inch (1 cm) squares. Chop the onions into small pieces and the potato into $\frac{1}{2}$ inch (1 cm) dice. Lift out the tripe and leave it to cool. Strain the stock into a tall glass jug if possible so you can easily see which is fat and which is stock, and remove most of the fat, leaving only 1 to 2 tablespoons according to taste. Clean the pan, and fry the bacon and onion in it gently over a low heat for 10 minutes. Cut the tripe into $\frac{1}{2}$ inch (1 cm) squares. Stir the flour into the bacon and onion mixture and add $\frac{1}{2}$ pint (300 ml) stock by degrees, stirring thoroughly between each addition. Now add the milk and bring back to the boil. Add the tripe and the potato, salt and more pepper, and simmer for 10 to 15 minutes. If the soup becomes too thick, add more milk. Taste, and adjust seasoning. Serve with the chopped parsley sprinkled on top.

Variations

1. According to taste and what is available, the soup can be made with all milk – $1\frac{1}{4}$ pints (750 ml) – or 1 pint (600 ml) stock and $\frac{1}{4}$ pint (150 ml) creamy milk.
2. A piece of lean boiled bacon can be substituted for the back rashers, in which case fry the onion in a little butter or lard before adding the chopped bacon.

257

ZUPPA DI TRIPPA ALLA MILANESE

Tripe aficionado friends point out that, because of my childish antipathy to its consistency, my recipes tend not to be tripey enough. If you are a real fan you can substitute more tripe for the haricot beans. The soup keeps and freezes well, but add the cabbage only 5 minutes before serving.

For 3 pints (1.75 l):
8 oz (225 g) tripe
2 tablespoons vinegar *or* lemon juice and water to soak the tripe
2 oz (60 g) white haricot beans, soaked overnight
2 pints (1.2 l) bacon or ham stock and 2 pints (1.2 l) water *or* 4 pints (2.3 l) water and 2 ham stock cubes
1 bay leaf
2 sprigs of thyme or marjoram
2 cloves *or* 6 allspice berries
8 to 10 peppercorns
2 pints (1.25 l) water to cook the beans
freshly milled pepper
2 large, red tomatoes
1 medium leek
3 to 4 oz (90 to 110 g) white cabbage
1 stick celery
salt
3 tablespoons grated Parmesan, fresh if possible

Trim away any hard parts from the tripe, and put it to soak in the vinegar or lemon juice and water for 10 minutes. If you forget to soak the beans overnight, put them in a pan, cover them with cold water, bring to the boil, turn off the heat, cover the pan and leave for 45 minutes. Then proceed with the recipe. Put the piece of tripe in a heavy pan with the water and stock and bring to the boil. Skim off the grey scum as it rises to the surface. Then add the bay leaf, cloves or allspice and peppercorns. Simmer for between 1 and 1½ hours (see p.256), until the tripe is tender. Cook the beans separately in water with pepper but no salt. Meanwhile peel and core the tomatoes (see p.247) and chop roughly. Finely slice the leek, put to soak in plenty of cold water, and finely slice the cabbage and celery. Lift out the cooked tripe and leave till it is cool enough to handle. Strain the stock, preferably into a tall glass jug, and skim off excess fat, leaving only 2 to 4 tablespoons according to taste. Wash the pan and return the stock to it; if you have more than 2 pints (1.2 l) reduce by fast boiling, if less make it up with water. Drain the cooked haricot beans. Cut the tripe into ½ inch (1 cm) squares and add them to the stock with the leeks, celery and tomato. Bring to the boil and simmer for 15 minutes. Taste and add salt and plenty of pepper. At this point the soup can be cooled and stored overnight in the fridge, or frozen. Bring the soup back to the boil, add the finely sliced white cabbage and simmer for 5 minutes. Serve with the grated Parmesan.

Variations

1. This is a stew-like, main course soup. For a lighter starter, either use the same quantities of tripe and vegetables with 3 pints (1.75 l) cooking liquid instead of 2 pints (1.2 l), or reduce the amount of tripe and vegetables by a quarter or so.
2. The bacon stock and water in which the tripe is cooked would be enriched by the addition of a beef bone or veal knuckle.
3. Two ounces (60 g) cooked ham or bacon, or 2 rashers fried bacon, can be diced and added to the soup either as well as all the other ingredients, or instead of part of the tripe or cabbage.
4. A 7 oz (200 g) can of peeled tomatoes can be used instead of fresh ones. This will make a rather more tomato-flavoured soup, which might be a good thing if you are using stock cubes. Reduce the stock by $\frac{1}{4}$ pint (150 ml) and chop up the tomatoes roughly before adding them.
5. Red kidney beans or chestnuts – 1 oz (30 g) dried chestnuts or 6 oz (175 g) fresh, unpeeled – can be used instead of haricot beans, or 2 oz (60 g) small pasta thrown in 10 minutes before serving.

Turkey

TURKEY CHOWDER

This recipe and the Devilled Turkey Soup that follows are of course intended to be eaten around 28 or 29 December, when the Christmas turkey has been reduced to a skeleton. Ideally these recipes use leftover breast meat and leg meat respectively, but any part of the bird will do. What is essential is a good, rich stock, made from the cooked carcass of the turkey and the vegetables and herbs as for chicken stock (see pps.116-17). If you have the ingredients at hand, it is worth making several times the quantity given of the soup, since it keeps for days and makes a good holiday lunch.

1 small onion
2 small sticks celery
1 oz (30 g) butter
1 pint (600 ml) turkey stock
½ bay leaf threaded on a clove
salt
freshly milled pepper
1 large or 2 small potatoes – reds or Edwards

6 to 8 tablespoons milk, $^1/_5$ pint (120 ml)
7 oz (200 g) can of whole or creamed sweetcorn
up to ¼ pint (150 ml) sour cream
2 to 4 oz (60 to 110 g) cooked turkey meat – white for preference

Dice the onion and celery small or large, depending on whether you want an elegant soup or a main course. Melt the butter in a heavy pan and sweat the onion and celery in it gently for a few minutes, stirring occasionally. Add the turkey stock and bring to the boil with the bay leaf and clove and a little salt and pepper. Boil steadily for 15 minutes, until the stock has reduced by half. Peel the potato, dice on the same scale as the onion and celery and add it to the stock with the milk. Simmer for about 10 minutes, until the potato is nearly done. Now add the sweetcorn and simmer for a minute. Taste, adjust the seasoning, then lastly stir in the sour cream and the diced turkey meat. If you think the chowder too thick, add a little more milk, stock or water. Serve at once, or cool and store overnight. The flavour is at its best the next day.

Variations

1. If you can't find the time to make turkey stock, a very pleasant soup can be made with all milk and, if you like, ½ a chicken stock cube.
2. The soup can be served with chopped parsley or chives, and grated nutmeg substituted for the bay leaf and clove. If you have allspice (Jamaica pepper), 4 crushed berries or ¼ teaspoon would be pleasant.
3. So long as the chowder has turkey, milk and potatoes, and to a lesser extent sweetcorn, the other ingredients are up to you. Carrots, leeks, mushrooms, frozen peas or beans, or a little parsnip or turnip could all be used, and even cauliflower or white cabbage, but not sprouts, which have too strong a flavour.
4. For a low fat soup the butter and sour cream can be left out.

DEVILLED TURKEY SOUP

The turkey bones with a bit of leg meat, the scrapings from the roasting tin or leftover turkey gravy, and a snifter from the Christmas madeira or port, combined with a few vegetables, make a warm, spicy soup which keeps and freezes very well. If you have these leftover scrapings or turkey gravy, use them in place of an equal quantity of stock. During the rest of the year the recipe will adapt to chicken or rabbit.

1 medium onion
1 carrot
1 stick celery
1 oz (30 g) turkey fat or butter *or* 2 tablespoons oil
1 clove garlic, peeled and crushed
½ teaspoon garam masala and ¼ flat teaspoon cayenne *or* 1 flat teaspoon curry powder

1 rounded tablespoon flour
1½ pints (900 ml) turkey stock
salt
2 oz (60 g) mushrooms, flat for preference
about 2 heaped tablespoons diced, cooked turkey
freshly milled pepper
5 tablespoons madeira or port

Dice the onion, carrot and celery large or small according to your taste. Put the turkey fat, butter or oil in a heavy pan and add the diced vegetables and garlic. Cook them over quite a high heat for 10 minutes or so, stirring them a little but allowing them to brown. Add the spice and cayenne or curry powder, and the flour; stir all the time as the flour browns, which will take about 5 minutes. When it is nut coloured, start to add the turkey stock by degrees, stirring each addition smooth before pouring in more. Let the soup come to the boil, add a little salt, then turn the heat very low, partly cover the soup and leave to simmer. Slice or dice the mushrooms and the cooked turkey meat. After the soup has simmered for 30 minutes add the mushrooms and continue simmering for another 5 minutes. Add salt, pepper and spice to taste, and finally the turkey meat and the madeira or port. Serve at once, or cool and store; the flavour will be at its best on the following day.

Variations

1. There is little point in making this soup without a good stock, but

you could substitute mild ham stock for turkey.

2. The spices can be varied according to what is available. A freshly ground mixture of cumin, coriander and chili with a few cardamom seeds would produce a very elegant flavour.

3. The basic vegetables can be varied as you like. Parsnip would be tasty, or more celery and no carrot, or the mushrooms can be left out and other ingredients increased proportionately.

4. One ounce (30 g) long grain white rice can be cooked with the soup instead of the flour. A couple of tablespoons of leftover chestnut, or even chestnut and prune, stuffing could be used instead of the flour. Add them either in bits or pounded to a mush near the end of the cooking time. If you have prunes, the madeira or port may be unnecessary.

See also:
Purée of Duck and Celery, Variation 1
Duck and Cucumber Soup, Variation 1

Turnip

CREAM OF TURNIP SOUP

Because turnips can sometimes be very coarsely flavoured, this recipe uses an equal quantity of potatoes. If you have some divinely flavoured, perfect little turnips, though, any of the recipes for other root vegetables – Jerusalem artichokes, celeriac, parsnips and so on – can be used instead of this one.

1 medium turnip	freshly milled pepper
1 largish potato	nutmeg
$\frac{1}{2}$ pint (300 ml) water	1 pint (600 ml) creamy milk
1 small onion *or* the white part of a leek	grated rind of $\frac{1}{4}$ lemon or orange garnish of plain croûtons (see
1 oz (30 g) butter	p.27)
salt	

If you are really worried about the flavour of your turnip, slice it and boil for 5 minutes in 1 pint (600 ml) water, then drain and proceed with the recipe. (If you do this, you may like to use all turnip and omit the potato.) Put the sliced turnip and sliced potato in the water so that they do not discolour. Meanwhile slice the onion and sweat it in a heavy pan in the butter; don't let it brown or the final soup colour will be spoilt. Add the vegetables and water, a little salt, pepper and a scrape or two of nutmeg. Cover the pan, bring to the boil and simmer for 15 minutes or until the vegetables are just breaking up. Remove from the heat and add the milk. You can leave the soup lumpy like this, or put it through the food mill. If you blend it, the consistency may be very gluey for a couple of hours afterwards, and anyway the texture will be dull. Ideally, use the medium plate of the food mill. At this point the soup can be cooled and stored overnight in the fridge. Pour the soup into a clean pan and reheat with the lemon or orange rind. When hot, taste it and adjust the seasoning. Serve with crisply fried croûtons.

Variations

1. The soup can be made with all water or vegetable broth, in which case you may like to add ½ teaspoon sugar, or meat or poultry stock or game stock. For a special occasion, the ultimate version of this soup would include game stock, with ¼ pint (150 ml) double cream stirred in a minute or two before serving.
2. A ½ teaspoon curry powder, cumin seeds or garam masala can be added to the onion. The soup can be garnished with chopped parsley, chives or marjoram.

Vegetables

VEGETABLE STOCK AND BROTH

It is not always possible to make meat, poultry or fish stock when you want it, because the particular ingredients are not on hand or you have too little time. A vegetable stock can be made in a little over 30 minutes and uses very basic ingredients, which can be varied with more exotic vegetables according to what you have in the house. It is not, however, so good-natured as a meat or poultry stock, and will quickly lose its fresh flavour if left sitting about in the pan in a warm kitchen. It should be strained and cooled as soon as possible after making. Vegetable stock will keep for a day or two in the fridge and can be frozen, though some of the fresh flavour is lost. Instead of using whole vegetables, you can make use of clean, fresh trimmings, with all the brown or bad bits cut away. Increase the quantity if you are using trimmings only.

For 2 pints (1.2 l) stock:
1 large onion
3 sticks celery
2 medium carrots
1 medium potato (optional)
3 pints (1.75 l) water
2 parsley stalks

2 bay leaves
1 sprig of marjoram or thyme *or*
   1 teaspoon dried marjoram or
   thyme
1 clove garlic, peeled and
   crushed
6 peppercorns

Wash the vegetables thoroughly, slice them roughly and cover with cold water. Add the herbs and seasonings, bring to the boil, and simmer for 30 minutes. Strain, pressing out all the juice from the vegetables. If not required at once, store in the fridge.

Vegetable Broth

Make the vegetable stock as described above, including the optional potato and adding 2 large, ripe, halved tomatoes or $\frac{1}{4}$ pint (150 ml) tomato juice. When the stock is cooked, pass as much as possible through the medium plate of the food mill, or through a sieve, pressing it with the back of a ladle. Taste the broth and add salt, soy sauce and freshly milled pepper. Serve plain or with dumplings (pps.32-3), pasta (p.22), ravioli (pps.36-7) or a vegetable garnish or enrichment (pps.31-2).

Variations

1. Shallots or leeks can be used instead of onion.
2. Replace one of the carrots with 1 to 2 oz (30 to 60 g) parsnip or turnip. If you really enjoy their strong flavours, use more.
3. Celeriac, bulb fennel or Jerusalem artichokes can be used instead of celery.
4. The carrots can be left out and 8 oz (225 g) fresh tomatoes or a 7 oz (200 g) can of peeled ones used instead.
5. The seasonings can be varied with fennel, tarragon, basil, orange and lemon peel, nutmeg, allspice etc.

MINESTRONE

The Italians and expatriates living in Italy to whom I have talked, and the cookery books I have consulted, all agree that the only essential ingredient of Minestrone is beans – red kidney in Turin, white haricot in Genoa and Rome. The word itself means 'big soup' and the ingredients can vary according to season and locality. The overcooked pasta and tomato gunk with minute pieces of vegetable that is sold as Minestrone by soup manufacturers is not only nasty but incorrect, since tomatoes are generally quite a minor ingredient and pasta usually absent altogether.

For 3 pints (1.75 l) soup:
2 oz (60 g) red kidney beans, soaked overnight
2 pints (1.2 l) water to cook the beans
freshly milled pepper
3 pints (1.75 l) water to cook the soup
1 medium onion
2 sticks celery
2 cloves garlic, peeled and crushed with a little salt

8 or so roughly chopped fresh basil leaves *or* 1 teaspoon dried basil (optional)
2 or 3 ripe, red tomatoes
2 small courgettes
2 oz (60 g) French beans
1 small potato – Edward or new
4 tablespoons fruity olive oil
salt
4 heaped tablespoons or more freshly grated Parmesan

If you forget to soak the beans, cover them with 2 pints (1.2 l) water in a heavy pan, bring to the boil, turn off the heat, and leave for 45 minutes. Then boil them in the water with pepper but no salt for 1 to 2 hours, until just tender. Drain them and use the bean water as part of the liquid needed for the soup.

Put the soup water in a large stainless or enamelled pan and bring to the boil. Chop the onion and celery in ½ inch (1 cm) cubes and add them to the water with the garlic and basil. Cook for 15 minutes. Meanwhile peel the tomatoes – drop them in the soup for a minute, lift out with a draining spoon, cool and peel. Remove the cores and chop roughly. Cut the courgettes in rounds and put in a bowl, sprinkled with salt. Top and tail the beans by holding them upright in a bunch and tapping them until the bottom ends are level; cut these off, reverse the beans and repeat. Cut the beans in 2 or 3 pieces. Add the potato, cubed, the red beans and the tomatoes, and cook the soup for another 10 minutes. Add the green beans, rinsed courgettes and olive oil, and simmer for 5 minutes. If the soup has reduced too much add water to make about 3 pints (1.75 l). Taste, adjust seasoning and serve, with the Parmesan either stirred in or sprinkled on top.

Variations

1. Bacon or ham stock (watch the saltiness) or a bacon bone or piece of rind from a bacon or ham joint can be used to flavour the soup.
2. A small piece of boiling bacon – say 4 oz (110 g) – can be cooked with the soup from the beginning and sliced into it just before serving. One or two French, German or Italian all-pork sausages can be browned in hot oil for a couple of minutes, then added to the soup with the onion and celery. Lift out, slice and return to the soup just before serving; 1 to 2 oz (30 to 60 g) good salami, cut in small cubes, can be added with the green beans – this is unorthodox but tasty. If using meat, leave out the oil.
3. A little small pasta or long grain white rice – 1 to 1½ oz (30 to 40 g) – can be added to the soup instead of potato. Add about 10 to 12 minutes before serving.
4. Green cabbage can be used instead of courgettes; broad beans or peas instead of French beans; carrots instead of celery; leeks instead of onion. The courgettes could also be replaced by mushrooms, or even pumpkin or marrow. In fact select from what is in seson the items that will create an interesting contrast of flavour and texture.

PISTOU

This soup is the French half-brother to the better-known Minestrone. It is also, Frenchmen would be swift to point out, more sophisticated and more luxurious. Since the essence of this soup is its fresh, just-cooked flavours and textures, it is a pity to keep it or freeze it. It can be made even more substantial with the addition of pork sausages (Variation 1), or into an elegant dinner party soup (Variation 2).

For 3 pints (1.75 l):
2 oz (60 g) white haricot beans, soaked overnight
2 pints (1.2 l) water to cook the beans

3 pints (1.75 l) water to cook the soup
1 small carrot
1 small onion
salt

freshly milled pepper

1 small potato – waxy potatoes such as new ones or Edwards are best

2 small courgettes

3 oz (90 g) French beans

8 oz (225 g) ripe, red tomatoes *or* a 7 oz (200 g) can peeled tomatoes

12 or so leaves fresh basil *or* 1½ teaspoons dried basil

2 cloves garlic

5 to 6 tablespoons good, fruity olive oil

1 oz (30 g) small pasta – vermicelli, shells or broken spaghetti

If you forget to soak the beans, put them in a pan with their cooking water, bring to the boil, turn off the heat, cover and leave for 45 minutes. Then boil them for 1 to 2 hours until just tender. You can use the haricot bean water as part of the soup water or not as you choose. Put the soup liquid in a large stainless or enamelled pan with the sliced carrot and onion and bring to the boil. Add a little salt and pepper and simmer for 15 minutes.

Meanwhile cut the potato into cubes ½ inch (1 cm) square. Cut the courgettes into rounds, put in a bowl and sprinkle with salt. Hold the French beans in a bunch like pick-a-sticks until all the bottom ends are level, then lay the bunch down and cut off the bottom ends. Reverse the beans and do the same with the other end. Cut the beans into 2 or 3 pieces. Peel and core the tomatoes (see pp.247-8) and chop them roughly. Chop the fresh or dried basil to a pulp with the garlic and a little salt. Mix this in a bowl with the tomatoes and olive oil. Add plenty of pepper. Add the potato and the cooked haricot beans to the soup and boil a further 10 minutes. Throw in the pasta, stir, and cook for another 5 minutes. Rinse the courgettes in cold water, add them with the French beans, and cook 5 minutes more. Add a ladleful of soup to the tomato mixture and whisk it in. If you are using a tureen, pour this mixture into the warmed tureen, otherwise turn off the heat under the soup and whisk in the tomato mixture gently. Taste, and adjust the seasoning. Serve at once with hot French bread.

Variations

1. If you can get French, German or Italian all-pork sausages, brown one or two for a few minutes in hot oil, then slice and add to the soup with the potato; don't add salt until the last minute. A little good salami – 2 oz (60 g) – cut in small cubes and added a minute or two before serving the soup makes a good substitute; a British

banger does not.

2. For a lighter, more tomato-flavoured and very elegant soup, use 1 lb (450 g) tomatoes or 8 oz (225 g) fresh tomatoes and a 7 oz (200 g) can peeled tomatoes. Leave out the haricot beans. Use only 2¼ pints (1.4 l) water and add the tomatoes with the pasta. Meanwhile mix the crushed garlic and basil with 2 egg yolks and beat well. Mix in the olive oil by degrees to form a mayonnaise, or use 4 tablespoons good bought mayonnaise. Add this to the Pistou as described in the main recipe.

3. Broad or runner beans can be used instead of French.

4. Celery or mushrooms can replace carrots and courgettes.

For Carribean vegetables see under:
Beef: Jamaican Red Pea Soup
Beef: Pepperpot Soup

For Chinese vegetables see under:
Duck and Cucumber Soup, Variation 3
Chinese Chicken Soup, Variation 2

GARBURE

This is a relative of Minestrone. It comes from southern France, but not so far south as Pistou, and the ingredients are much cheaper for our northern pockets. The original recipes sometimes contain preserved goose or duck, which add wonderful savour, but bacon or salt pork makes a delicious and very filling one-pot meal.

For 3 pints (1.75 l):

8 oz (225 g) boiling bacon or salt belly of pork
1 oz (30 g) lard – if you are using lean meat
3½ pints (2 l) water
6 to 8 allspice berries *or* 2 cloves and 1 bay leaf
freshly milled pepper
2 small carrots

1 medium onion
2 cloves garlic, peeled and crushed with a little salt
2 oz (60 g) French beans
6 oz (175 g) green or white cabbage
1 large new potato
1 small red pepper
slices of wholemeal bread

Soak the bacon or salt pork overnight to remove excess salt. Turn the oven on high and put the meat in a roasting tin with the optional lard, if required, and roast for 10 to 15 minutes, turning once, until brown and crisp. Put the pork or bacon and scrapings from the tin in a large stainless or enamelled pan with the water, and bring to the boil. Add the spices and pepper but no salt. Chop the carrots and onion roughly and add them to the pot with the crushed garlic. Simmer for 30 minutes or until the bacon is nearly cooked. Meanwhile top and tail the beans by holding them upright in a bunch and tapping them until the bottom ends are level. Cut off the bottom ends, reverse the beans and repeat the process. Chop the beans into 1-inch lengths. Cut the cabbage into small pieces, say $\frac{1}{2}$ inch (1 cm) square, and the potato into large cubes. Slice the pepper into small strips. Add the potato and pepper to the soup and cook gently for 10 minutes. Throw in the beans and cook 5 minutes longer; lastly add the cabbage. Bring back to the boil, taste and add salt and pepper as required. Lift out the bacon and slice it; traditionally it is served on a separate plate. Put a slice of wholemeal bread in the bottom of each soup plate and pour or pile the stew-like soup on top. Accompany it with the sliced bacon or salt pork and a young red wine, a little of which can be poured into the soup as you progress down the bowl.

Variations

1. Your own cured belly of pork or ham will give a far, far better flavour than a commercially cured one unless you buy the very best Wilsthire or imported ham. However, rashers of good bacon could be used. Cut them up with their rinds on and fry them in a little lard or bacon fat for a minute or two, then add to the soup with the carrot and onion.
2. Two ounces (60 g) white haricot beans or dried chestnuts, or 8 oz (225 g) fresh chestnuts, can be used instead of potatoes (see p.1.2 for information on peeling and cooking chestnuts).
3. Broad beans, runner beans, or peas can be used instead of French beans.
4. Turnip or parsnip can be used instead of carrot.

GOULASCHSUPPE

When I was an au pair in Heidelberg this soup used to be sold from stalls on street corners for one mark. The soup part was hot and tasty, and the big knackwurst with its head and feet sticking out over the edges of the bowl was fresh and well-flavoured. A roll was included in the price. It was much tastier and considerably better value than the evil-smelling and outrageously priced hot dogs sold as fast food nowadays. Goulaschsuppe is quick and easy to make and can be varied endlessly. The south German version of my youth is described in Variation 1.

1 small onion	chopped into dice
1 small carrot	1 dessertspoon paprika
2 small Jerusalem artichokes *or* 1 small parsnip	$\frac{1}{2}$ teaspoon dill weed or dill seeds salt
1 clove garlic, peeled and crushed with a little salt	freshly milled pepper 3 ripe tomatoes
3 to 4 oz (90 to 110 g) smoked bacon, rinded, boned and	

Chop or slice all the vegetables except the tomato. Put the sliced vegetables with the garlic and bacon in a heavy pan and fry them all gently for 10 minutes, stirring occasionally to prevent sticking. Add the paprika, dill and seasoning. Meanwhile peel and core the tomatoes (see pps.247-8) and cut into chunks. Add the bacon or ham stock to the vegetable mixture and bring to the boil. Simmer for 10 minutes. Add the tomatoes and simmer for 10 minutes more. Adjust the seasoning and serve.

Variations

1. Omit the bacon and fry the vegetables with 2 tablespoons oil. Knackwurst or other cooked German sausage, or chunks of cooked ham, can be added to the soup with the tomatoes.
2. For a really hearty soup, add 1 oz (30 g) small pasta or rice or suet dumplings (see p.32) about 10 to 12 minutes before serving the soup. If you want to use brown rice add it right at the beginning or pre-cook it.
3. Little meat balls can be made from fresh pork in the same way as the beef balls on p.33, and added 10 to 15 minutes before serving.
4. In Germany the soup is traditionally served with noodles. For a special occasion make and add fresh noodles (see p.37).

Venison

RICH VENISON SOUP WITH PORT

The Shorter Oxford Dictionary defines venison as 'the flesh of an animal killed in the chase or by hunting ... now generally refers to species of deer'. It is as well to bear this definition in mind before laying out a lot of money for venison in some smart game dealer's shop, for deer are now farmed in England and the resulting flesh is bland and dull, lacking the gamey flavour of a wild animal. This soup is adapted from an early Victorian recipe and is best suited to a well-hung piece of genuine venison. It keeps and freezes well.

For the stock:
1 lb (450 g) breast or shin of
    venison, meat and bones
3 pints (1.75 l) water
12 juniper berries
1 piece of mace *or* ½ teaspoon
    ground mace or nutmeg
10 peppercorns
peelings from the vegetables

To finish the soup:
2 small onions
2 small carrots
2 sticks celery
2 rashers streaky bacon, 2 oz
    (60 g) after trimming
2 tablespoons port
2 tablespoons wine vinegar
1 slice wholemeal bread
    (optional thickening)
salt
freshly milled pepper

Put the venison in a heavy pan and cover with the water. Bring to the boil and skim off any scum that rises. Add the spices and vegetable trimmings and simmer for 2 hours, with a bubble breaking the surface only every second or so. This may also be done very successfully in a slow cooker or in an oven preheated to 325°F (170°C, Gas 3). It will take 6 to 8 hours in the slow cooker and about 3 hours in the oven. Strain the stock; you will need about 1¼ pints (750 ml).

Dice or chop the vegetables and bacon finely and put them all in a heavy-bottomed pan. Brown them over a very low heat, stirring often to prevent burning; they will gradually shrivel and go nut brown – the process takes about 30 minutes. Add the stock, port and vinegar and bring to the boil. If you think the soup too thin, add the slice of bread, crumbled. Lower the heat and simmer for 15 minutes. Meanwhile remove the bones and gristle from the venison and cut the meat in neat dice or strips. Taste the soup and add salt, pepper and more juniper, mace, port and vinegar as you like. The soup should possess aromatic and sweetly acid flavours to balance the gamey venison. It is best cooled and stored for several hours or overnight. Add the venison pieces when the soup is cold, and reheat. Serve plain, from a tureen if you have one, or with fried croûtons (see p.27).

Variations

1. Other tough cuts of game such as fore parts of hare, or legs and back of grouse, partridge, pheasant etc. can be used instead of venison.
2. If you have a well-flavoured game stock but no meat, use half as much vegetable again or 3 to 4 oz (90 to 110 g) flat mushrooms, sliced and added a few minutes before serving.
3. A little oatmeal – 1 to 2 oz (30 to 60 g) – fried with the vegetables and bacon for the last 10 minutes can be used as an alternative thickening agent. This method gives an interesting texture if no venison meat is available to provide it.
4. If you have no juniper, use 2 cloves, or 1 large bay leaf, or 6 to 8 allspice berries.

Vichyssoise

See under:
Cream: Crème Vichyssoise
Leek and Potato Soup, Variation 1

Walnuts

See under:
Celery, Almond and Walnut Cream
Iced Cucumber and Yogurt Soup, Variation 1

Watercress

CHOOSING AND USING

The peppery flavour of watercress goes exceptionally well with starchy and creamy soups, besides giving an attractive colour contrast. It is also rich in iron, which the British diet tends to lack. Watercress dries and yellows very quickly after picking, so don't let the greengrocer whip a bunch into a bag before you have had time to examine it. The stalks and leaves should be a uniform dark green.

Watercress stores well if you first run it under a cold tap, then shake off the excess water, put it into a plastic bag, press out the air and seal the bag with a wire twist. It will keep fresh in the bottom of the fridge for several days if given this treatment. If you have been lumbered with a yellowing bunch, cut away all the yellow and use just the green tops, supplementing them if necessary with a few shredded lettuce leaves.

CREAM OF WATERCRESS SOUP

While watercress can be used to pep up almost any bland soup, it has quite enough character to stand on its own. This soup is about as simple as you can get, but very pretty and delicious. The soup base can be made in advance and the chopped watercress leaves added just before serving.

1 fresh, dark green bunch watercress	salt
½ bunch spring onions	scrape of nutmeg
1½ oz (40 g) butter	5 tablespoons thick cream
1½ oz (40 g) plain flour	squeeze of lemon juice
1 pint (600 ml) milk	freshly milled pepper

Hold the watercress in its bunch while you wash it, then cut off any yellow bits and slice the stalks very finely to the base of the leaves. Cut the leaves once or twice. Chop the spring onions finely. Melt the butter in a stainless or enamelled pan over a low heat, stir in the flour and continue stirring the roux for 2 to 3 minutes. Add the milk by degrees, stirring thoroughly to perfect smoothness between each addition. If you do end up with lumps, don't worry – the soup can be milled or blended later. Bring the soup to the boil, but don't let it boil over. Add the spring onions and watercress stalks, a little salt and nutmeg. Turn the heat as low as possible, or put the pan on a stove mat, and leave it to simmer for 20 minutes. If the soup has flour lumps in it or the watercress stalks are very stringy, it can be blended or put through the medium plate of a food mill. At this point the soup can be cooled and stored overnight in the fridge, or frozen.

Reheat in a clean stainless or enamelled pan with the watercress leaves, cream and lemon juice. Taste when hot, and add more salt, nutmeg and some pepper if necessary. Serve with a chewy, well-flavoured, whole grain bread.

Variations

1. For a low calorie, low animal fat soup, sweat the watercress stalks and spring onions in 1 teaspoon butter or oil or in their own moisture; add the milk and thicken the soup with $1\frac{1}{2}$ tablespoons rice flour or potato flour, stirred into 2 to 3 tablespoons cold milk and added when the soup has simmered for 15 minutes. Add 3 tablespoons cottage or curd cheese to the soup just before blending or milling it. The whole milk can be replaced with dried low fat milk and water.
2. Chicken or other light meat or fish stock or vegetable stock can be used instead of milk.
3. For a thicker soup, use 2 to $2\frac{1}{2}$ oz (60 to 75 g) butter and 2 to $2\frac{1}{2}$ tablespoons plain flour.
4. Eight ounces (225 g) fresh spinach or a small packet of frozen leaf spinach can be used instead of watercress; alternatively try a $\frac{1}{2}$ bunch of watercress and $\frac{1}{2}$ a small head of letuce, or 3 to 4 oz (90 to 110 g) fresh wild sorrel, or 8 oz (225 g) young nettle tops, picked in May or early June.

See also:
Almond Cream Soup, Variation 2
Haricot Bean and Watercress Soup
Cauliflower and Watercress Soup
Chicken, Egg and Lemon Soup, Variation 3
Green Leaves: Zuppa di Verdura
Leek and Potato Soup, Variation 4
Purée of Lettuce with Sour Cream, Variation 2
Potato and Parsley Soup with Cream, Variation 3
Spinach: Crème Florentine, Variation 3

Woodcock

Yogurt

Techniques for Rescuing Failed Soups

Some seemingly major mistakes in soup-making are easily put right. Others, such as a really pervasive burnt taste, are not, and it is as well to know which are which before wasting further good ingredients. Here are some suggestions for dealing with the commoner mistakes. The more reversible ones come first, and the more or less hopeless cases at the end.

TOO SALTY

How completely this problem can be rectified depends on how far in advance of the meal you make the unwelcome discovery. Perfect success can be achieved without any wastage if you have enough time and ingredients to make another batch of the soup, this time totally salt-free. Mix the salty with the unsalty until you have the right balance. Any salty soup left over can be used as a sauce for salt-free vegetables, pasta etc, or as a liquid base for an otherwise salt-free stew.

If the saltiness is found out only 15 minutes, say, before you intended to serve the soup, add raw, grated or diced vegetables, rice, small pasta or dumplings as appropriate, or cut up a peeled potato or two, cook in the soup, and remove before serving. Adding vegetables or grains will absorb a moderate excess of salt.

For a really appalling surfeit of salt, or if you only realize you have this problem a few minutes before serving, you may have to resort to this method. Pour $\frac{1}{2}$ pint (300 ml) milk, stock or water into another pan. Knead 1 oz (30 g) butter with 1 heaped tablespoon flour. Put the liquid on to boil. When it is very hot, whisk in the butter and flour paste to make a thin sauce. Immediately start adding the salty soup, a little at a time, until it tastes right. Serve at once. If you have really overdone the salt it may be necessary to start with $\frac{3}{4}$ to 1 pint (450-600 ml) milk or stock and $1\frac{1}{2}$ to 2 oz (40 to 60 g) butter and flour, in which case the soup will be pretty dull.

Finally, it is worth remembering that iced soups need more seasoning than hot ones. What is too salty as a hot soup may be just right very cold, though of course this is no help to you if you discover the fault at a late stage, for you will then have no time to ice the soup.

TOO PEPPERY OR TOO HOT WITH CURRY

Any of the ideas for disguising excess saltiness may be used, or the soup can be served with a boiled potato, a spoonful of cooked rice or a garnish of finely sliced, raw, sweet vegetables in each bowl. It can also be accompanied by plenty of yogurt or sour cream, or with pitta bread or chapattis.

TOO ACID

Any of the remedies for salty soups can be tried, as appropriate. Richness covers acidity to a certain extent, so cream, butter or oil can be added. Sugar is a useful addition only in an acid fruit soup; in other cases it merely makes the soup both too acid and too sweet.

Soups and other dishes are eaten extremely tart or lemony in hot climates since the sharp taste has a cooling, refreshing effect, so a rather drastic solution to a too acid soup might be to heat the dining-room to a sub-tropical temperature, when the soup may well be thought perfectly seasoned by your dripping guests!

TOO RICH

If there is time to chill the soup, fat will rise to the surface and can be skimmed or lifted off. This will not happen if the fat is held in suspension by flour or other starch, as in a velouté soup. In this case, follow the most appropriate remedy for too salty soups, and/or add wine, lemon juice or wine vinegar by degrees until the taste satisfies you.

THE SOUP BASE CONTAINS FLOUR LUMPS

This is easily cured by putting the soup through the medium or fine plate of a food mill, or blending it thoroughly. Both methods, however, will result in a thin, smooth soup. This can be corrected by adding grated or finely diced vegetables, or rice or small pasta as appropriate, or by kneading 1 oz (30 g) butter with 1 tablespoon flour and whisking this paste into the soup, a little at a time, just before serving.

TOO THIN OR TOO THICK

See Basic Processes, pps. 20-2 and 22 respectively.

The following faults are more difficult to put right.

TOO BITTER

If aubergines or courgettes have been used without sufficient salting and draining of the juices (see p.52) an unpleasant bitterness may pervade the soup. Young courgettes do not need to be drained but aubergines and mature courgettes do. The bitter flavour sometimes diminishes if the soup is kept for a day or two, and a cover-up job can be attempted with extra garlic, olive oil, spices and herbs and even a teaspoon of sugar, but complete success is unlikely.

CURDLING

This term denotes the separation of a fluid substance into

solids and liquids, as in curds and whey. It occurs in various ways, three of which are relevant to soup-making.

1. If yogurt is added directly to hot soup it will separate, as will unpasteurized cream. Page 21 gives instructions on how to add raw cream and yogurt, but if the worst has happened a partial cure can be effected by blending the soup with about 1 dessertspoon rice or potato flour. The texture of the soup will still be granular and a little heavy with the flour, but it will be an improvement on the original state.

2. When making an oil-based enrichment such as aillade or pesto, the oil may separate from the other ingredients. If the enrichment contains egg yolk, put another yolk in a clean bowl and add the curdled mixture drop by drop, beating thoroughly between each addition. If the mixture is without egg, for instance rouille or pesto, blend it again and/or beat in 1 tablespoon fresh breadcrumbs.

3. If egg yolks are being added as a final thickening and enrichment it is all too easy to miss that critical moment when the egg has thickened but not scrambled. If you do end up with little bits of scrambled egg, it is impossible to reverse. If the soup is a smooth one it can be blended, but the texture will still be granular. If the soup already has pieces of meat, fish or vegetable in it, cut your losses and serve it.

SOUP WHICH HAS STUCK TO THE PAN BOTTOM AND BURNT

Thick liquids, especially those containing flour, have a strong propensity for sticking to the pan. It is therefore very important to use pans with thick bottoms, so that the heat is well distributed.

As soon as you notice that the soup is sticking to the bottom, pour it into a clean pan and discard the stuck bits. If the sticking has been prolonged, a burnt flavour will pervade the soup. In a very hearty, strongly flavoured soup the problem may be partially disguised with spices, pepper or alcohol as appropriate, but if it is a delicate or creamy one there is really nothing to do except throw it out and start again.

SOUP WHICH TASTES FLAT OR DEAD

It is tempting to use leftovers or rather old ingredients for soup, but the liquefying of an ingredient will not disguise its flavour. A cover-up job can be attempted with the aid of lemon juice, sherry, madeira or port, curry, or other spices and fresh herbs, but the soup will be only fairly acceptable in the end. If fresh ingredients have been used and the result is still flat, it may be that the proportions were wrong or that they are overcooked. There may, of course, be too many ingredients. 'When in doubt leave it out' is a good basic motto for empirical cooks.

Soups Which Work Well in Large Quantities

This list is for people who have to prepare soup by the gallon rather than by the pint.

The soups can all be prepared at least some hours in advance of being served. They can be re-heated and kept waiting while hot without much deterioration. Last minute adjustments are quick and easy.

Since variations of an ounce or so, which pass unnoticed in a small quantity of soup, can make a big difference when multiplied by 20, and since one person's medium onion is another's whopper, here is a rough guide to the quantity of an ingredient meant by a certain phrase in the recipe.

onions	large, 4 oz (110 g) after peeling
	medium, 3 oz (90 g) afer peeling
	small, 2 oz (60 g) after peeling
	very small, 1 oz (30 g) after peeling
carrots	medium, 2 oz (60 g) after peeling and trimming
	small, 1½ oz (40 g) after peeling and trimming
leeks	medium, 3-4 oz (90-110 g) after peeling and trimming
turnips	small, 2 oz (60 g) after peeling
parsnips	small, 2 oz (60 g) after peeling and coring
poatoes	large, 6 oz (175 g) after peeling
	small 3 oz (90 g) after peeling
sweet pepper	medium, 4 oz (110 g) after coring
	small, 3 oz (90 g) after coring

courgettes	small, 1½ oz (40 g) after trimming
tomatoes	average, 2 oz (60 g) after peeling and coring
celery	small stick, 1 oz (30 g) after trimming
	stick, 1½ oz (40 g) after trimming

Almond Cream Soup
Bacon or Ham Stock
Broad Bean and Mushroom Soup
Broad Bean – Purée of Broad Beans with Toasted Almonds
Beans, Dried Mixed – Harira
Beans, Red Kidney – Red Bean and Bacon Soup
Bean, White Haricot – Basic Purée
Beef Stock and Broth
Beef Consommé
Beef – Pot Au Feu
Beef – Oxtail, Bacon and Vegetable Soup
Beef – Wedding Soup
Carrot and Coriander Soup
Celery, Almond and Walnut Cream
Celeriac – Basic Purée
Chicken Stock and Broth
Chicken and Chestnut Soup
Chicken, Egg and Lemon Soup
Chicken, Pumpkin and Peanut Butter Soup
Chicken – Cream of Chicken Soup
Crab and Red Pepper Bisque
Crab and Mushroom Chowder
Cucumber – Purée of Cucumber and Fennel
Duck – Purée of Duck and Celery
Fish Stock
Fish Stew with Garlic, Tomatoes and Olive Oil
Haddock – Smoked Haddock Cream
Lamb or Mutton – Mutton Rice and Apricot Soup
Lamb or Mutton – Scotch Broth
Lobster – Bisque d'Homard
Mushroom – Black Mushroom Soup
Onion – Cream of Onion Soup
Onion – French Onion Soup
Pea, Dried Split – Split Pea and Bacon Soup
Pheasant and Lentil Purée
Potato and Parsley Soup with Cream
Rabbit and Cider Cream
Shrimp and Salmon Cream

Tripe – Zuppa di Trippa alla Milanese
Tripe Chowder
Turkey Chowder
Turkey – Devilled Turkey Soup
Vegetables, Mixed – Garbure
Vegetables, Mixed – Minestrone
Venison – Rich Venison Soup with Port

Easy Soups

Soups in this list are either made in one process by adding ingredients one by one to a basic liquid (e.g. Fish Slice and Mushroom Soup), or involve more than one process but a very short total preparation and cooking time (e.g. Peach and Blackberry Soup).

Artichoke – Cream of Artichoke Soup
Iced Avocado Cream
Broad Beans – Basic Purée
Bean, White Haricot – Basic Purée
Beetroot – Jewish Borscht
Cabbage – Hungarian Cabbage Soup
Cabbage – Majorcan Cabbage Soup
Carrot and Coriander Soup
Carrot and Lemon Soup
Cauliflower Cheese Soup
Cheese – Fontina, Egg and Milk Soup
Chestnut and Milk Soup
Chicken Liver – Cream of Chicken Liver and Madeira
Corn Chowder
Courgette Chowder
Eels – Jellied Eels
Finnish Fish Soup
Fish Slice and Mushroom Soup
Green Leaves – Zuppa di Verdura
Haddock – Smoked Haddock Chowder
Lettuce – Porage du Père Tranquill
Mackerel and Lemon Cream
Mackerel – Smoked Mackerel Soup
Oatmeal and Vegetable Soup
Oyster Cream

Parsnip – Spiced Parsnip Purée
Pea, Dried Split – Quick Split Pea Soup
Peach and Blackberry Soup
Potato – Potage Bonne Femme
Potato, Mushroom and Sour Cream Soup
Potato and Parsley Soup with Cream
Shellfish Cream
Tomato, Onion and Potato Soup
Tomato and Orange Soup
Turnip – Cream of Turnip Soup
Vegetable Stock and Broth
Watercress – Cream of Watercress Soup

Soups Which Freeze Successfully

My freezer is about as primitive and inadequate as possible, consisting of the freezing compartment of a small fridge, the compartment having lost its door some years ago. Therefore anyone with really superior freezing equipment will be able to freeze more of the soups in this book than are listed here. These are only the sure-fire freezers.

Asparagus Purée with Cream
Bean – Broad Bean and Mushroom Soup
Bean – Basic Purée of Broad Beans
Beans, Dried Mixed – Harira
Bean, Dried – Mung Bean and Black Olive Soup
Bean Dried White Haricot – Basic Purée
Beef Stock and Broth
Beef – Big Beef Broth
Beef – Jamaican Red Pea Soup
Bean, Green – Green Bean and Cashew Nut Cream
Beef – Meatball and Tomato Soup
Beef – Pepperpot Soup
Celery, Almond and Walnut Cream Soup
Celeriac or Root Celery – Basic Purée of Celeriac
Chestnut, Bacon and Cabbage Soup
Chicken Stock, Broth and Glaze
Chicken, Egg and Lemon Soup (base only)

Chicken, Pumpkin and Peanut Butter Soup
Chicken – Cream of Chicken Soup
Duck – Purée of Duck and Celery
Hare Soup with Madeira and Bread Balls
Lamb or Mutton – Scotch Broth
Lentil and Sausage Soup
Lentil – Spicy Lentil and Vegetable Soup
Peas, Dried Split – Quick Split Pea Soup
Peas, Dried Split – Split Pea and Bacon Soup
Peas, Green – Green Pea and Ham Soup
Pheasant and Lentil Purée
Pork Gravy and Madeira Soup
Rabbit and Cider Cream Soup
Shrimp and Green Pea Soup
Spinach – Crème Florentine
Tomato and Red Pepper
Tripe – Zuppa di Trippa alla Milanese
Venison – Rich Venison Soup with Port

Soups to Serve Chilled or Iced

The average Briton is not nuts for iced soups unless the weather is really scorching so this list is shorter than it could be. If you enjoy chilled soups, many of the vegetable purées can be adapted very successfully, but bear in mind that oil should be used in the recipe instead of butter or other hard fat, that the soups should be made rather thinner than the hot version and that chilled soups need more seasoning.

Bean – Broad Bean Purée (Variation 3)
Beef Consommé (Variation 1)
Beetroot – Jewish Borscht
Chicken Broth
Chicken – Cream of Chicken (Variations 1 and 2)
Cream – Crème Vichyssoise
Iced Cucumber and Yogurt Soup
Leek and Potato Soup (Variation 1; this is real Vichyssoise)
Iced Melon and Green Ginger Soup
Peach and Blackberry Soup (Variation 1)

Plum – Iced Plum Soup with Sour Cream
Raspberry – Iced Raspberry and Yogurt Soup
Tomato – Gazpacho
Tomato and Orange Soup (Variation 1)

Main Course Soups

Mostly chunky and filling soups containing a variety of proteins, vitamins and minerals.

Apple, Rye and Sour Cream Soup (especially Variation 4)
Bass, Vermouth and Garlic Soup
Bean, Dried Mixed – Harira
Bean, Dried – Mung Bean and Black Olive
Bean, Dried Red – Red Bean and Bacon
Beef – Big Beef Broth
Beef – Jamaican Red Pea Soup
Beef – Pot au Feu
Bean Dried White Haricot – Haricot Bean and Watercress
Beef – Meatball and Tomato Soup
Beef – Oxtail, Bacon and Vegetable Soup
Beef – Pepperpot Soup
Beef – Wedding Soup
Beetroot – Borscht with Mushrooms and Sour Cream
Cabbage – Hungarian Cabbage Soup (Variation 1)
Cabbage Soup with a Meat Crust
Cheese – Fontina Egg and Milk Soup
Chestnut, Bacon and Cabbage Soup
Chicken and Chestnut Soup
Chicken Noodle Soup
Chicken, Pumpkin and Peanut Butter Soup
Chicken – Chinese Chicken Soup
Crab Gumbo
Duck and Cucumber Soup
Fish – Atlantic Fish Chowder
Fish – Cod and Prawn Velouté
Finnish Fish Soup
Fish Stewed with Garlic Tomatoes and Olive Oil
Fish – Schchi (Russian Fish and Spinach Soup)
Haddock – Smoked Haddock Chowder

Hare Soup with Madeira and Bread Balls
Lamb or Mutton – Mutton Rice and Apricot Soup
Lamb or Mutton – Scotch Broth (Variation 4)
Lentil and Sausage Soup
Mussels – Moules Marinière
Pea, Green – Green Pea and Ham Soup (Variation 3)
Rabbit and Cider Cream Soup (Variation 1)
Salmon – Green Salmon Soup
Shrimp and Salmon Cream
Tripe Chowder
Turkey Chowder
Vegetables, mixed – Garbure
Vegetables, mixed – Goulaschsuppe
Vegetables, mixed – Minestrone
Vegetables, mixed – Pistou

Slimming Soups

Fat, sugar and alcohol are now thought to be the major food factors in excess weight, while those old enemies of the waistline – bread, potatoes and rice – have been reinstated with little halos. Therefore while some of the recipes and variations below are very low in calories (stock and broths without fat or thickenings have none to speak of) others are quite bulky and filling but low in fat, especially animal fats.

Apple, Rye and Sour Cream Soup
Asparagus Purée with Cream
Bean – Broad Bean and Mushroom Soup (Variation 3)
Bean Broad – Basic Purée (Variation 1)
Beef Consommé
Beef – Meatball and Tomato (Variation 4)
Beef – Wedding Soup (Variation 4)
Beetroot – Jewish Borscht
Cabbage – Majorcan Cabbage Soup
Carrot and Lemon Soup
Celeriac or Root Celery – Basic Purée
Celery and Tarragon Mousseline (Variation2)
Chicken Broth

Chicken Egg and Lemon Soup (Variation 2)
Chicken – Chinese Chicken Soup
Chicken – Cream of Chicken Soup (Variation 5)
Chicken – Mulligatawny
Cream – Crème Vichyssoise (Variation 2)
Cucumber – Iced Cucumber and Yogurt Soup (Variation 2)
Duck and Cucumber Soup
Eel Soup
Fish Stewed with Garlic Tomatoes and Olive Oil (Variation 6)
Fish Slice and Mushroom Soup
Green Leaves – Spinach, Green Pea and Lettuce Purée (Variation 2)
Hare Soup with Madeira and Bread Balls (Variation 4)
Lamb and Mutton – Scotch Broth (Variation 3)
Leek and Lemon Soup
Leek and Potato Soup (Variation 5)
Lettuce – Potage du Père Tranquill (Variation 1)
Mackerel, Lemon and Cream Soup (Variation 4)
Iced Melon and Green Ginger Soup
Black Mushroom Soup (Variation 3)
Mussels – Moules Marinière
Parsnip – Spiced Parsnip Purée (Variation 4)
Pea Green – Green Pea and Ham Soup (Variation 4)
Pea, Green – Purée of Green Peas and their Pods
Potato, Mushroom and Sour Cream Soup (Variation 2)
Raspberry – Iced Raspberry and Yogurt Soup
Salmon – Green Salmon Soup
Tomato – Gazpacho (Variation 2)
Tomato and Orange Soup
Tomato and Red Pepper Soup (Variation 4)
Turkey Chowder (Variation 4)
Watercress – Cream of Watercress Soup (Variation 1)

Vegetarian Soups

Soups made only from vegetables, fruit, grain and milk products.
The definition of vegetarianism I have used for this list includes milk
products (though plenty of vegan soups and variations will be found
amongst the soups listed) but does not include eggs poultry or fish in
any form. Thus Mung Bean and Black Olive Soup, among others, has
been omitted from this list because of the egg garnish, but could
easily be adapted.

287

Almond Cream Soup (Variation 1)
Artichoke – Cream of Artichoke Soup
Asparagus Purée with Cream
Aubergine and Red Pepper Soup
Avocado – Iced Avocado Cream (Variation 2)
Bean, Broad – Broad Bean and Mushroom Soup
Bean, Mixed Dried – Harira
Bean Dried White Haricot – Basic Purée
Bean, Green – Green Bean and Cashew Nut Cream (Variation 1)
Bean, Dried White Haricot – Haricot Bean and Watercress Soup
Beetroot – Jewish Borscht (Variation 1)
Cabbage – Majorcan Cabbage Soup
Carrot and Coriander Soup
Carrot and Lemon Soup
Cauliflower Cheese Soup
Cauliflower and Watercress Soup
Celery, Almond and Walnut Cream (Variation 2)
Celeriac, or Root Celery – Basic Purée
Celeriac and Chestnut Soup (Variation 1)
Chestnut and Milk Soup
Corn Chowder
Courgette Chowder
Cucumber – Crème Vichyssoise
Cucumber – Iced Cucumber and Yogurt Soup
Green Leaves – Spinach, Green Pea and Lettuce Purée
Green Leaves – Zuppa di Verdura
Leek and Lemon
Leek and Potato
Lentil – Spicy Lentil and Vegetable
Melon – Iced Melon and Green Ginger Soup
Mushroom – Black Mushroom Soup
Mushroom – Cream of Mushroom Soup
Oatmeal and Vegetable Soup
Onion – Cream of Onion Soup
Onion _ French Onion Soup (Variations 2 and 3)
Parsnip – Spiced Parsnip Purée
Peach and Blackberry Soup
Plum – Iced Plum Soup with Sour Cream
Potato – Potage Bonne Femme
Potato, Mushroom and Sour Cream Soup
Potato and Parsley Soup with Cream (Variation 1)
Raspberry – Iced Raspberry Soup and Yogurt Soup
Spinach – Crème Florentine (Variation 1)

Tomato – Cream of Tomato Soup
Tomato – Gazpacho
Tomato, Onion and Potato Soup
Tomato and Orange Soup
Tomato and Red Pepper Soup
Turnip – Cream of Turnip Soup
Vegetable Broth
Vegetables, Mixed – Minestrone
Vegetables, Mixed – Pistou
Watercress – Cream of Watercress Soup

Using Precooked Foods in Soups

There is quite a widespread belief among British cooks that soups can be used like 'Shepherd's Pie' in bad canteens – as a final resting place for the week's little left-overs. Although the left-overs may disappear from view in the soup, their stale taste will predominate, dulling even the flavours of fresh foods used as well. On the other hand there is no reason why a well-organised cook should not save himself a separate job by cooking extra beans, pasta or chestnuts with the next day's soup in view.

Fish and green vegetables, being very delicate in both consistency and flavour do not respond well to pre-cooking, but meat, poultry, starchy vegetables and grains can be pre-cooked successfully provided that they are used while still really fresh.

In fact cooked meat and poultry are used so often in the book that there's no point making a separate list. Look up the soups listed under the meat or fowl you have on hand. Alternatively, small quantities of freshly cooked poultry can be added to some green vegetable soups, and meat or game to grain and bean soups.

Cooked Chestnuts

Chinese Celeriac and Chestnut Soup
Tripe: Zuppa di Trippa alla Milanese
Devilled Turkey Soup
Vegetables: Garbure

Cooked Pasta or Noodles

Bacon and Ham: Goulaschsuppe
Beef: Meat Ball and Tomato Soup
Chicken Broth
Chicken Noodle Soup
Green Leaves: Zuppa di Verdura
Tripe: Zuppa di Trippa alla Milanese

Cooked Red Beans

Red Bean and Bacon Soup
Beef: Jamaican Red Pea Soup
Tripe: Zuppa di Trippa alla Milanese
Vegetables: Minestrone

Cooked White Haricot Beans

Dried Mixed Beans: Harira
Basic Bean Purée
Haricot Bean and Watercress Soup
Tripe: Zuppa di Trippa alla Milanese
Vegetables: Minestrone
Vegetables: Pistou

Cooked Rice

Beef; Pot au Feu (Variation 4)
Chicken: Cock-a-Leekie
Mutton, Rice and Apricot Soup
Cream of Onion Soup
Tomato, Onion and Potato Soup (Variation 6)
Tomato and Red Pepper Soup
Devilled Turkey Soup

Cooked Potatoes

Beef: Meat Ball and Tomato Soup
Chicken: Cock-a-Leekie
Smoked Haddock Cream
Green Pea and Ham Soup
Garnishes and Accompaniments: potato dumplings, p.33

Index